Neighborhoods, Communities, and Urban Marginality

Series Editors
Carol Camp Yeakey
Washington University in St. Louis
St. Louis, MO, USA

Walter R. Allen
University of California
Los Angeles, CA, USA

This series examines the ecology of neighborhoods and communities in not only twenty-first century America, but across the globe. By taking an ecological approach, the study of neighborhoods takes into account not just structures, buildings and geographical boundaries, but also the relationship and adjustment of humans to highly dense urban environments in a particular area or vicinity. As the violent events of the past year in marginalized urban neighborhoods and communities across the country have demonstrated, "place matters." The series contain original research about the power of place, that is, the importance of where one lives, how public policies have transformed the shape and geography of inequality and disparity in our metropolitan areas, and, the ways in which residents impacted by perceived inequality are trying to confront the problem.

More information about this series at
http://www.palgrave.com/gp/series/15097

Sheri R. Notaro

Marginality and Global LGBT Communities

Conflicts, Civil Rights and Controversy

palgrave
macmillan

Sheri R. Notaro
Washington University in St. Louis
St. Louis, MO, USA

Neighborhoods, Communities, and Urban Marginality
ISBN 978-3-030-22414-1   ISBN 978-3-030-22415-8   (eBook)
https://doi.org/10.1007/978-3-030-22415-8

Cover credit: Yuri Alexandre/Moment/Getty Images

This Palgrave Macmillan imprint is published by the registered company Springer Nature Switzerland AG
The registered company address is: Gewerbestrasse 11, 6330 Cham, Switzerland

With gratitude for their everlasting love and support, I dedicate this book to my husband, Paul C. Notaro, and my son, Paul M. Notaro.

To the LGBT community, I dedicate this book in deepest thanks for your perseverance, resiliency and quest for human dignity. Your fight to live, to love, and to simply be is the universal struggle for humanity that unites us all.

SERIES EDITORS' PREFACE

This year marks a propitious time in our nation's history as we celebrate, in June 1969, the violent confrontations at the Stonewall Inn in Greenwich Village, in Manhattan, in New York City. Little did we know that the Stonewall riots, from fifty years ago, would become the signal event of the modern LGBT rights movement, a previously marginalized group on the periphery of social, political and economic life in America. Once ostracized and hidden from public view, we now see symbols of LGBT pride in both public and private venues. Notaro's timely volume, *Marginality and Global LGBT Communities—Conflict, Civil Rights and Controversy*, examines just how far the LGBT movement has come and how much more remains to be accomplished in their quest for equal justice under the law. Nowhere is LGBT pride more evident than on college campuses, where lavender graduations have now become commonplace, as an end of the year ceremony which celebrates the achievements of graduating LGBT college students, who, at times, faced challenges and discrimination during their college years. According to the Human Rights Campaign, the color lavender is important to the LGBT community for several reasons. First, lavender represents the pink triangle that gay men were forced to wear in concentration camps. Second, the black triangle designates lesbians who were political prisoners in Nazi Germany. The LGBT rights movement combined them to make symbols and vivid colors to denote pride and a sense of community. Notaro's book cover is endemic of this sense of pride, and of community. Where appropriate, *Marginality and Global LGBT Communities—Conflict, Civil*

Rights and Controversy, provides a lens by which to view LGBT issues not just in the United States, but in differing nation states as well.

As co-editors of the series, *Neighborhoods, Communities and Urban Marginality*, we welcome this volume as we now see the globalization of the LGBT community and their fight for just and legal recognition and accommodation. The extent to which any community of persons is marginalized and not afforded basic human rights is the extent to which the rights of us all are denied.

Carol Camp Yeakey
The Marshall S. Snow Professor
of Arts and Sciences
Washington University in St. Louis
St. Louis, USA

Walter R. Allen
Distinguished Professor of Education
of Sociology and African American Studies
Allan Murray Cartter Chair in Higher Education
University of California at Los Angeles
Los Angeles, USA

ACKNOWLEDGEMENTS

This book is a product of family, friends, and colleagues and their unwavering confidence in me.

My mother, Joyce Gail Marshall Wynn, always put my needs before her own, never letting me know of the sacrifices she made for me on a daily basis. To see and remember her joy in my accomplishments inspired me to always reach higher. When I lost her, my second mother took on the role of loving me unconditionally. Thank you Aunt Tine.

My husband, Paul C. Notaro, has shared his life with me as a loving and dedicated partner who can always make me laugh. He stands beside me in all things, reviewing copious drafts, boosting my confidence, and cooking the best meals I've ever tasted. His devotion to our son, Paul M. Notaro, knows no bounds.

My dear friend, Carol Camp Yeakey, saw something special in me so many years ago. Because of her faith in me, I have learned to recognize my potential and to strive for excellence in all things.

I also want to thank Rachel Daniel, Madison Allums, and the entire Palgrave Macmillan staff for supporting this book from inception to publication.

Contents

LIST OF FIGURES

LIST OF TABLES

CHAPTER 1

Objectives and Significance of the Volume

Alice Walker, a poet and writer, provides a lens into the main objectives of this volume:

> Please remember, especially in these times of group-think and the right-on chorus, that no person is your friend (or kin) who demands your silence, or denies your right to grow and be perceived as fully blossomed as you were intended. (Alice Walker, 1983, *In Search of Our Mothers' Gardens: Womanist Prose*)

This volume has several objectives, all of which focus on the marginality of persons identifying as lesbian, gay, bisexual, and transgender (LGBT) both in the United States and globally. The volume will illuminate the ways in which health disparities and inequities experienced by the LGBT population stem from historical and political struggles and at times violent persecutions faced by LGBT persons throughout the world. Specifically, the objectives of the volume are to illuminate the marginalization of the LGBT community in its many forms and societal structures while also discussing progress and movement from the margins of society to the mainstream in both the United States and globally.

This chapter will present the origins, definition of homosexuality, estimates of the LGBT population, an abridged history of homosexuality, and the foundation for LGBT civil rights formed by the Stonewall Inn riots.

© The Author(s) 2020
S. R. Notaro, *Marginality and Global LGBT Communities*,
Neighborhoods, Communities, and Urban Marginality,
https://doi.org/10.1007/978-3-030-22415-8_1

This chapter explicates that although the Stonewall Inn was a turning point and catalyst for gains in LGBT civil and political rights, the remainder of the volume will demonstrate that significant challenges stemming from discrimination, bias, and stigmatization persist among the LGBT community in the United States and globally. The ensuing chapters of the volume will provide ample evidence of significant barriers to full inclusion of the LGBT community into society, with focused attention on legal challenges, access to health care, health disparities, and violence (e.g., U.S. Department of Health and Human Services [DHHS], 2010).

Throughout the volume, care will be taken to emphasize and analyze the variations within this community that influence the uneven distribution of both health risk and protective factors and resiliency. The topic of LGBT marginalization is relevant and timely given that the 50th anniversary of the Stonewall Inn uprising provides a moment to pause and reflect upon ways in which the struggles for human rights of one group are indicative of the struggles for us all. Full inclusion of LGBT persons affects the lived experiences of all peoples. Limitations of the volume include the sometimes uneven focus on the United States, given the lack of comparative data sets globally as well as the inability to capture the full breadth of experience of individuals within the LGBT community.

The minority stress model (e.g., Meyer, 2003, 2010) will be discussed throughout the volume as an important conceptualization of the ways in which marginalization negatively impacts health outcomes. The model offers a framework for understanding and examining the impact of bias, discrimination, homophobia, and marginality on the unequal and poor health outcomes of LGBT individuals. Meyer (2003) emphasizes that minority stress theory is based upon several sociological and psychological theories (e.g., Allport, 1954; Goffman, 1963) that discuss the negative effects of social conditions such as prejudice and discrimination. Minority stress theory posits that health disparities among LGBTQ individuals or sexual minorities (e.g., psychological distress, substance use, HIV risk) can be partially explained by the stressors associated with experiencing a lifetime of homophobia, discrimination, bias, and harassment (Meyer, 2010). The minority stress theory posits that these stressors are not experienced by majority or non-stigmatized groups, are chronic, and are socially based in terms of institutional structures (Meyer, 2003). The model explores the variability within sexual minority communities by explicitly investigating the intersectional and overlapping identities within the LGBTQ community—e.g., LGBTQ individuals of color who hold unified identities as racial/ethnic minorities as well as sexual minorities. Research has demonstrated that, at least in the United States, LGBT individuals of color have a long and rich history of involvement in the "mainstream" gay rights movement (e.g., Stonewall), as well as within LGBT communities of color (Meyer, 2010). These communities of support serve as protective factors or buffers against homophobia, harassment, and discrimination and in turn, lower the risk of health disparities (Meyer, 2010).

Origins of Homosexuality

The origins of homosexuality have been formally debated among psychologists and psychiatrists for decades, with some claims that homosexuality results from unhealthy relationships between parents and children (Edsall, 2003). While research has examined a number of biological, genetic, and cultural factors that may influence sexual orientation, no definitive conclusions have been reached on this issue (American Psychological Association, 2016). There is fairly widespread agreement, however, that both biological and environmental factors impact the development of sexual orientation, leaving the individual with little or no choice in the matter (American Psychological Association, 2016). It was not until 1973 that the American Psychiatric Association ceased to classify homosexuality as a mental illness. The decision to remove homosexuality from the Diagnostic and Statistical Manual (DSM) was partly influenced by gay activism as well as the failure of established psychiatric tests such as the Rorshach to distinguish heterosexual men and women from homosexual men and women.

Defining Homosexuality

The origins of the terms *homosexuality* and heterosexuality are attributed to a letter written in 1869 by Karl Maria-Kertbeny, a Hungarian journalist and human rights activist The terminology applied to the homosexual community has changed over time and put into view the struggle to positively self-define one's community in the face of discriminatory and pejorative labels imposed by anti-gay sentiment. In an attempt to mitigate stigma associated with the term homosexual, some gay and lesbian activists in the late 1940s and early 1950s created the "homophile" or "loving the same" movement (Carter, 2004). In direct opposition to the homophile attempt at positive self-identification, Carter (2004) details terminology applied to homosexuals that suggested either weakness (e.g., "fag" and "limp-wrist") or inappropriate expressions of gender (e.g., "drag queens" and "transvestites" who favored women's clothing and makeup; "scare queens or flame queens" who adopted men's clothing and makeup; and "butch lesbians" who sometimes favored men's clothing).

While the label of "gay" was associated with any persons who did not self-identify as heterosexual from the 1930s to the 1960s, activists identifying themselves as "gay" chose to link the term with their struggles for civil rights and social services beginning in the 1960s (Los Angeles Conservancy, 2016). The next change in terminology occurred in the 1970s when women who identified as "gay" sought a distinctive way to signal solidarity with heterosexual feminists by adopting the term "lesbian." Early in the 1980s the LGB (lesbian, gay, bisexual) acronym overtook the term "gay" as more of the homosexual community sought a way to better represent their diversity of sexual identities (Los Angeles Conservancy, 2016).

In today's lexicon, homosexuality is considered as one type of sexual orientation or the patterns of emotional, romantic, and sexual attractions to men, women, or both sexes (American Psychological Association, 2016). According to evidence from numerous research studies conducted since the middle of the twentieth century, sexual orientation can be conceptualized on a continuum, from exclusive attraction to the other sex to exclusive attraction to the same-sex (American Psychological Association, 2016). Despite this view of a continuum of sexual orientation, it is commonly discussed in terms of three categories: heterosexual (having emotional, romantic, or sexual attractions to members of the other sex), homosexual or gay/lesbian (having emotional, romantic, or sexual attractions to members of one's own sex), and bisexual (having emotional, romantic, or sexual attractions to both men and women) (American Psychological Association, 2016). Sexual orientation may also include one's identity based on attractions and behaviors as well as membership in a community who shares those attractions and behaviors (American Psychological Association, 2016). It is important to note that sexual orientation is distinct from biological sex (the anatomical, physiological, and genetic characteristics associated with being male or female), gender identity (the psychological sense of being male or female), and social gender role (the cultural norms that define feminine and masculine behavior) (American Psychological Association, 2016).

Various cultures and societies throughout the globe have described this continuum of sexual attractions and behaviors, with some applying identity labels to describe persons exhibiting these attractions and behaviors and others choosing not to apply any labels (American Psychological Association, 2016). According to the Los Angeles Conservancy (2016), in the United States the most frequent labels for this community are represented by the initialism of LGBTQIA which includes "lesbians" (women attracted to women); "gay" men (men attracted to men); "bisexual" persons (men or women attracted to both sexes); "transgender" persons (individuals whose personal identities and gender do not correspond to their birth sex); "queer" persons (those who identify as queer or questioning their sexual identity); "intersex" persons (those who do not fit the typical definitions of exclusively male or exclusively female bodies); and "asexual" persons (those who identify as someone who is not attracted to anyone and who has no sexual orientation).

The changes in the LGBTQIA acronym signify the continual evolution in the views and self-perceptions represented within the homosexual community. For example, transgender was added to the acronym to signal the inclusion of those persons who did not identify as "cisgender" wherein there exists a match or congruency between gender identity and gender assigned at birth. Similarly, while the term "queer" was originally defined as "strange," queer scholars reclaimed the term to embrace sexual and gender minorities who do not identify as heterosexual or cisgender (Los Angeles Conservancy, 2016). In addition to asexual, the "A" also represents allies who support the rights of LGBTQIA individuals, but who themselves may not identify as part of this community. To maximize inclusivity, LGBTQ+ is used to represent the full spectrum and range of gender and sexuality. What is clear in research focusing on LGBT communities is the fluidity of sexual and gender identity as well as potential intersections of sexual orientation and gender identity (Ranji, Beamesderfer, Kates, & Salganicoff, 2017). For example, an individual may identify sexually along a spectrum that does not necessarily fit a specific category of lesbian, gay, or bisexual (Ranji et al., 2017). A transgender individual may identify sexually as heterosexual, lesbian, gay, bisexual, or along a spectrum of sexual identity (Ranji et al., 2017). Finally, it is important to understand how sexual and gender identity intersect with race/ethnicity, social economic status, and class, as these complexities then shape and influence the experiences of LGBT individuals in positive and negative ways (Ranji et al., 2017).

One final note on sexual orientation and gender identity labels should be mentioned. Some researchers take issue with the use of such labels for a variety of reasons, including the differences in the ways that societies have defined sexual orientation identities and to the changing meanings of words such as "queer." Research has shown that some societies embrace same-sex acts while others ignore them, assigning no labels to their existence. These nuances and variations necessitate a careful specification of terminology and context in research concerning the LGBT community.

LGBT Population Estimates in the United States and Globally

To provide context for the struggles and achievements of the LGBT community in a variety of arenas including political, health, economic, and social, it is important to gain a sense of the size of this population both within the United States and globally. The data estimating the size of the LGBT population is complicated and flawed for several reasons. First, data collected regarding sexual orientation may only inquire about some of the elements (e.g., attraction, identity, behavior, and membership in a community) that form this construct (American Psychological Association, 2016). For example, some studies focus on same-sex sexual behaviors and attractions while others inquire about identification as gay, lesbian, bisexual, or transgender. This discrepancy is especially impactful to the validity of LGBT population estimates given that many studies conducted in the United States and internationally have suggested that fewer subjects identify as lesbian, gay, bisexual, or transgender as compared to those who report engaging in same-sex sexual behaviors and attractions (Gates, 2011). Additionally, data integrity is further compromised by nonrepresentative studies with small sample sizes, differences in survey administration (e.g., online versus face-to-face), issues of incidence versus prevalence of sexual behaviors, and respondents' concerns regarding confidentiality and privacy (Gates, 2011).

Data from the nationally representative 2017 Gallup Daily Tracking Survey and the Gallup-Sharecare Well-Being Index Survey provide estimates of the percentage of adults in the United States who self-identify as lesbian, gay, bisexual, or transgender. The Gallup data are based on telephone interviews conducted from January 2 to December 30, 2017 with a random sample of 360,604 adults, aged 18 or older, living in all fifty states and the District of Columbia. The Gallup estimates were derived from affirmative answers to the question "Do you personally identify as lesbian, gay, bisexual, or transgender?".

Table 1.1 shows the total percentage of self-identifying LGBT persons, as well as the percentages by sex, race, and birth cohort from 2012 when Gallup began collecting this information to 2017.

Table 1.1 Percent of U.S. adults identifying as LGBT by sex, race/ethnicity, and birth cohort, 2012–2017

	2012	2013	2014	2015	2016	2017
Total percent LGBT	3.5	3.6	3.7	3.9	4.1	4.5
Sex						
Male	3.4	3.5	3.6	3.7	3.7	3.9
Female	3.5	3.6	3.9	4.1	4.4	5.1
Race/ethnicity						
White, non-hispanic	3.2	3.3	3.4	3.5	3.6	4.0
Black, non-hispanic	4.4	4.0	4.6	4.5	4.6	5.0
Hispanic	4.3	4.7	4.9	5.1	5.4	6.1
Asian, non-hispanic	3.5	3.3	4.2	4.9	4.9	4.9
Birth cohort						
Millennials (1980–1999)	5.8	6.0	6.3	6.7	7.3	8.2
Generation X (1965–1979)	3.2	3.3	3.4	3.3	3.2	3.5
Baby boomers (1946–1964)	2.7	2.7	2.7	2.6	2.4	2.4
Traditionalists (1913–1945)	1.8	1.8	1.9	1.5	1.4	1.4

Note Author created using information adapted from U.S. Adults Identifying as LGBT, 2012–2017; Percentage of Americans Identifying as LGBT, by Birth Cohort; Percentage of U.S. Adults Identifying as LGBT by Gender and Birth Cohort, 2012–2017; Gallup Daily Tracking Survey and Gallup-Sharecare Well-Being Index Survey; Release Date May 22, 2018; Retrieved from https://news.gallup.com/poll/234863/estimate-lgbt-population-rises.aspx

Overall, the percentage of U.S. adults identifying as LGBT has increased from 3.5% in 2012 to 4.5% in 2017 (Newport, 2018). According to Gallup, the expanded total LGBT identification percentage is predominantly a function of the increase in LGBT identification among the millennial birth cohort (born between 1980 and 1999) whose percentage increased from 7.3 to 8.7 from 2016 to 2017, and from 5.8 since 2012. By comparison, the Generation X cohort (born between 1965 and 1979) increased its LGBT identification 0.2% from 2016 to 2017, while there was no change in identification from 2016 to 2017 for baby boomers (born between 1946 and 1964) or traditionalists (born before 1946).

In terms of gender, as shown in Table 1.1, estimates of LGBT identification are higher among women, as demonstrated in the 2017 expansion of this gender gap (Newport, 2018). The change in LGBT identification for men has been minimal from 2012 to 2017, whereas the change in LGBT identification for women increased from 3.5% in 2012 to 5.3% in 2017, with the largest increase occurring between 2016 and 2017 (Newport, 2018). Estimates of LGBT identification among race/ethnicity reveal increases since 2012, with the largest increases among Hispanics and Asians. Overall, in 2017 the largest LGBT percentage was found among Hispanics (6.1%) while the lowest percentage was found among Whites (4.0%). In terms of income, since 2012, LGBT identification has consistently been more common among those with lower incomes with 2017 data revealing the largest ever income gap (6.2% for those earning less than $36,000 versus 3.9% for those earning $90,000 or more). No significant differences in LGBT identification have emerged by educational attainment.

GLOBAL ESTIMATES OF THE LGBT POPULATION

Turning toward global estimates of the LGBT population presents additional data challenges. First concepts of "gay" that are common in Western nations including the United States, are not as prevalent in non-Western nations. For example, some men who have sex with men do not relate to the term "gay" or "homosexual" and do not consider sex with other men as sexual activity, instead conceptualizing sexual activity as sex with women. Some men in Africa and Latin America for example, refer to themselves as heterosexual although they may engage in sexual relationships with other men (e.g., Anyamele, Lwabaayi, Nguyen, & Binswanger, 2005; Gonzalez, 2007), leading to challenges in gathering data concerning the identity component of sexual orientation. In terms of Latin America, the 2010 Brazil national census identified 60,000 same-sex couples in a population of 190.7 million (Institute of Brazil Geography and Statistics, 2010).

In Africa, men who have sex with men typically also have sex with women, get married, and have children. Most African countries legally prohibit sex between those of the same gender as such laws were introduced during colonization (Anyamele et al., 2005). Stigma and discrimination against those who have sex with partners of the same-sex leads to a great deal of underreporting of the behavioral aspect of sexual orientation (Anyamele et al., 2005). Some limited survey data regarding the behavioral aspects of sexual orientation in sub-Saharan Africa found that 18% of males and 44% of females in a Sengalese survey reported a homosexual experience (Brody & Potterat, 2003). In a 2002 survey of men who have sex with men (MSM) in Dakaar, the vast majority reported having had sex with women, 13% were married and 25% had children (Niang et al., 2002).

Regarding western European countries, a review of recent available nationally representative survey data sheds light on the identity aspect of

Table 1.2 Percentages of self-identified LGB adults in selected Western European countries

Country	Survey year	LGB percentage estimate (range for both sexes) (%)
Australia	2012–2013	1.3–2.2
Israel	2012	4.8–8.2
New Zealand	2013	1.1–3
Britain	2014	1.6–2.6

Note Author created using information adapted from Richters et al. (2014), Smith, Rissel, Richters, Grulich, and De Visser (2003), Mor and Davidovich (2016), Dickson, van Roode, Cameron, and Paul (2013), and Office for National Statistics (2014)

sexual orientation. Data from Australia, Israel, New Zealand, and Britain is shown in Table 1.2.

The data are quite consistent across these selected countries, and are overall lower than estimates obtained in the United States. It is important to note that the available global data represents the entire population as compared with recent Gallup data from the United States that provides additional analyses of LGBT identification by gender, birth cohort, race/ethnicity, income, and educational attainment. These differences in data richness make comparisons between LGBT identification in the United States and internationally problematic.

While the aforementioned estimates of the current domestic and international LGBT and LGB population are instructive, it is important to note that historically, estimates of this population have not been based on representative data in the United States or abroad. In fact, the discrimination and bias faced by those identifying as LGBT was a significant and often insurmountable barrier to accurately gauging the size of this population; moreover, nationally representative samples in both the United States and globally did not consistently include a standard set of sexual orientation items until relatively recently (e.g., Institute of Medicine, 2011; U.S. DHHS, 2010).

Overview of the History of Homosexuality

As the origins, definition, and size of the LGBT population have been presented, it is informative to also consider an abridged history of homosexuality, as an exhaustive and complete delineation is beyond the scope of this volume. The history of homosexuality reveals a shifting sense of society's view of same-sex relationships and same-sex behaviors that depend upon historical and political context, place, and time period. Societal attitudes have ranged from widespread engagement in same-sex relationships to acceptance, to viewing such relationships as sinful, to formally declaring same-sex sexual behaviors as illegal and even punishable by death. Over time, the history of homosexuality demonstrates that innumerable individuals have suffered from discrimination, bias, stigmatization, and violence due to their sexual orientation.

The history of homosexuality reveals a shifting sense of society's view of same-sex relationships and same-sex behaviors that depend upon historical and political context, place, and time period. Societal attitudes have ranged from widespread engagement in same-sex relationships to acceptance, to viewing such relationships as sinful, to formally declaring same-sex sexual behaviors as illegal and even punishable by death. Over time, the history of homosexuality demonstrates that innumerable individuals have suffered from discrimination, bias, stigmatization, and violence due to their sexual orientation. Before providing a brief, abridged version of homosexuality, first it is important to discuss the origins and definition of homosexuality as well as estimates of the size of the homosexual population within the United States and globally.

LGBT history begins with ancient civilizations around the globe, as evidenced by art, literary, music, and other cultural and political references. The historical record reveals centuries of discrimination, bias, and persecution of LGBT individuals and communities, leading to secrecy and shame as well as to resiliency and hope. From ancient Greece and Rome come the earliest documents referencing same-sex relationships. In Greece, it was common practice for older free men to have a younger same-sex lover who could be a slave or free, with such relationships sometimes described as a valued method of mentoring and teaching (Skinner, 2014). Similarly to ancient Greece, evidence exists of same-sex relationships in ancient Rome between older free men and young males who were slaves or free; however, by the time of the reign of Emperor Justinian in 558 homosexuality was declared illegal and an affront to God (Skinner, 2014). Shifting to Asia reveals references in ancient Chinese literature to homosexuality since approximately 600 BC with some scholars concluding that homosexuality was common among emperors in several dynasties including the Han, Song, Ming, and Qing (Dynes, 2015).

Painting and literature from ancient Japan, Thailand, India, Mesopotamia, and Melanesia refer to the practice of homosexuality, often among royalty and within religious rituals, dating back over one thousand years (Dynes, 2015). In ancient Israel, homosexuality was forbidden by God and punished severely as depicted in the story of Sodom and Gomorrah, in which God destroyed the city in retribution for an attempted homosexual rape (Dynes, 2015). Although the legal definition of sodomy encompasses oral sex, anal sex, and bestiality (sex between humans and animals), over time and in practice the term sodomy has become associated with homosexual sexual activity that was deemed immoral and unnatural (Newton, 2009).

Turning toward the Middle East finds disputes among Egyptologists and historians regarding the status and practice of homosexuality in ancient Egypt as evidence of homosexuality during that era is considered vague and speculative. In Middle Eastern Muslin cultures, since ancient times homosexuality has been practiced but not sanctioned, with same-sex sexual behaviors labeled as illegal and punishable by death in some countries such as Saudi Arabia, Iran, Qatar, United Arab Emirates, and Yemen (Mooney, Knox, & Schacht, 2017). In the Americas prior to European colonization, evidence suggests that individuals of homosexual and gender variant identities were included in the social and ceremonial aspects of their communities, perhaps occupying respected spiritual and social duties as "Two Spirit" people in some Indigenous cultures (Leland, 2006). As Spain colonized Native Americans throughout the Americas, the Spanish colonizers attempted to end same-sex sexual behavior through severe and violent penalties including public execution and burning (Leland, 2006).

Similarly to ancient Greece and Rome, the Renaissance era (1300–1600) included the common practice of same-sex sexual behavior; however, the Roman Catholic Church led the shift from homosexual activity being legal throughout most of Europe to being punishable in violent and cruel means such as removal of the testicles and penis, burning, stoning, mutilations, and execution (Dynes, 2015). By 1533 King Henry VIII had declared all sexual activity between males punishable by death (Dynes, 2015). Moving forward in time to the late eighteenth and nineteenth century Europe reveals that the new field of psychology often cast homosexuals as criminals, degenerates, and psychopaths (Dynes, 2015). In 1791, France decriminalized homosexual acts, including sodomy, between consenting adults, becoming the first West European country to do so (Dynes, 2015). During the late nineteenth century and up until Adolph Hitler's Third Reich or rule of Germany, Berlin was known for its robust LGBT rights movement as typified by Magnus Hirschfelf, a Jewish doctor, who in 1897 founded the first gay rights organization which sought to legalize sodomy and socially recognize homosexual and transgender men and women (Dynes, 2015). During the 1920s Berlin was home to bars, clubs, newspapers, and demonstrations that benefited gay men and lesbians (Dynes, 2015). As the Third Reich ushered in Hitler's brutality in 1933, evidence exists of the sentencing of nearly 50,000 men to concentration camps where many of these vulnerable prisoners died from extreme persecution levied by German soldiers and other prisoners (Dynes, 2015).

In the United States, prior to the American Civil War, most of the country was rural, providing less visibility and opportunities to build community among homosexual persons. Additionally, laws in the United States regarding homosexuality were initially based on British laws which levied the ultimate penalty of execution for the crime of sodomy. Later in the eighteenth century in 1786, Pennsylvania became the first state to remove the death penalty for the practice of sodomy, with all other states following suit within a generation (Dynes, 2015). The repeal of the death penalty for sodomy was accompanied by a shift in language from references to religious damnation to that of abomination (Dynes, 2015). Further, beginning in the twentieth century, some states began to legalize anal intercourse among heterosexual persons while still codifying homosexual anal intercourse as illegal (Dynes, 2015).

In the early twentieth century after World War I, society's awareness and acceptance of homosexual culture was growing, especially in cities such as New York where large numbers of homosexual persons developed communities within the Greenwich Village and Harlem neighborhoods (Carter, 2004). By the mid-1930s, societal mores had shifted once more to conservative Victorian values, which promoted "purity" campaigns, censorship laws, the codification of homosexuality as a mental illness, and large-scale arrests of suspected homosexuals (Dynes, 2015). During this period, LGBT persons were viewed as diseased but curable with treatments such as castration, lobotomies, and electroshock therapy (Dynes, 2015).

The opportunity for nearly 250,000 women to serve in the armed forces in World War II also opened the possibility for lesbians to meet partners, some of whom identified with "masculine" appearances and "men's" occupations such as mechanics and engineers (Dynes, 2015). After the war, many women, including lesbians, chose to remain in nontraditional gender roles, providing support for nascent social movements including the women's movement and the gay liberation movement (Dynes, 2015).

HOMOSEXUALITY AS A SOCIAL MOVEMENT 1950S AND 1960S

In the post-war era, the United States was fueled by a fierce anti-communism embodied by the Army-McCarthy hearings led by Senator Joseph McCarthy in 1954. The hearings sought to expose supposed security risks, including those persons labeled as communists, anarchists, and homosexuals in the U.S. government, military, and other government-funded institutions (Carter, 2004). These hearings led to the denial of and dismissal from federal jobs and to the dishonorable military discharges of thousands of U.S. citizens (Adam, 1987). Homosexual persons were given the right to serve openly in the military a half-century later when then President Barack Obama signed a directive in 2010 (Bumiller, 2011). During the 1950s and 1960s, the Federal Bureau of Investigation (FBI), local police departments, and the U.S. postal service continued to persecute and discriminate against homosexuals on several fronts including maintaining lists and postal addresses of "known" homosexuals (Edsall, 2003).

New York City during the 1950s and 1960s offers a prime example of the discrimination that local police levied at the homosexual community. "Gay" bars known to be frequented by homosexuals were often raided and closed while local newspapers printed the names of the customers (Bausum, 2015). Similarly, undercover transit authority police attempted to entrap and arrest homosexuals for soliciting sex in public spaces such as beaches and parks (e.g., Adam, 1987; Carter, 2004). In 1964, Robert Wagner Jr., the mayor of New York City, sought a "tough on crime" reputation by revoking the liquor licenses and closing all of the gay bars as the city geared up for the 1964 World's Fair and ensuing national and global publicity (Bausum, 2015).

The election of Mayor John Lindsay in 1965 ushered in a less restrictive attitude toward and more positive treatment of the homosexual community and pioneering homophile activist groups such as the New York City Mattachine Society (Bausum, 2015). While the original goals of the Mattachine Society and a similar organization for lesbians, the Daughters of Bilitis, focused on educating and unifying homosexuals and assisting with legal issues, that approach was considered radical at the time and was replaced by efforts to convince heterosexuals of their "normality," similarity to hetero-sexuals, and respectability through silent protests and educational lectures (Carter, 2004). In 1966 bowing to pressure emanating from protests such as a sit-in or "sip-in" at Julius' Bar in Greenwich Village led by Dick Leitsch and Craig Rodgwell, New York City Mattachine Society's president and vice president respectively, Mayor Lindsay ended the sanctioned practice of police entrapment at gay bars and soon thereafter ordered the removal of questions regarding homosexuality on employment applications in New York City (Bausum, 2015). Although police and fire departments refused to enact the new policy, the changes in law, the increased acceptance of freedom of sexual expression, and continued activism by the Mattachine Society paved the way for a more radical and empowering social movement ignited by the 1969 Stonewall Inn riots.

The Stonewall Inn: Respite and Refuge

In 1969 both licensed and unlicensed "gay" bars operated in Greenwich Village, a neighborhood of Manhattan, New York City (Bausum, 2015). One of the most popular unlicensed gay bars was the Stonewall Inn which began operating in 1967 in Greenwich Village at the address of 51 and 53 Christopher Street (Bausum, 2015).

> For me, there was no bar like the Stonewall, because the Stonewall was like the watering hole on the savannah. You know, it's just, everybody was there. We were all there. (M. Boyce, personal interview, Bausum, 2015, *Stonewall: Breaking Out in the Fight for Gay Rights*, p. 23)

Although police entrapment of gay patrons at licensed bars was no longer formally sanctioned, the practice continued this practice into the late 1960s, creating a climate wherein organized crime operated unlicensed gay bars such as the Stonewall Inn (Bausum, 2015).

Carter (2004) describes several aspects, features, and historical realities which led to the immense popularity of the Stonewall Inn. First, same-sex couples were allowed to dance together, despite a local law prohibiting same-sex dancing and "masquerading" or wearing clothing identified as the opposite sex's clothes (Carter, 2004). Second, the bar's two dance floors with jukeboxes and flashing lights added to the ambience while also serv-ing as a warning sign of impending and routine police raids that resulted in arrests of the patrons and the collection of briberies from the bar's owners

(Carter, 2004). The Stonewall was unique among other gay bars in that it provided a place for customers with intersectional identities along a spectrum of sexuality, gender, race, and ethnicity to find respite, friends, and lovers (Carter, 2004). Carter (2004)'s interviews with some customers of the Stonewall Inn also revealed bitterness that routine societal, police, and local governmental discrimination and bias left them with few to no other options besides the Stonewall Inn.

In fact the customers of the Stonewall Inn sought out refuge in this space despite its physical dangers and indignities (e.g., no fire exits, unsanitary conditions, exorbitant liquor prices, and routine police raids) in exchange for a space to find common ground (Carter, 2004). Indeed, in 1969 in New York City, to avoid ridicule and possible arrest, it was rare for homosexuals to openly express their sexuality in public or show any signs of affection for same-sex partners (Bausum, 2015).

> The closet door was so tight back then. (D. Garvin, personal interview, Carter, 2004, *Stonewall: The Riots That Sparked the Gay Revolution*, p. 49)

The Riots Begin

Bausum (2015) and Carter (2004) describe the details of the Stonewall Inn riots and their significance in igniting the modern-day gay rights movement. The riots occurred over a period of six days, beginning at about 1 a.m. on Friday, June 27, 1969 in response to a police raid by the Public Morals Squad. In contrast to prior raids which usually resulted in arrests followed by the quick reopening of the bar, this raid sought to resolve an alleged mafia extortion scheme involving some Stonewall Inn patrons by permanently closing the Stonewall Inn. Unlike prior raids in which patrons cooperated with police who checked their identification and the sex of customers dressed as women, on the night of the riots, men and women customers refused to follow the police's orders within the bar and lingered outside of the bar without dispersing. This atypical resistance resulted in the police's attempts to transport nearly 200 customers to the police station. As patrons exited the bar but remained outside, a fight ensued between the police and one of the lesbian patrons of the Stonewall Inn. The police's attack of the woman with a club spurred the anger and frustration of local inhabitants of Greenwich Village, including many members of the LGBT community who routinely suffered from discrimination, bias, and harassment associated with their intersectional identities (Carter, 2004). The thousands of people in the crowd engaged with the police by lighting trash on fire and throwing debris, rocks, and bottles as "the tension of the night and countless previous nights and hundreds of lifetimes of abuse burst the dams of person after person" (Bausum, 2015).

The Tactical Patrol Force (TPF), whose purpose was to control riots, failed to disperse the crowds who used their knowledge of the area's many one-way streets to taunt and confront the police in non-traditional and unexpected ways including forming kick lines and singing (Carter, 2004). The riots continued for several additional days, as bystanders and even tourists joined in the battle against the police. The publicity surrounding the riots was mostly due to the strategic-thinking of Craig Rodwell, one of the leaders of the Mattachine Society New York, who successfully garnered coverage in three local newspapers (Carter, 2004). Ironically, one of the local papers, *The Village Voice*, which is known today for its support of gay civil rights and the annual Gay Pride parade, demonstrated bias and derogatory coverage of the riots as evidenced by the outlet's use of the terms "the Sunday fag follies" and "Limp wrists" (Carter, 2004).

The Stonewall Inn riots had both immediate and long term consequences. Clendinen and Nagourney (1999) summarize the sense of transformation resulting from the resistance:

> Before the riots, homosexuals were "a secret legion of people, known but discounted, ignored, laughed at or despised...But that night, for the first time, the usual acquiescence turned into violent resistance...From that night the lives of millions of gay men and lesbians, and the attitude toward them of the larger culture in which they lived, began to change rapidly. People began to appear in public as homosexuals, demanding respect." (p. 12)

The intense reaction to years of police harassment launched a sustained and long-lasting movement for change, dignity, and equal treatment under the law. At the same time, it is important to note that some of the more "traditional" members of the gay community expressed dismay that drag queens singing and dancing in the streets undermined their efforts of gaining heterosexual's acceptance into society (Carter, 2004). The momentum from the Stonewall riots gave rise to new gay rights organizations such as the Gay Liberation Front or GLF (Carter, 2004). Although the GLF, the first group to include "gay" in its name, withstood the strain of conflicting strategic goals and principles for only a few months, activists soon formed the Gay Activists Alliance (GAA) to focus exclusively on gay civil rights. The GAA became known for their masterful use of the "zap," a public, political, and theatrical technique used to advocate for gay rights (Carter, 2004). One interesting aftershock of the Stonewall riots was the closing of the Stonewall Inn, attributed to the damage to the building as well as to boycotts against its mafia-ownership (Carter, 2004).

The Stonewall Inn riots were first commemorated on June 28, 1970 by Craig Rodwell and other gay activists as the first Christopher Street Liberation Day, which were attended by nearly 5000 participants marching peacefully up Sixth Avenue in New York City (Carter, 2004). The national publicity and interest in this initial march grew over time and eventually became known as Gay Pride events throughout the United States and countries across the globe (Carter, 2004). The rainbow gay pride flag, the universal and global symbol of the struggle for gay civil rights created in 1978 by Gilbert Baker, was first displayed at a march protesting the assassination of Harvey Milk, a prominent gay rights activist and politician in San Francisco (Wickman, 2013). Ironically, Baker created the flag at the request of Milk, who had sought an enduring symbol for gay pride (Bausum, 2015). Milk had a prescient understanding that his open fight for gay rights could lead to his untimely death, as he expressed in 1977 taped interview that he requested be played in the event of his assassination:

> If a bullet should enter my brain, let that bullet destroy every closet door. (quoted in Shilts, 1982, *The Mayor of Castro Street: The Life and Times of Harvey Milk*)

The 1970s ushered in both unity and calls for increased acceptance of the LGBT community as well as disagreements and struggles segmented by race, class, and gender (Carter, 2004). Rifts between lesbians and gay men surfaced as lesbians pointed out multiple areas of misalignment, including the patriarchal attitudes among some gay men as well as the focus on issues of police entrapment that did not resonate within the lesbian community (Carter, 2004). The societal acceptance of homosexuality once again shifted by the late 1970s as renewed religious conservatism led to new anti-gay sentiment marked by discrimination, harassment, and bias toward the LGBT community (Bausum, 2015).

The 1980s and 1990s gave rise to a proliferation and growth of thousands of gay rights activist groups in both the United States and globally

(Carter, 2004). Many of these groups still pay homage to the Stonewall Inn riots, as is the case with Stonewall Equity Limited or Stonewall, a British LGBT rights charity founded in 1989 and named for the Stonewall Inn riots. This group has paid tribute to British lesbian, gay, and bisexual people as well as allies since 2006 ("Stonewall: Acceptance without exception", 2015).

During the presidency of Barack Obama, the LGBT community found expanded recognition and acceptance as evidenced by President Obama's recognition of the contributions of the transgender community in the fight for LGBT rights. In a 2009 proclamation, President Obama acknowledged the importance of LGBT Pride Month as a way of honoring the Stonewall legacy and confirmed his support for LGBT civil and political rights (Obama, 2009). President Obama's actions spoke volumes for his support of the transgender community in 2010 when he appointed Amanda Simpson, the first openly transgender person to serve in a U.S. government post, as the Senior Technical Advisor to the Commerce Department (Tapper, 2010). Simpson's gratitude and hope for sustained progress was captured in her quote at the time of her appointment, as she said that "as one of the first transgender presidential appointees to the federal government, I hope that I will soon be one of hundreds, and that this appointment opens future opportunities for many others" (Tapper, 2010). President Obama continued to demonstrate unprecedented executive branch support for the LGBT community by creating the first American memorial to honor LGBT civil rights. According to President Obama, the Stonewall National Monument, which occupies the same space that was once home to the Stonewall Inn, "changed the nation's history. The quest for LGBT equality after Stonewall evolved from protests and small gatherings into a nationwide movement" (Obama, 2016). President Obama's support for diversity and inclusion were apparent as he addressed the crowd gathered to celebrate the new monument:

> I'm designating the Stonewall National Monument as the newest addition to America's National Park System. Stonewall will be our first national monument to tell the story of the struggle for LGBT rights. I believe our national parks should reflect the full story of our country, the richness and diversity and uniquely American spirit that has always defined us. That we are stronger together. That out of many, we are one. (Obama, 2016, para. 3)

STRUCTURE OF THE VOLUME

This chapter provided historical context and perspective for the remainder of this volume. After presenting the origins, definition of homosexuality, and estimates of the LGBT population, the chapter provided an abridged history of homosexuality which demonstrated that homosexuals throughout the globe have faced continuous and severe prejudice, discrimination, and violence from ancient times until today. The chapter described the Stonewall Inn riots as the catalyst for the modern-day gay liberation movement. The remainder of the volume argues that the failure to extend equitable civil and political rights and equal protection under the law to LGBT individuals as well as efforts to reverse gains in such rights has and will continue to be associated with stress, bias, stigma and discrimination experienced within this community, both in the United States and globally. In turn, this sustained stress, bias and stigma are consistently and strongly associated with a host of LGBT civil, political, and health inequalities.

As discrimination against lesbian, gay, and bisexual people in a variety of arenas remains widespread, Chapter 2 focusses on the legal status of homosexuality regarding same-sex sexual behavior, same-sex marriage and adoption, anti-discrimination laws and legal protections in military service and refugee rights, and remedies for hate crimes. Chapter 3 discusses the impacts on the health of the LGBT community emanating from their struggles to access culturally competent health care and adequate health insurance.

Chapter 4, which focuses on the history, transmission, risk-factors, prevention and intervention of HIV/AIDS, provides context for the devastation and loss of life among the LGBT community that in many ways resulted from discrimination, stigmatization, and bias. Chapter 5 discusses substance use and abuse in the LGBT population with a specific focus on alcohol, cigarettes, and prescription drugs. Mental health is featured in Chapter 6, with attention given to psychological distress, suicide, homelessness, reparative therapies, and resiliency and protective factors. Given numerous surveys and reports indicating that physical abuse is still commonly experienced among lesbian, gay, and bisexual people, Chapter 7 discusses violence within the LGBT community in several forms and spaces including among incarcerated individuals and victims of human trafficking.

Each chapter will also discuss the variability within and between LGBT individuals and communities that include both protective factors and supports that may form important components of intervention and prevention strategies aimed at reducing health disparities among the LGBT community domestically and throughout the globe. While the volume is not exhaustive in its scope, it provides a cogent examination of the negative and sometimes dire consequences stemming from deliberate, consistent and sustained unfair and unequal treatment based solely on sexual orientation. The conclusion of the volume provides a framework for future reflection as challenges to the civil rights, health, and well-being of the LGBT population continue to mount.

References

Adam, B. (1987). *The rise of a gay and lesbian movement.* Woodbridge, CT: Twayne Publishers.

Allport, G. (1954). *The nature of prejudice.* Reading, MA: Addison-Wesley.

American Psychological Association. (2016). *Answers to your questions: For a better understanding of sexual orientation and homosexuality.* Retrieved from http://www.apa.org/topics/lgbt/orientation.aspx.

Anyamele, C., Lwabaayi, R., Nguyen, T. V., & Binswanger, H. (2005). *Sexual minorities, violence and AIDS in Africa* (Africa Region Working Paper Series No. 84). Retrieved from http://documents.worldbank.org/curated/en/665071468001786948/pdf/342450PAPER0Sexual0minorities0wp84.pdf.

Bausum, A. (2015). *Stonewall: Breaking out in the fight for gay rights.* New York, NY: Speak.

Brody, S., & Potterat, J. (2003). Assessing the role of anal intercourse in the epidemiology of AIDS in Africa. *International Journal of STD and AIDS, 14,* 431–436.

Bumiller, E. (2011, July 22). Obama ends 'Don't Ask, Don't Tell' policy. *The New York Times.* Retrieved from http://www.nytimes.com/2011/07/23/us/23military.html?_r=0.

Carter, D. (2004). *Stonewall: The riots that sparked the gay revolution.* New York, NY: St. Martin's Griffin.

Clendinen, D., & Nagourney, A. (1999). *Out for good: The struggle to build a gay rights movement in America.* New York, NY: Simon & Schuster.

Dickson, N., van Roode, T., Cameron, C., & Paul, C. (2013). Stability and change in same-sex attraction, experience, and identity by sex and age in a New Zealand birth cohort. *Archives of Sexual Behavior, 42*(5), 753–763.

Dynes, W. (Ed.). (2015). *Encyclopedia of homosexuality* (Vol. 1). New York, NY: Routledge.

Edsall, N. (2003). *Toward Stonewall: Homosexuality and society in the modern western world*. Charlottesville: University of Virginia Press.

Feray, J., & Herzer, M. (1990). Homosexual studies and politics in the nineteenth century: Karl Maria Kertbeny. *Journal of Homosexuality, 19*(1), 34–35.

Gates, G. (2011). *How many people are lesbian, gay, bisexual, and transgender?* The Williams Institute, UCLA School of Law. Retrieved from http://williamsinstitute.law.ucla.edu/wp-content/uploads/Gates-How-Many-People-LGBT-Apr-2011.pdf.

Goffman, E. (1963). *Stigma: Notes on the management of spoiled identity*. New York, NY: Touchstone.

Gonzalez, M. (2007). Latinos on da down low: The limitations of sexual identity in public health. *Latino Studies, 5*(1), 25–52.

Institute of Brazil Geography and Statistics. (2010). *Atlas of the 2010 Population Census*. Retrieved from http://censo2010.ibge.gov.br/apps/atlas/.

Institute of Medicine. (2011). *The health of lesbian, gay, bisexual, and transgender people: Building a foundation for better understanding*. Washington, DC: National Academies Press. Retrieved from http://www.ncbi.nlm.nih.gov/books/NBK64806/. https://doi.org/10.17226/13128.

Leland, J. (2006, October 8). A spirit of belonging: Inside and out. *The New York Times*.

Los Angeles Conservancy. (2016). *Explanation of LGBTQ terms*. Retrieved from https://www.laconservancy.org/explanation-lgbtq-terms.

Meyer, I. (2003). Prejudice, social stress, and mental health in lesbian, gay and bisexual populations: Conceptual issues and research evidence. *Psychological Bulletin, 129*, 674–697.

Meyer, I. (2010). Identify, stress, and resilience in lesbians, gay men, and bisexuals of color. *Counseling Psychologist, 38*(3), 1–9.

Mooney, L., Knox, D., & Schacht, C. (2017). *Understanding social problems* (10th ed.). Boston, MA: Cengage Learning.

Mor, Z., & Davidovich, U. (2016). Sexual orientation and behavior of adult Jews in Israel and the association with risk behavior. *Archives of Sexual Behavior, 45*(6), 1563–1571.

Newport, F. (2018, May 22). *In U.S., estimates of LGBT population rises to 4.5%* [Web log post]. Retrieved from https://news.gallup.com/poll/234863/estimate-lgbt-population-rises.aspx?version=print.

Newton, D. (2009). *Gay and lesbian rights: A reference handbook* (2nd ed., Contemporary World Issues). Santa Barbara, CA: ABC-CLIO.

Niang, C. I., Diagne, M., Niang, Y., Mody, M. A., Gomis, D., Diouf, M., … Castle, C. (2002). *Meeting the sexual health needs of men who have sex with men in Senegal*. Horizons Program, USAID. New York: Population Council Inc. Retrieved from http://www.who.int/hiv/topics/vct/sw_toolkit/men_sex_men_senegal.pdf.

Obama, B. (2009, June 1). *Lesbian, gay, bisexual and transgender pride month.* Retrieved from https://www.whitehouse.gov/the-press-office/presidential-proclamation-lgbt-pride-month.

Obama, B. (2016, June 24). *President Obama designates Stonewall National Monument.* Retrieved from https://www.whitehouse.gov/blog/2016/06/24/president-obama-designates-stonewall-national-monument.

Office for National Statistics. (2014). *Integrated Household Survey.* Retrieved from http://webarchive.nationalarchives.gov.uk/20160105160709, http://www.ons.gov/uk/ons/dcp171778_418136.pdf.

Ranji, U., Beamesderfer, A., Kates, J., & Salganicoff, A. (2017, August). *Health and access to care and coverage for lesbian, gay, bisexual, and transgender individuals in the U.S.* Retrieved from http://files.kff.org/attachment/Issue-Brief-Health-and-Access-to-Care-and-Coverage-for-LGBT-Individuals-in-the-US.

Richters, J., Altman, D., Badcock, P., Smith, A., de Visser, R., Grulich, A. E., … Simpson, J. (2014). Sexual identity, sexual attraction and sexual experience: The second Australian study of health and relationships. *Sexual Health, 11*(5), 451–460.

Shilts, R. (1982). *The Mayor of Castro Street: The life and times of Harvey Milk.* New York, NY: St. Martin's Press.

Skinner, M. (2014). *Sexuality in Greek and Roman culture.* Sussex, UK: Wiley.

Smith, A., Rissel, C., Richters, J., Grulich, A., & De Visser, R. (2003). Sex in Australia: Sexual identity, sexual attraction and sexual experience among a representative sample of adults. *Australian and New Zealand Journal of Public Health, 27*(2), 138–145.

Stonewall: Acceptance without exception. (2015). *Ian McKellen, Stonewall co-founder, hosts the tenth and final Stonewall Awards.* Retrieved from http://www.stonewall.org.uk/news/ian-mckellen-host-stonewalls-final-awards-ceremony.

Tapper, J. (2010, January 4). *President Obama names transgender appointee to commerce department* [Web log post]. Retrieved from http://blogs.abcnews.com/politicalpunch/2010/01/president-obama-names-transgender-appointee-to-commerce-department.html.

U.S. Department of Health and Human Services, Office of Disease Prevention and Health Promotion. (2010). *Healthy people 2020.* Washington, DC. Retrieved from http://www.healthypeople.gov/2020/default.aspx.

Walker, A. (1983). *In search of our mothers' gardens: Womanist prose.* San Diego, CA: Harcourt.

Wickman, F. (2013, June 26). *A rainbow marriage: How did the rainbow become a symbol of gay pride?* [Web log post]. Retrieved from http://www.slate.com/articles/life/explainer/2012/06/rainbows_and_gay_pride_how_the_rainbow_became_a_symbol_of_the_glbt_movement_.h.

CHAPTER 2

Legal Status and Challenges to Homosexuality

Chapter 1 of this volume provided an abridged account of the history of homosexuality from ancient times until present day, highlighting the constant theme of discrimination, bias, and persecution levied upon the LGBT community. This chapter will first provide a brief overview of the perception of and consequences of same-sex sexual behavior while also discussing recent legal gains in marriage and adoption rights for same-sex couples.

> Once I knew this kid who very bravely and bossily came out of the closet when she was only fourteen years old. She told me then that we can't choose who we love. We just love the people we love, no matter what anyone else might want for us. Wasn't that you? (from Madeline George, 2012, *The Difference Between Me and You*)

Next, this chapter will focus on selected additional national and international legal challenges faced by the LGBT community including discrimination and legal challenges in employment, housing, education, public accommodations, military service, refugee protections, and hate crimes.

© The Author(s) 2020
S. R. Notaro, *Marginality and Global LGBT Communities*,
Neighborhoods, Communities, and Urban Marginality,
https://doi.org/10.1007/978-3-030-22415-8_2

SAME-SEX SEXUAL BEHAVIORS IN THE UNITED STATES AND GLOBALLY

Chapter 1's historical review of homosexuality included numerous references to same-sex sexual behavior, often codified as sodomy. While the term sodomy originates from the homosexual activities of men in the story of the city of Sodom and Gomorrah in the *Bible*, over time, sodomy became associated with oral and anal sex among homosexuals that was deemed unnatural and perverse by courts of law and societies across the globe (The Free Dictionary, 2016). Sodomy was classified as a felony throughout the United States with the exception of Illinois until the 2003 U.S. Supreme Court decision, *Lawrence v. Texas*, in which the Court ruled that sexual activities between two consenting adults were legal.

Next, the timeline of the changes in the legal status of homosexuality throughout the globe will be summarized. For example, in France in 1791 during the French Revolution, sodomy was decriminalized along with other "victimless-crimes" including heresy, witchcraft, and blasphemy (Dynes, 2015). Similarly, during the nineteenth century, homosexual acts were decriminalized throughout most of the countries in Europe ruled by France, Brazil, and the Ottoman Empire (Dynes, 2015). During the early twentieth century after Lenin and Trotsky's Bolshevik Revolution, Russia decriminalized homosexuality, only to have it criminalized again under Stalin's rein in the 1920s (Dynes, 2015). While Britain had criminalized homosexual activity in 1885, a series of arrests, prosecutions, and sensational trials of alleged homosexuals immediately after World War II as well as the results of a report from a governmental committee chaired by Sir John Wolfenden led to the 1957 legalization of consensual homosexual behavior in the United Kingdom (Dynes, 2015).

As of 2018, sodomy has been decriminalized throughout Europe, North America, South America, Israel, Japan, Kazakhstan, the Philippines, and Thailand. Despite this trend, some nations continue to criminalize homosexual activity including parts of the Caribbean (e.g., Antigua and Barbuda, Barbados, Dominica, Grenada, Guyana, Jamaica, Saint Kitts and Nevis, Saint Lucia, and Saint Vincent and the Grenadines). Life imprisonment is imposed for homosexual activity in several African (e.g., Sierra Leone, Tanzania, Uganda) and Asian (e.g., Bangladesh, the Maldives, Myanmar) countries. The ultimate punishment of death is meted out in the African countries of Mauritania, Sudan, Nigeria, Somalia, and the Asian countries of

Afghanistan, Pakistan, Qatar, Brunei, Iran, Iraq, Saudi Arabia, the United Arab Emirates, and Yemen.

The history of China's treatment of same-sex sexual behaviors is worthy of examination, given that China and several other Asian countries (e.g., Taiwan, North Korea, South Korea, Vietman) have never had Western-style sodomy laws (Dynes, 2015). As discussed in Chapter 1 of this volume, homosexuality and same-sex sexual behaviors have been documented in art, culture, and music in China since ancient times; however, in China same-sex sexual activity was illegal until 1997 and classified as a mental illness until 2001. Currently, reports of overt crimes against homosexuals is rare; however, the government does not promote gay issues in China, choosing instead to support a policy of ambivalence and in some cases censorship of same-sex sexual behaviors as portrayed in entertainment outlets such as film, television, and the internet. On December 31, 2015, the China Television Drama Production Industry Association officially banned the depiction of "abnormal sexual relationships and behaviors, such as incest, same-sex relationships, sexual perversion, sexual assault, sexual abuse, sexual violence, and so on" (Lu & Hunt, 2016).

SAME-SEX MARRIAGE AND ADOPTION IN THE UNITED STATES AND GLOBALLY

Related to the acceptance or rejection of same-sex sexual behaviors, is the topic of same-sex marriage and the legal rights associated with marriage. In 2015, marriage between same-sex couples was declared legal in every state as a result of the United States Supreme Court decision in *Obergefell v. Hodges*. The Supreme Court ruled in a 5–4 decision that the right to marry is guaranteed to same-sex couples by both the Due Process Clause and the Equal Protection Clause of the Fourteenth Amendment to the United States Constitution. Since March 2016, same-sex married couples may legally adopt children nationwide (Barbash, 2016) as a result of a ruling by Mississippi U.S. District Court judge Daniel P. Jordan III. In the case, *Campaign for Southern Equality v. Mississippi Department of Human Services* (2016), Judge Jordan ruled that Mississippi's state ban on same-sex adoption was unconstitutional, violating the Equal Protection Clause of the United States constitution and denying the full benefits of marriage, including adoption, to same-sex couples. As Mississippi's law prohibiting same-sex adoption was the last such state ban in the United States, Judge

Jordan's ruling effectively cleared the way for same-sex adoption throughout the United States (Barbash, 2016).

In terms of the global landscape for same-sex marriage, Fig. 2.1 demonstrates the range of the legal status and recognition of unions between same-sex individuals in countries worldwide. Some countries prohibit all same-sex unions, while others recognize limited aspects of same-sex unions including partnership certificates, residency rights, and civil unions. As of 2018, 25 countries, all of which are classified as developed or developing democracies, recognized same-sex marriage and all of the legal rights associated with marriage.

As is the case with homosexuality broadly, China's prohibition against same-sex marriage and adoption demonstrates resistance in granting full civil and legal rights to the LGBT community. In fact, several attempts by Chinese activists in 2000, 2004, 2006, and 2007 failed to gain the required support for a bill in the National People's Congress that would have legalized same-sex marriage. Today in China the tradition of family obligations to carry on the family line continues to exert pressure on homosexuals and gay men in particular to hide their sexual orientation and instead to marry an opposite-sex partner and have a child.

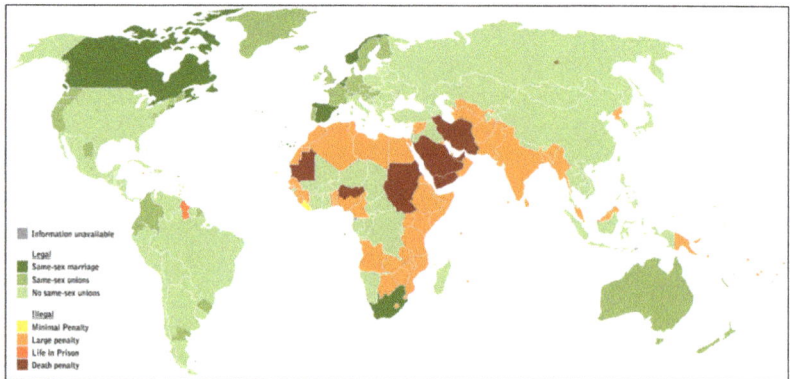

Fig. 2.1 World laws pertaining to homosexual relationships and expression (Courtesy of Southern, Wikimedia Commons at https://commons.wikimedia.org/wiki/File:World_homosexuality_laws.png)

Fig. 2.2 Sexual orientation employment anti-discrimination map (Courtesy of Adrian Frith, Wikimedia Commons at https://commons.wikimedia.org/wiki/File:Sexual_orientation_employment_anti-discrimination_map.svg)

The Legal Status of Anti-discrimination Laws and Remedies

Discrimination and bias levied against the LGBT community in the United States and globally has a long history, as chronicled within the realms of housing, employment, higher education, public accommodations, military service, refugee asylum, and hate crimes. In 2011, the United Nations passed its first resolution aimed at bringing awareness to LGBT rights while laying the foundation for later reports documenting violations of these rights. Across the globe, very few countries prohibit discrimination against homosexuals. For example, Fig. 2.2 demonstrates the lack of laws throughout the world that protect homosexuals from employment discrimination.

Housing and Employment Discrimination in the United States

In terms of housing discrimination, the federal Fair Housing Act protects renters and home buyers in both publicly assisted and privately owned housing from discrimination based on race, color, religion, sex, national origin, disability, and familial status; however, no federal laws ban housing discrimination on the basis of sexual orientation or gender identity ("Ending Housing Discrimination," 2016). Despite this lack of federal protection, many state, city, and county laws ban discrimination based on sexual orientation and gender identity ("Ending Housing Discrimination," 2016). Since 2012, the U.S. Department of Housing and Urban Development's Office of Fair Housing and Equal Opportunity has prohibited discrimination based on sexual orientation and gender identity in federally assisted housing programs ("Ending Housing Discrimination," 2016).

Regarding employment, the U.S. Equal Employment Opportunity Commission enforces bans on employment discrimination based on race, color, sex, religion, national origin, age, disability, and genetic information in federal, private, state, and local employment; however, no federal law exists to address employment discrimination based on sexual orientation or gender identity ("Facts About Discrimination," 2016). Protections are extended, however, at the state and local levels, with many cities, counties, and states plus Washington, D.C. and Puerto Rico banning discrimination based on sexual orientation and gender identity or expression ("Employment Law Guide," 2009). Supporting the anti-discrimination LGBT employment laws at the state and local levels are two rulings from the U.S. Equal Employment Opportunity Commission. In 2012, the U.S. Equal Employment Opportunity Commission issued a ruling that Title VII of the Civil Rights Act of 1964 does not allow employment discrimination based on gender identity because it is a form of sex discrimination ("Facts About Discrimination," 2016).

Higher education is one area of employment where gains in protection for the LGBT community have been realized over time; however, there remain significant challenges and need for improvement in the daily lives of LGBT faculty, students, and staff on college campuses across the United States (Rankin, Weber, Blumenfeld, & Frazer, 2010). Recent estimates (Trammell, 2014) suggest that there are nearly 1 million self-identified LGBT students and more than 160,000 faculty and staff members at universities across the United States. The history of harassment and discrimination against the LGBT community on U.S. college campuses is unfortunately shameful in many respects (Trammell, 2014). In the 1920s Harvard University supported a secret committee which exposed and then expelled gay faculty members, staff, and students. In the 1950s and 1960s some universities in Florida utilized the "Johns Committee" state legislative committee investigations to harass gay and lesbian faculty members and students.

Fortunately, the circumstances for LGBT individuals on college campuses across the United States have improved over time (Trammell, 2014), but there remain difficult and painful challenges that require the commitment and focus of the leaders of college campuses. The 2010 Campus Pride's *State of Higher Education for LGBT People* report is a national research study which documents the experiences or "campus climate" of 5, 149 undergraduate and graduate students, faculty members, staff members, and administrators who identify as LGBTQQ (lesbian, gay, bisexual, transgender, questioning, and queer). This 2010 report builds on and replicates the findings of prior campus climate surveys (e.g., Dolan, 1998; Rankin, 2003) which documented the self-reported "chilly" or unwelcoming climate on many college campuses throughout the United States.

Specifically, the 2010 report found that LGBTQQ respondents (23%) reported significantly greater harassment and discrimination than heterosexual respondents (12%) and were more than seven times more likely (83% versus 12%) to indicate that the harassment was based on sexual identity. Some of the discriminatory and harassing acts included derogatory remarks, being ignored deliberately or excluded, stared at, and singled out as a resident authority due to their identity. LGBTQQ respondents (70%) were significantly less likely than heterosexual respondents (78%) to feel comfortable or very comfortable with the overall campus climate, their department or work unit climate, and classroom climate. Among the LBGTQQ respondents, faculty (60%) were significantly less likely than their student (70%) and staff counterparts (73%) to feel very comfortable or comfortable with the overall campus climate and with their department/work unit climate. Finally, LGBTQQ respondents more often seriously considered leaving their institution and feared for their physical safety due to their sexual identity, and avoided disclosure of sexual identity due to intimidation and fear of negative consequences.

The report concludes with suggested best practices designed to improve the climates on college campuses for those in the LGBTQQ community. Highlights include developing inclusive policies that explicitly welcome LGBTQQ faculty, staff, and students, integrating the concerns of all members of the community through inclusive wording in campus documents, recognizing the contributions of LGBTQQ scholars in all disciplines, and supporting the study of gender and sexuality-specific topics.

PUBLIC ACCOMMODATIONS

In contrast to the gains described above, President Donald Trump's administration has actively sought to reverse and weaken the civil and political rights of LGBT individuals, with the rights of transgender persons most impacted. In May of 2016, the Obama administration-led Justice and Education departments issued a "Dear Colleague" letter to k-12 school districts to provide guidance in the interpretation of Title IX (Kamenetz & Turner, 2017). The letter advised school districts that Title IX, which prohibits sex discrimination in education, also protects the rights of transgender students. Compliance with Title IX required school districts to ensure that transgender students were not treated differently from students of the same gender identity (Kamenetz & Turner, 2017). Controversial outcomes of this guidance included ensuring that transgender students were allowed to use the bathroom of their choice that corresponded to their gender identity and allowing all students to attend prom and graduation in clothing of their choice (Kamenetz & Turner, 2017).

In February of 2017, the Trump administration rescinded the Obama administration's guidance providing states with more flexibility in interpreting Title IX and whether and how they accommodate transgender students (Kamenetz & Turner, 2017). On the same day that the guidance was rescinded, the American Academy of Pediatrics (ACP) issued a statement disagreeing with the Trump administration's interpretation (Stein, 2017). The ACP argued that because transgender children's emotional and physical health is already at risk in the school-setting, the Trump administration's guidance to no longer allow them to use restrooms corresponding to their gender identity might subject these children to more harm, stigmatization, and exclusion (Stein, 2017).

Trump's revised guidance regarding the interpretation of Title IX and the protection for gender identity has specific consequences for one particular transgender high school student, Gavin Grimm (Kamenetz & Turner, 2017). In 2015, before the start of his sophomore year, Grimm and his mother notified Gloucester High School in eastern Virginia that he was transgender, having legally changed his name to Gavin, and should be referred to with male pronouns (ACLU of Virginia, 2017). Gavin Grimm had been diagnosed with severe gender dysphoria, in which individuals experience a conflict between their physical or assigned gender and their gender identity. This conflict may then be expressed in several ways including the desire to wear gender-identified clothing, to use appropriate gender pronouns and bathrooms, and to medically transition with sex-affirmation surgery and/or hormone treatment (Parekh, 2016).

When Grimm sought to use the boy's bathroom at school, he was initially allowed to use the boys' bathroom until parents and others complained, resulting in the school board enacting a new policy requiring bathrooms to be used by students according to their "corresponding biological gender" (ACLU of Virginia, 2017). To protest this policy and the requirement that Gavin and other transgender students use unisex bathrooms, Gavin obtained representation by the American Civil Liberties Union (ACLU) and filed a lawsuit (*G.G. v. Gloucester County School Board*) in June 2015 against the Gloucester County School Board (ACLU of Virginia, 2017). The lawsuit was based on the ACLU's assertion that the Gloucester School Board's policy violates Title IX's prohibition of sex discrimination in public schools that receive federal funds (ACLU of Virginia, 2017). In September 2015 the district court denied Gavin's request for a preliminary injunction that would allow him to use the boys' restroom pending a final decision on the case (ACLU of Virginia, 2017). That decision was appealed before the U.S. Court of Appeals for the Fourth Circuit. The Fourth Circuit Court of Appeals overturned the lower court's decision in August 2016 based on the Obama administration's guidance on Title IX that has now been rescinded (ACLU of Virginia, 2017). The Fourth Circuit's decision would have allowed Gavin to use the boys' bathroom pending a final decision on the case; however, the Gloucester County School Board responded by requesting a Writ of Certiorari to the Supreme Court of the United States to review the Fourth Circuit's decision (ACLU of Virginia, 2017).

In March 2017, the Supreme Court refused to hear the case and sent it back to the Fourth Circuit Court of Appeals citing Trumps' rescinding of the Obama era Title IX guidance (ACLU of Virginia, 2017). Grimm's case had been stalled in the appeal process as the focus was on the preliminary injunction and whether the case is moot given that Grimm has since graduated from high school (Marimow, 2017). The ACLU continues to argue that Grimm's intention to attend future school events provides enough of a connection to the school to allow the court to continue to consider the case (Marimow, 2017). The school board refutes the ACLU's argument claiming that their bathroom policy does not necessarily apply to alumni of the school (Marimow, 2017). More broadly, the legal limbo and uncertainty of Grimm's case means that states and school districts may determine whether or not Title IX and its protections regarding "sex" should include gender identity and whether or not they provide equal access to facilities on the basis of gender identity (Kamenetz & Turner, 2017). The lack of unresolved constitutional issues may result in an increase in persons on both sides of the issue suing school districts (Brown & Balingit, 2017). As of March 2017, 14 states and the District of Columbia explicitly provided protections for transgender students (Brown & Balingit, 2017).

North Carolina is one prominent example of a state with a turbulent history regarding the LGBT community as it holds the distinction of being the only state in the U.S. to prohibit transgender people's right to use the bathroom of their choice (Hanna, Park, & McLaughlin, 2017). In 2016, the state of North Carolina passed House Bill 2 (HB2), commonly known as the "bathroom bill" (Hanna et al., 2017) which required people to use bathrooms and locker rooms at government-funded facilities that corresponded to the sex on their birth certificate, if the rooms are multi-occupancy (Hanna et al., 2017). HB2 was controversial from the outset, generating more than a year of protests from internal and external constituencies including LGTBQ advocacy groups, businesses and organizations (e.g., the NCAA, the ACC, and the NBA) who left the state or refused to hold major conferences and events there (Hanna et al., 2017). In March of 2017, the state legislature of North Carolina partially repealed HB2 by removing the requirement that individuals must use the bathroom corresponding to the sex on their birth certificate in government facilities; however, it retained the state legislature's regulation of bathroom access without ceding any control to local governments until December 2020 (Hanna et al., 2017). This "compromise" bill, HB142, failed to satisfy LGBTQ advocacy groups who allege that the revised law still discriminates against LGBT residents by preventing local governments from passing ordinances similar to the one passed by the Charlotte, North Carolina City Council in February 2016 which added gender identity to the city's protections against discrimination in public accommodations including bathrooms (Hanna et al., 2017). In 2015, the Justice Department under the Obama administration filed a lawsuit challenging HB2, but in March 2017, the Trump administration-led Justice Department dropped the lawsuit in a shift that would allow states and local governments to determine the rights of transgender individuals to access public accommodations including bathrooms (Drew, 2017).

Lamba Legal and the ACLU continued their separate federal lawsuit on behalf of six plaintiffs, arguing that HB142, the replacement law, still violated the rights of transgender individuals, in part by leaving them confused on which bathrooms they could use. (Drew, 2017). In October 2017, the Governor of North Carolina, Roy Cooper, and transgender rights advocates settled the federal lawsuit through a proposed consent decree (Fausset, 2017). Cooper, elected in part due to his opposition to HB2, had previously called the revised law, HB142, a first step to increasing transgender rights in North Carolina (Fausset, 2017). Along with the consent decree that would allow transgender people to use the bathrooms that matched their gender identity, Cooper also issued an executive order offering protections based on sexual orientation and gender identity to state government employees (Fausset, 2017). Cooper's executive order was met with considerable opposition from some conservative groups including the NC Values Coalition who argued that the settlement represents an attempt to take authority and power away from the state legislature who alone has the authority to institute such changes (Fausset, 2017).

DISCRIMINATION WITHIN THE MILITARY

In 2010, President Barack Obama finalized his decision to repeal the "Don't Ask, Don't Tell" executive order implemented eighteen years earlier by President Bill Clinton which had prevented gay men and women from revealing their sexual orientation and gender identities while serving in the military (Bumiller, 2011). President Obama's administration had planned to start enlisting transgender troops in all branches of the military by July 1, 2017; however, the Trump administration postponed and then canceled the policy entirely in another attempt at reversing gains made by transgender individuals (McLaughlin, 2017). In August 2017 President Trump issued a series of tweets and a memo formally ordering the Pentagon to ban transgender people from serving in the United States military by immediately prohibiting their "accession" or enlistment in the military and most likely discharging those transgender individuals currently serving no later than March 23, 2018 (McLaughlin, 2017). President Trump tweeted that the United States military's ability to be decisive in victory should not be impacted by the burden, expensive medical costs, and disruption of transgender military personnel (McLaughlin, 2017). The memo also required the Pentagon to stop funding all new gender-related surgeries and granted former Secretary of Defense Jim Mattis six months to create a policy on how to handle the issue of transgender individuals who were already serving in the U.S. military (McLaughlin, 2017). Mr. Mattis assembled a panel to advise him on appropriate policy regarding transgender individuals serving in the military (McLaughlin & Martinez, 2018). In September 2017, General Joseph Dunford, the chairman of the Joint Chief of Staffs, provided testimony to the Senate Armed Services Committee in which he asserted that any individuals who meet physical and mental standards and who is currently serving should be allowed to continue to serve; further, Dunford informed Congress that he had privately recommended that transgender individuals be allowed to continue serving in the military (Mclaughlin, 2017).

In response to President Trump's directive, four federal lawsuits were filed resulting in the U.S. Department of Justice's attempt to have one of the lawsuits dismissed due to it being premature in light of the Defense department's revue of President Trump's directive to ban transgender personnel from the military (Sands & Seyler, 2017). The lawsuits drew upon data, including that furnished by the RAND Corporation, to argue against the Trump administration's rationale for banning transgender military personnel. The RAND Corporation estimated in 2016 that there were approximately 2450 transgender personnel serving in the active portion of the U.S. military out of about 1.3 million active personnel and about 1510 serving in the reserves (Schaefer et al., 2016). Of those transgender military personnel, the RAND report estimated that between 29 and 129 individuals serving in the active portion of the military would seek transition-related or gender confirmation surgery that could impede their ability to deploy (Schaefer et al., 2016). Further, the cost of such health care was estimated to increase the military's active component health care costs by $2.4 million to $8.4 million annually, representing a .04 to .13% increase (Schaefer et al., 2016). At the time of the 2016 RAND study, 18 close allies of the United States, including England, Israel, Canada and Australia, allowed transgender individuals to serve openly in the military (McLaughlin & Martinez, 2018).

In October 2017 Judge Colleen Kollar-Kotelly blocked the Trump administration's ban on enlisting and retaining transgender military personnel, asserting that the plaintiffs who filed the federal lawsuit demonstrated that the directive would cause injury from inequality and from the risk of discharge and denial of enlistment (de Vogue, 2017). Judge Kollar-Kotelly, who ordered the government to begin enlisting transgender individuals as of January 1, 2018, also criticized President Trump's use of Twitter to announce the new policy, as this mode of communication did not conform to the typical formal processes that accompany a major policy change with such a wide impact (de Vogue, 2017). Further, in her 76-page opinion, Judge Kollar-Kotelly asserted that the reasons offered by Mr. Trump for banning transgender military personnel were contradicted by conclusions and studies conducted over a year-long period by the military (de Vogue, 2017). Two significant outcomes of this ruling include the judge's conclusion that the Constitution limits federal discrimination against transgender individuals and that the President's tweets may be viewed as official presidential policies (de Vogue, 2017). On December 11, 2017, Judge Kollar-Kotelly declined the Trump administration's request to put her order on hold that would allow transgender individuals to enlist in the military beginning January 1, 2018. The Pentagon asserted that it was prepared to follow Judge Kollar-Kotelly's court order as of January 1, 2018, allowing transgender individuals to join the military if they met strict criteria including certifications from a medical provider about the status of their health (McLaughlin & Martinez, 2018). Two transgender individuals are already under contract to serve in the U.S. military since that court ruling (McLaughlin & Martinez, 2018).

Despite their claim of compliance with the court ruling, the Justice Department appealed the judge's ruling to a federal appeals court based in the District of Columbia (Crawford & de Vogue, 2017). On March 23, 2018, President Trump rescinded his previous memorandum banning all transgender service in the military (Geidner, 2018). The second version of the ban prohibits most transgender people from serving in the military if they undergo gender transition or affirmation surgery, with some exceptions for about 900 transgender people who are already serving openly and for others who would agree to serve without undergoing gender transition surgery (Marimow, 2018). The revised ban further states that transgender individuals who had received a diagnosis of gender dysphoria would be prohibited from serving except under limited circumstances (McLaughlin & Martinez, 2018). On November 23, 2018 the Justice Department asked the Supreme Court to review three cases challenging the Trump administrations' efforts to bar transgender people from serving in the military based on his revised ban (Geidner, 2018). The request is viewed as unusual as it requests that the Supreme Court review the cases before appeals courts have had an opportunity to rule on the matter (Geidner, 2018).

In January 2019 the Supreme court ruled that Trump's ban on transgender troops serving openly in the military could take effect pending ongoing litigation (Tillet, 2019). As of April 12, 2019, transgender troops, including those diagnosed with gender dysphoria, are prohibited from serving in the U.S. military unless they are willing to serve in their "biological" sex without surgery or hormone treatment (Tillet, 2019). Troops who had already transitioned or who had requested gender reassignment surgery prior to the April 12, 2019 deadline were allowed to continue serving in the military. The Defense Department estimates that up to 15,000 troops identify as transgender and are thus subject to this policy.

Overall, the Trump administration has attempted to reverse the gains in transgender individual's civil rights that were afforded under the Obama administration, including the right to access public accommodations and to serve openly in the United States military. The transgender community had many allies including LGBT rights groups such as Lambda Legal and the ACLU, who have filed federal lawsuits on behalf of transgender plaintiffs. After months of litigation, the results are mixed for the transgender community. In terms of transgender students enrolled in k-12 publicly funded schools who sought the right to use bathrooms corresponding to their gender identity, as of October 2018 Gavin Grimm's lawsuit against the Gloucester County School board is now back at the trial court and is in the discovery phase (ACLU of Virginia, 2019). In North Carolina, a consent decree will allow transgender individuals to use the publicly funded restrooms and facilities of their choice; furthermore, the rights of the transgender community have been bolstered by Governor Cooper's sweeping executive order providing protections for sexual orientation and gender identity to state employees. Finally, Mr. Trump's most recent memo of March 2018 outlining his policy regarding transgender troops took full effect as of April 12, 2019.

In contrast to the erosion of civil rights for the LGBT community under the Trump administration, some recent gains in political representation in the United States have been achieved by LGBT politicians in state and local elections. In Virginia, former journalist Danica Roem was elected to the state legislature in 2017, becoming the nation's first openly transgender woman elected to a state legislature (Stracqualursi & Chavez, 2017). Roem defeated incumbent Robert Marshall who described himself as a homophobe and allegedly referred to Roem with male pronouns during the campaign (Stracqualursi & Chavez, 2017). Roem asserted in her acceptance speech that "No matter what you look like, where you come from, how you worship, who you love, how you identify…if you have good public policy ideas, if you're well qualified for office, bring those ideas to the table, because this is your America too" (Stracqualursi & Chavez, 2017). Also in

2017 Andrea Jenkins was elected to a council seat in Minneapolis, becoming the first African American transgender woman to win a council seat in a major city (Stracqualursi & Chavez, 2017). Jenkins' statement after her win expressed her feelings of marginalization and exclusion, stating that transgender individuals… "don't just want a seat at the table. We want to set the table. My election is what resistance looks like. It's also about hope" (Stracqualursi & Chavez, 2017). Seattle, Washington elected its first openly lesbian mayor and first female mayor in 90 years as Jenny Durkan ascended to the position after serving as the first openly gay U.S. attorney (Stracqualursi & Chavez, 2017). Durkan was appointed by former President Obama in 2009 to the Western District of Washington (Stracqualursi & Chavez, 2017). In April 2019, Jane Castor became Tampa, Florida's first openly LGBTQ mayor as she defeated her opponent with 73% of the votes cast (Weinberg, 2019). As of 2019, it is estimated that 38 openly LGBTQ mayors are serving nationwide (Weinberg, 2019).

GLOBAL ADVANCES AND CHALLENGES IN LGBT CIVIL RIGHTS

Refugees and Asylum Seekers in the United States and Globally

As previously discussed in this chapter, homosexuality remains illegal and even punishable by death in many parts of the globe. Thus, it is imperative to examine the plight of sexual and gender minority "refugees" who are searching for safe havens to escape persecution and to secure a safer life (Sherwood, 2017). Those individuals who claim persecution for their sexual orientation and gender identities constitute a portion of the estimated 21 million refugees worldwide (Kushner, 2017). The United Nations High Commissioner For Refugees (UNHCR) is the body designated to process refugee status and aid those seeking asylum (Kushner, 2017). The UNHCR interviews asylum seekers who make it to a refugee camp and then decides which among them to prioritize for resettlement in a very limited number of slots in nations in Europe and North America (Kushner, 2017). The decisions are difficult forcing the UNHCR officials to choose among those who identify as political and economic refugees; families, individuals, the elderly, and the disabled forced to flee their homes due to wars and famine; and sexual and gender minorities escaping persecution (Kushner, 2017). If a refugee is chosen for resettlement by the UNHCR, then the lengthy process of security and medical vetting and processing begins before the host country determines admittance (Kushner, 2017).

In 2014, an estimated 105,000 people, or a small portion of the 866,000 applicants, were approved for resettlement (Kushner, 2017). Historically, the United States has admitted more refugees than any other country, as evidenced in 2014 when the U.S. accepted about 49,000 people or about two-thirds of the total 77,331 that the UNHCR helped to resettle (Kushner, 2017). In Canada, approximately 2200 refugees applied for asylum based on their sexual orientation between 2013 and 2015, with about 70% of the claims being granted as compared to about 63% of claims granted to all refugees (Bielski, 2017). In May of 2017, for the first time, Canada formalized the guidelines, which were crafted with guidance from LGBT advocates, lawyers, social workers, and researchers, regarding LGBTQ refugees (Bielski, 2017). The guidelines must be followed by the refugee boards throughout Canada (e.g., the Immigration and Refugee Board of Canada) who decide on whether or not to grant asylum to LGBT individuals who consider themselves as "persecuted minorities" in their home countries, based on proof of same-sex relationships including texts, letters, photographs, or other artifacts such as prison records. These requirements are an added burden on many LGBT individuals seeking asylum as most spend the majority of their lives hiding their sexual orientation, romantic relationships, and other "indicators" to avoid persecution, torture, jail, and even death (Beilski, 2017).

As asylum seekers navigate the refugee guidelines over months and even years, some are in such immediate danger and desperate straits that in June 2017 Canada began a secret program to evacuate gay men from Chechnya, a republic within the Russian Federation, into Canada (Ibbitson, 2017a). The secret program is controversial as it is not sanctioned by conventional international law and places further strain on the tense relationship between Russia and Canada (Ibbitson, 2017a). Despite the political ramifications, Canada's Liberal government decided it must take action given the recent practice of Chechen security forces placing gay men in detention centers, prisons, and other undisclosed locations, beating them, and demanding the names of sexual partners (Walker, 2017). Several survivors of such torture have claimed that upon their release, they were "outed" to family members who expressed hostility and condemnation of homosexuality (Ibbitson, 2017a). At least two reports of familial beatings and "honor" killings for a few of these men have surfaced but cannot be confirmed (Ibbitson, 2017a).

While NGOs or nongovernmental organizations dedicated to protecting and advancing the civil rights of LGBT individuals across the globe have called upon other governments to provide asylum to gay Chechens, the matter is complicated because homosexuality is technically legal in Russia despite President Putin's ban of gay "propaganda" in 2012 (Ibbitson, 2017a). Further, other countries have not been willing to make the exception to international laws that refugee claimants must leave their home countries before seeking refugee status (Ibbitson, 2017a). Canada acknowledged the need for the exception, allowing gay refugee claimants who were still located in Russia—mostly in safe houses operated by the Russian LGBT Network, to be evacuated immediately and allowed to enter Canada (Ibbitson, 2017a). The exact number of gay men who have been affected by the Chechnyan "pogrom" or deliberate persecution is unknown; however, the Russian LGBT Network bases its estimate of 75 affected gay men on the number of calls received at a hotline that the organization established when reports of the persecution first surfaced (Ibbitson, 2017a).

Violence within spaces designed to provide sanctuary and safety are often dangerous places for LGBT people, as is the case in the Kakuma Refugee camp in Kenya. The Kakuma camp hosts approximately 180,000 refugees from several African countries including Burundi, the Democratic Republic of Congo, Ethiopia, Sudan, South Sudan, Somalia, and Uganda (e.g., Onyulo, 2018). Of the purportedly 200 self-identified LGBT refugees living in the camp, many claim that they are victims of homophobic acts of violence perpetrated by other refugees who are encouraged by religious leaders in the camp who oppose homosexuality and urge LGBT refugees to change their sexual orientation (Onyulo, 2018).

One South Sudanese Pentecostal pastor who resides within the camp, Peter Long, asserted that LGBT refugees might influence heterosexual refugees within the camp to experiment with or embrace a LGBT sexual orientation (Onyulo, 2018). LGBT refugees claimed that the refugee camp officers separated them from the other refugees in worse conditions with sparse accommodations and supplies (Onyulo, 2018). While some of the LGBT individuals have attempted to form their own church and pray together, they live in fear of the other refugees as well as from Kenyans outside the camps (Onyulo, 2018). Given this dangerous environment, LGBT refugees have expressed their desire to relocate to the U.S. or Europe where they believe they will be protected (Onyulo, 2018).

In another stride forward for LGBT civil rights, several countries, including Australia, England, Germany, and Canada, have issued apologies in various forms and in some cases reparations, to individuals in the LGBT community who were persecuted and/or prosecuted for homosexuality prior to the decriminalization of homosexual acts (Ibbitson, 2017b). In May 2016 the Victorian parliament in Australia became the first government to apologize to men who had been convicted for homosexuality (Ibbitson, 2017b). In his address to Parliament, Australian Premier Daniel Andrew stated:

> I move that this house apologize for laws that criminalized homosexuality in this State, laws which validated hateful views, ruined people's lives and forced generations of Victorians to suffer in fear, silence, and isolation. These laws did not just punish homosexual acts, they punished homosexual thought. They had no place in a liberal democracy. They have no place anywhere. The Victorian Parliament and the Victorian Government were at fault. For this we are sorry. (Andrew, 2016, para. 4)

By the summer of 2017, Britain and Germany had both issued their own apologies to LGBT individuals who had been discriminated against, with Germany promising to compensate those affected as well as to overturn convictions for homosexuality (Ibbitson, 2017b). In the fall of 2016 Canada's Prime Minister, Justin Trudeau, appointed Randy Boissonnault, a Liberal Member of Parliament, to frame an apology and possible reparations for those individuals who had been convicted and imprisoned prior to 1969, when homosexuality was illegal in Canada (Ibbitson, 2017b). Although the apology had been discussed since the 1980s and two other countries (Britain and Germany) had both issued apologies by the summer of 2017 to gay men who had been prosecuted under anti-homosexuality laws, Canada did not formally issue its apology or accompanying reparations until November 28, 2017 (Ibbitson, 2017b).

The final catalysts for the apology can be partially attributed to the 2016 attack on a gay nightclub in Orlando, in which 49 people were killed, and a report prepared by the Egale Canada Human Rights Trust, known as Egale (Ibbitson, 2017b). Egale, describing itself as the "only national charity promoting lesbian, gay, bisexual, and trans human rights," urged the Canadian government to apologize to those who had been imprisoned, fired from jobs, or persecuted because of their sexuality (Egale, 2016). At the time that Trudeau was nearing his decision to make a formal apology, some

LGBT individuals were participating in a class action lawsuit that sought financial compensation and redress for their loss of jobs during the Canadian "gay purge" conducted between 1950 and the early 1990s, which focused mostly on occupations within national security, the military, and public service (Egale, 2016). Mr. Trudeau's apology issued in the House of Commons was made on behalf of all Canadians to lesbian, gay, bisexual, transgender, and queer individuals who had been imprisoned, fired, or persecuted in other ways due to their sexuality (Catungal, 2017). The apology was also accompanied by a promised sum of $145 million dollars, the largest amount provided by any government to compensate the LGBT community (Ibbitson, 2017b). The funds will be allotted to individual compensation and to the cost of a memorial in Ottawa and educational activities throughout Canada (Ibbitson, 2017b).

Although acknowledging the importance of these various apologies from several countries, some activists and scholars have emphasized the need to for continued action and commitment to long term financial and political support for the LGBT community (Catungal, 2017). Catungal (2017) further stressed that the inequalities within the LGBT community necessitate a varied response, with careful attention given its most vulnerable members including transgender women and transgender people of color. Catungal (2017) argued for stronger policies and legislation to combat the disproportionate violence suffered by transgender individuals in schools, the workplace, and in the community.

HATE CRIMES

A hate crime is defined as a crime (e.g., physical or verbal assault, bullying, harassment) that is motivated by bias or hate directed toward victims who are members of particular races or social groups including sex, sexual orientation, gender identity, ethnicity, disability, language, nationality, and religion (Stotzer, 2007). Incidents that are motivated by hate but classified as noncriminal are often referred to as bias incidents. As hate crimes targeting the LGBT community occur throughout the world, in 2014, the United Nations Human Rights Council passed its first resolution condemning violence and discrimination on the basis of sexual orientation and gender identity (Howard, 2014). The United States strongly supported the resolution which was sponsored by Uruguay, Columbia, Brazil, and Chile (Howard, 2014).

Although the term "hate crime" did not become a common part of the English lexicon in the United States until the 1980s, the term often refers to events such as the killing of millions of Jewish people during the Holocaust as well as lynchings of African Americans during reconstruction and the civil rights movement that occurred well before the term was popularized. Hate crimes have numerous psychological effects on victims including feelings of terror, vulnerability, powerlessness, depression, and anxiety. Reasons for committing hate crimes often overlap. Some motivations for committing such crimes include seeking excitement and thrills; protecting a community from perceived threats; retaliating or seeking revenge as in the case after terrorist attacks; and defending a mission or particular ideology (Burke, 2017).

Hate crime laws are designed to deter crimes based on bias and hatred by several means including the enhancement of penalties associated with existing crimes, the classification of some acts as distinct crimes or classes of civil actions, and the collection of hate crime statistics (Stotzer, 2007). In 1968 in the United States a federal statute was included in the Civil Rights Act which codified the first modern hate crime legislation aimed at protecting victims who were targeted based on race, color, religion, and national origin. The U.S. Supreme Court has upheld hate crime laws as long as the crimes are associated with threats of injury or death.

In the United States, 20 states and the District of Columbia address hate or bias crimes based on sexual orientation and gender identity while 11 states have laws against hate or bias crimes based on sexual orientation only. Fifteen states have laws addressing hate or bias crimes but do not include protections based on sexual orientation or gender identity. Finally, three states have no laws concerning hate crimes based on sexual orientation or gender identity, but do collect data on such crimes.

In 2009, the Matthew Shepard and James Byrd, Jr. Hate Crimes Prevention Act augmented the federal definition of hate crimes by adding actual or perceived gender, gender identity, sexual orientation, and disability. The Act also removed the prerequisite that the victim had to be engaging in federally protected activity such as attending school, using public accommodations, applying for employment, serving as a juror, or voting (Human Rights Campaign, 2010). Although this expanded version of hate crimes legislation was introduced in the United States House of Representatives and Senate in 1997, it was not until 12 years later that the bill was passed and signed into law by President Barack Obama (Human Rights Campaign, 2010). The Act assigned the United States Justice Department jurisdiction over the investigation and prosecution of hate crimes and also provided funding and technical assistance for the local and state investigation and prosecution of hate crimes.

The Mathew Shepard and James Byrd, Jr. Hate Crimes Prevention Act was named to honor the victims of two especially heinous and gruesome murders. On October 9, 1998, near Laramie, Wyoming, Matthew Shepard, a college student, was brutally beaten, burned, and tied to a fence where he was found 18 hours later. He subsequently died after five days in the hospital. The prosecution provided evidence that Matthew's killers murdered him because he was gay (Human Rights Campaign, 2010). On June 7, 1998, in Jasper, Texas, James Byrd Jr., an African American man, was murdered by three white men because of their hatred against African Americans. Of the three convicted assailants, two were members of white supremacist groups called the Aryan Nations and Confederate Knights of America, an offshoot of the Ku Klux Klan. James Byrd was kidnapped, driven to a wooded area, beaten, and chained by the ankles to the back of one of the assailant's truck. His severed head, neck, and right arm were discovered about one mile from where his torso was eventually dumped (Human Rights Campaign, 2010). According to the Federal Bureau of Investigation, hate crimes in the United States increased 4.6% from 2015 to 2016 and 17% between 2016 and 2017 (Federal Bureau of Investigation, 2017).

Hate Crimes and Discrimination Globally

While data regarding hate crimes, discrimination, and harassment of LGBT individuals has not been consistently collected throughout the globe, some information on this matter is available from surveys conducted by the European Union Agency for Fundamental Rights or FRA. As depicted in Fig. 2.3 twenty-eight member states located primarily in Europe comprise the European Union (EU), a political and economic entity whose goals are to support an internal single financial market and common policies regarding trade, development, and laws.

Since 2008 the FRA has conducted research examining intolerant attitudes and behaviors including verbal and physical attacks suffered by the LGBT community throughout the EU. Within the EU, sexual orientation-based discrimination is prohibited by law only in the realm of employment while gender identity is also protected if the discrimination is related to gender reassignment (FRA, 2019).

Fig. 2.3 European Union map (Courtesy of the US Central Intelligence Agency Library)

In 2012 the FRA conducted the EU LBGT online survey with 93,079 persons aged 18 years or over living in the EU or Croatia who self-identified as lesbian, gay, bisexual, or transgender. The FRA acknowledges that the survey was not representative of all LGBT persons living in the EU; however, at the time the survey was the largest of its kind providing a view into experiences of the LGBT community. The anonymous online survey focused on self-reported discrimination, violence and harassment of LGBT people living in the EU in the domains of employment, education, health-care, housing and other services (FRA, 2019).

A consistent finding across all countries surveyed was the relationship between perceptions about the level of offensive language about LGBT people by politicians and self-reports of feeling personally discriminated against or harassed based on sexual orientation (FRA, 2019). Specifically, results demonstrated that in 14 out of the 17 countries in which fewer than half of the respondents reported discrimination or harassment based on sexual orientation in the year before the survey, the majority of respondents reported that offensive language about LGBT people by politicians was rare. The survey revealed differences by age, gender identity, and gender. The youngest age group (18–24 years) were the least likely to have disclosed their sexual orientation and the most likely to report being victims of violence or discrimination based on sexual orientation. Respondents who self-identified as transgender reported a more hostile environment and more discrimination in employment and healthcare than that experienced by lesbian, gay and bisexual respondents (FRA, 2019). Respondents identifying as women were much more likely than men respondents to report that the most recent attack that they experienced in the 12 months prior to the survey was sexual in nature.

Given the results of this survey, the FRA published several recommendations designed to bolster responses to and reductions in discrimination targeting the LGBT community living within the EU. For example, the FRA encouraged the EU to develop and execute plans to increase respect for LGBT people by integrating their needs into national human rights plans and strategies. As the results pointed to harsher environments and higher incidences of self-reported discrimination based on age and gender identity, the FRA urged special focus on the youngest respondents and those self-identifying as transgender. Finally, FRA encouraged EU member states to facilitate dialogue among social and political institutions regarding LGBT rights and protections while increasing funding for national level research regarding discrimination targeting LGBT individuals.

Summary

This chapter illuminated the current legal status of LGBT persons both in the United States and across the globe. One area of progress within the United States and some countries worldwide is the legalization of same-sex marriage and adoption, which afforded all of the legal benefits enjoyed by opposite-sex couples to same-sex couples. Despite this positive outcome, this chapter provided ample evidence that discrimination, bias, and the denial of legal rights continue to plague the LGBT community as they attempt to access employment, housing, education, public accommodations, military service opportunities, refugee protections, and remedies for hate crimes based on sexual orientation and gender identity. Although no federal laws exist to protect the LGBT community from discrimination, some progress has occurred as individual states have passed laws prohibiting discrimination based on sexual orientation and gender identity. Sexual and gender minority refugees have been assisted by some countries including Canada, who recently took action to secretly evacuate gay men who were being attacked from the Russian Federation republic of Chechnya into Canada. Further progress for some homosexuals who had been persecuted and often jailed for homosexuality prior to the decriminalization of homosexuality came by way of recent apologies and in some cases reparations from several European countries. The Mathew Shepard and James Byrd, Jr. Crimes Prevention Act provided additional legal remedies for federal hate crimes by adding actual or perceived gender, gender identity, sexual orientation, and disability and removing the stipulation that the victim had to be engaging in federally protected activity such as attending school, using public accommodations, applying for employment, serving as a juror, or voting (Human Rights Campaign, 2010). Globally, discrimination in employment based on sexual orientation is prohibited within the European Union; however, a recent online survey reveals experiences of discrimination, bias, and violence within the EU's LGBT community. Overall, this chapter demonstrated that, at best, progress in gaining equality in the legal treatment and status of the LGBT community is mixed and in need of sustained efforts within the United States and globally.

References

ACLU of Virginia. (2017). *Gavin Grimm v. Gloucester County Public School Board: Right of transgender student to use appropriate bathroom* [Web log post]. Retrieved from https://acluva.org/en/cases/gavin-grimm-v-gloucester-county-public-school-board.

ACLU of Virginia. (2019). *G.G. v. Gloucester County School Board.* Updated [Web log post]. Retrieved from https://www.aclu.org/cases/gg-v-gloucester-county-school-board.

Andrew, D. (2016, May 24). *State apology: Victorian government.* Retrieved from https://www.vic.gov/au/equality/state-apology.html.

Barbash, F. (2016, April 1). Federal judge voids Mississippi ban on same-sex couple adoptions. *The Washington Post.* Retrieved from https://www.washingtonpost.com/news/morning-mix/wp/2016/04/01/federal-judge-voids-mississippi-ban-on-same-sex-couple-adoptions/.

Bielski, Z. (2017, November 12). *After a lifetime of hiding, gay refugees seeking protection in Canada are expected to prove their identity* [Web log post]. Retrieved from https://www.theglobeandmail.com/life/relationships/after-lifetime-of-hiding-gay-refugees-to-canada-expected-to-prove-theiridentity/article34858343/.

Brown, E., & Balingit, M. (2017, March 6). *Supreme Court's decision to pass on transgender bathroom case leaves schools, parents without answers* [Web log post]. Retrieved from https://www.washingtonpost.com/local/public-safety/case-of-virginia-transgender-teen-gavin-grimm-put-off-by-appeals-court/2017/08/02/4d49a254–77ad-11e7-8839-ec48ec4cae25_story.html?utm_term=.58e998937301.

Bumiller, E. (2011, July 22). Obama ends 'Don't Ask, Don't Tell' policy. *The New York Times.* Retrieved from http://www.nytimes.com/2011/07/23/us/23military.html?_r=0.

Burke, D. (2017, June 12). *The four reasons people commit hate crimes* [Web log post]. Retrieved from https://edition.cnn.com/2017/06/02/us/who-commits-hate-crimes/index.html.

Campaign for Southern Equality v. Mississippi Department of Human Services. (2016). Case 3:15-cv-00578-DPJ-FKB, Document 67.

Catungal, J. (2017, November 27). *Justin Trudeau's apology to LGBTQ people isn't enough* [Web log post]. Retrieved from https://www.usnews.com/news/best-countries/articles/2017–11-28/justin-trudeaus-apology-to-lgbtq-people-isnt-enough.

Crawford, J., & de Vogue, A. (2017, December 11). *DOJ appeals ruling that transgender people are free to enlist in US military* [Web log post]. Retrieved from http://www.cnn.com/2017/12/11/politics/us-pentagon-transgenderenlist/index.html.

de Vogue, A. (2017, October 30). *Judge blocks enforcement of Trump's transgender military ban* [Web log post]. Retrieved from http://abcnews.go.com/Politics/trump-administration-moves-dismiss-lawsuit-transgender-military-ban/story?id=50310395.

Dolan, J. (1998). Gay and lesbian professors: Out on campus. *Academe, 84*(5), 40–45.

Drew, J. (2017, April 14). *Justice Department drops North Carolina LGBT rights lawsuit* [Web log post]. Retrieved from https://www.apnews.com/1ea5569e41da4e48bba8e429fdaefd32.

Dynes, W. (Ed.). (2015). *Encyclopedia of homosexuality* (Vol. 1). New York, NY: Routledge.

Egale Canada Human Rights Trust. (2016). *The just society report.* Retrieved from https://egale.ca/wp-content/uploads/2016/06/FINAL_REPORT_EGALE.pdf.

Employment law guide: Laws, regulations, and technical assistance services. (2009). United States Department of Labor. Retrieved from https://www.dol.gov/compliance/guide/.

Ending housing discrimination against lesbian, gay, bisexual and transgender individuals and their families: Enriching and strengthening our nation. (2016). United States Department of Housing and Urban Development. Retrieved from http://portal.hud.gov/hudportal/HUD?src=/program_offices/fair_housing_equal_opp/LGBT_Housing_Discrimination.

Facts about discrimination in federal government employment based on marital status, political affiliation, status as a parent, sexual orientation, and gender identity. (2016). United States Equal Employment Opportunity Commission. Retrieved from https://www.eeoc.gov/federal/otherprotections.cfm.

Fausset, R. (2017, October 18). *Deal on North Carolina bathroom law would expand transgender protections* [Web log post]. Retrieved from https://www.nytimes.com/2017/10/18/us/north-carolina-bathroom-bill.html.

Federal Bureau of Investigation. (2017). United States Department of Justice. Criminal Justice Information Services Division. 2017 Hate Crime Statistics. Retrieved from https://ucr.fbi.gov/hate-crime/2017/topic-pages/tables/table-1.xls.

FRA. (2019, June 6). Rising inequalities and harassment as fundamental rights protection falters. *Press release.* Retrieved from https://fra.europa.eu/en/press-release/2019/rising-inequalities-and-harassment-fundamental-rights-protectionfalters.

Geidner, C. (2018, November 23). The Trump administration just asked the Supreme Court to let it enforce its transgender military ban. *BuzzFeed.News.* Retrieved from https://www.buzzfeednews.com/article/chrisgeidner/trump-transgender-military-ban-supreme-court.

George, M. (2012). *The difference between me and you.* New York, NY: Penguin Group.

Hanna, J., Park, M., & McLaughlin, E. (2017, March 30). *North Carolina repeals 'bathroom bill'* [Web log post]. Retrieved from http://www.cnn.com/2017/03/30/politics/north-carolina-hb2-agreement/index.html.

Howard, A. (2014, October 15). UN passes resolution on behalf of LGBT citizens around the globe. *MSNBC* [Web log post]. Retrieved from http://www.msnbc.com/msnbc/un-passes-resolution-behalf-lgbt-citizens-around-the-globe.

Human Rights Campaign. (2010). *Questions and answers: The Matthew Shepard and James Byrd, Jr. Hate Crimes Prevention Act* [Web log post].

Retrieved from http://www.hrc.org/resources/questions-and-answers-the-matthew-shepard-and-james-byrd-jr.-hate-crimes-pr.

Ibbitson, J. (2017a, November 12). *How Canada has been secretly giving asylum to gay people in Chechnya fleeing persecution*. Retrieved from https://www.theglobeandmail.com/news/canada-chechnya-gay-asylum/article36145997/?utm_source=Shared+Article+Sent+to+User&utm_medium=E-mail:+Newsletters+/+E-Blasts+/+etc.&utm_campaign=Shared+Web+Article+Links.

Ibbitson, J. (2017b, November 29). *Trudeau's LGBTQ apology: A globe guide to how we got here*. Retrieved from https://www.theglobeandmail.com/news/politics/trudeau-lgbtq-apology-backstory-explainer/article37109540/?utm_source=Shared+Article+Sent+to+User&utm_medium=E-mail:+Newsletters+/+E-Blasts+/+etc.&utm_campaign=Shared+Web+Article+Links.

Kamenetz, A., & Turner, C. (2017, February 23). *Trump and transgender rights: What just happened?* [Web log post]. Retrieved from https://www.npr.org/sections/ed/2017/02/23/516837258/5-questions-about-the-trump-administrations-new-transgender-student-guidance.

Kushner, J. (2017). Letter from Kakuma. *Nation, 304*(6), 12–16.

Lawrence v. Texas, 539 U.S. 558 (2003).

Lu, S., & Hunt, K. (2016, March 3). *China bans same-sex romance from TV screens* [Web log post]. Retrieved from https://www.cnn.com/2016/03/03/asia/china-bans-same-sex-dramas/index.html.

McLaughlin, E. (2017, September 26). *General Dunford: Transgender individuals should not be separated from service* [Web log post]. Retrieved from http://abcnews.go.com/US/gen-dunford-transgender-individuals-separated-service/story?id=50112896.

McLaughlin, E., & Martinez, L. (2018, March 23). *Trump orders ban on most transgender troops, although final policy rests in courts* [Web log post]. Retrieved from http://abcnews.go.com/Politics/trump-orders-ban-transgender-troops-final-policy-rests/story?id=53963411.

Marimow, A. (2017, August 2). Case of Virginia transgender teen Gavin Grimm put off by appeals court. *The Washington Post*. Retrieved from https://www.washingtonpost.com/local/public-safety/case-of-virginia-transgender-teen-gavin-grimm-put-off-by-appeals-court/2017/08/02/4d49a254-77ad-11e7-8839-ec48ec4cae25_story.html?utm_term=.58e998937301.

Marimow, A. (2018, December 10). Trump administration: It's 'extraordinary judges won't let military restrict transgender troops'. *The Washington Post*. Retrieved from https://www.washingtonpost.com/local/legal-issues/president-trumps-transgender-military-ban-is-back-in-court/2018/12/09/56a0c13a-f965-11e8-8c9a-860ce2a8148f_story.html?noredirect=on&utm_term=.9a1711be45ff.

Obergefell v. Hodges, 576 U.S. __ (2015).

Onyulo, T. (2018, September 20). *LGBT refugees say they face hostility, violence in Kenyan camp* [Web log post]. Retrieved from https://religionnews.com/2018/09/20/lbgt-refugees-say-they-face-hostility-violence-in-kenyan-camp/.

Parekh, R. (2016, February). *What is gender dysphoria?* American Psychiatric Association Expert Q&A. Retrieved from https://www.psychiatry.org/patients-families/gender-dysphoria/what-is-gender-dysphoria.

Rankin, S. (2003). *Campus climate for gay, lesbian, bisexual, and transgender people: A national perspective.* Washington, DC: Policy Institute of the National Gay and Lesbian Task Force. Retrieved from http://thetaskforce.org/downloads/reports/reports/CampusClimate.pdf.

Rankin, S., Weber, G., Blumenfeld, W., & Frazer, S. (2010). *2010 state of higher education for lesbian, gay, bisexual and transgender people.* Campus Pride 2010 National College climate survey. Retrieved from https://www.campuspride.org/wp-content/uploads/campuspride2010lgbtreportssummary.pdf.

Sands, G., & Seyler, M. (2017, October 6). *Trump administration moves to dismiss first lawsuit against transgender military ban* [Web log post]. Retrieved from http://abcnews.go.com/Politics/trump-administration-moves-dismiss-lawsuit-transgender-military-ban/story?id=50310395.

Schaefer, A., Iyengar, R., Kadiyala, S., Kavanagh, J., Engel, C., Williams, K., & Kress, A. (2016). *Assessing the implications of allowing transgender personnel to serve openly.* Retrieved from Rand Corporation website: https://www.rand.org/pubs/research_reports/RR1530.html.

Sherwood, M. (2017, June 19). *Canada: A safer haven for LGBT refugees* [Web log post]. Retrieved from https://www.theglobeandmail.com/news/national/worldpride/article19285991/.

Stein, F. (2017, February 23). *APA statement on protecting transgender youth* [Web log post]. Retrieved from https://www.aap.org/en-us/about-the-aap/aap-press-room/pages/AAP-Statement-on-Protecting-Transgender-Youth.aspx.

Stotzer, R. (2007, June). *Comparison of hate crime rates across protected and unprotected groups.* The Williams Institute. Retrieved from http://williamsinstitute.law.ucla.edu/wp-content/uploads/Stotzer-Comparison-Hate-Crime-June-2007.pdf.

Stracqualursi, V., & Chavez, P. (2017, November 8). *Democratic LGBT, other minority candidates see historic wins, but long-term impact on diversity unclear* [Web log post]. Retrieved from http://abcnews.go.com/Politics/democratic-lgbt-minority-candidates-historic-wins-long-term/story?id=51009433.

The Free Dictionary by Farlex. (2016). *Sodomy.* Retrieved from http://legal-dictionary.thefreedictionary.com/sodomy.

Tillet, E. (2019, April 12). *Controversial Trump administration ban on transgender troops goes into effect* [Web log post]. Retrieved from https://www.cbsnews.com/news/transgender-military-ban-trump-administration-ban-on-transgender-troops-goes-into-effect/.

Trammell, J. (2014, May/June). *LGBT challenges in higher education today: 5 core principles for success* [Web log post]. Retrieved from http://www.agb.org/trusteeship/2014/5/lgbt-challenges-higher-education-today-5-core-principles-success#.

Walker, S. (2017, October 16). *Victim of Chechnya's 'gay purge' calls on Russia to investigate* [Web log post]. Retrieved from https://www.theguardian.com/world/2017/oct/16/victim-chechnya-anti-gay-purge-urges-russia-investigate-maxim-lapunov.

Weinberg, T. (2019, April 24). *Jane Castor elected Tampa's first openly LGBTQ mayor* [Web log post]. Retrieved from https://abcnews.go.com/Politics/jane-castor-elected-tampas-openly-lgbtq-mayor/story?id=62597692.

CHAPTER 3

Access to Health Care

CULTURALLY COMPETENT HEALTH CARE

This chapter will discuss the significance of access to health care for LGBT persons, with a focus on the impact of health care reform which was codified into law via the Affordable Care Act (ACA) and attempts to repeal it.

> Nancy Pelosi says the angry opposition to health care reform is like the angry opposition to gay rights that led to Harvey Milk being shot. (P. J. O'Rourke, comedian and entertainer, n.d.)

The concept of culturally competent health care is the first area of importance in understanding health care outcomes for marginalized communities. Culturally competent health care is defined as the ability of providers and organizations to effectively deliver health care services that meet the social, cultural, and linguistic needs of patients (Butler et al., 2016). Educating providers to deliver culturally competent health care to LGBT patients has the potential to improve health outcomes and quality of care while eliminating health disparities among this community. While most health care providers do not receive specific training in LGBT health, protocols, and recommendations (Butler et al., 2016), there have been attempts to provide culturally competent LGBT health care training (Butler et al., 2016). Butler et al. (2016) sought to conduct a review of evaluations of such interventions, but found a paucity of studies that met their criteria which included only studies designed to better inform the average, nonspecialized

© The Author(s) 2020   53
S. R. Notaro, *Marginality and Global LGBT Communities,*
Neighborhoods, Communities, and Urban Marginality,
https://doi.org/10.1007/978-3-030-22415-8_3

provider and health care system of appropriate ways and strategies to improve the health of LGBT individuals. This approach explicitly excluded providers embedded in the so-called "parallel" system (e.g., public health, specialized LGBT clinics, and AIDS service organizations or ASOs) as the authors' goal was to evaluate efforts of providers who do not typically receive specialized training or have caseloads consisting mostly of LGBT individuals (Butler et al., 2016).

Butler et al. (2016) reviewed 11 studies, including 5 randomized controlled trials conducted from 2002 to 2013. The interventions provided culturally competent LGBT health care training in several areas targeting providers and patients, in inpatient, outpatient, and community settings (Butler et al., 2016). Intermediate outcomes included provider competencies, knowledge, changes in attitude, behaviors such as decision-making, and beliefs such as stereotypes; improved access to health services, utilization of health services, patient experience and satisfaction, patient health behaviors, and use of preventive services and other access to care (Butler et al., 2016). Final outcomes included the patient's physical and mental health outcomes (Butler et al., 2016).

One of the randomized control trials attempted to use culturally competent counseling to increase rates of breast self-examination and mammography among women who self-identified as lesbian or bisexual (e.g., Bowen, Powers, & Greenlee, 2006; Butler et al., 2016). The culturally competent approach included concordance between the patient and the provider such that participants were informed that all scientists, staff, and counselors involved with the study were self-identified as sexual minority women (e.g., Bowen et al., 2006; Butler et al., 2016). While the authors reported significant increases in both breast self-examination and mammography and significant decreases in perceived risk and cancer worry as compared to a waitlisted control group, they did not include a control group of providers whose sexual identity was not explicitly identified as lesbian or bisexual (e.g., Bowen et al., 2006; Butler et al., 2016).

Overall, Butler et al. (2016) concluded that research evaluating ways to reduce LGBT health disparities through cultural competency interventions are sparse and limited in terms of non-randomized designs, low sample size and response rates, and lack of tests of statistical significance (Butler et al., 2016). A much larger body of research has examined ways to deliver culturally competent HIV prevention for the LGBT population, and specifically to men who have sex with men (MSM), as compared to non-specialized systems of care (Butler et al., 2016). Butler et al. (2016) argue for a main-stream approach to delivering culturally competent care to LGBT individuals, ensuring that patients have the choice of where to obtain care that is not driven by stigma or lack of skill. Further, research into other areas of LGBT health disparities beyond HIV/AIDS, including obesity, mental health, substance abuse, and suicide, while also ensuring the inclusion of intersectional identities including sexual minority women, transgender people, and LGBT youth would be beneficial (Butler et al., 2016). Finally, more research focusing on the effectiveness of culturally tailored interventions versus patient-centered or individualized interventions would add to our understanding of the impact of these related approaches (Butler et al., 2016).

ACCESS TO HEALTH INSURANCE

In addition to the need for culturally competent care, LGBT individuals are seeking expanded access to health insurance. In response, recent United States Supreme Court decisions have expanded pathways to health insurance for the LGBT community (Kates, Ranji, Beamesderfer, Salganicoff, & Dawson, 2017). As discussed in Chapter 2 of this volume, perhaps the most influential of these decisions was the 2015 *Obergefell v. Hodges* ruling in which the United States Supreme Court cited both the Due Process Clause and the Equal Protection Clause of the Fourteenth Amendment in its recognition of same-sex marriages nationwide. Although the decision was not unanimous, former Justice Anthony Kennedy eloquently stated the majority opinion's reasoning for recognizing the legality of same-sex marriage:

> In forming a marital union, two people become something greater than once they were. As some of the petitioners in these cases demonstrate, marriage embodies a love that may endure even past death. It would misunderstand these men and women to say they disrespect the idea of marriage. Their plea is that they do respect it, respect it so deeply that they seek to find its fulfillment for themselves. Their hope is not to be condemned to live in loneliness, excluded from one of civilization's oldest institutions. They ask for equal dignity in the eyes of the law. The Constitution grants them that right. (Justice Anthony Kennedy, *Obergefell v. Hodges*, A. Soergel, 2015)

The Kaiser Family Foundation details a variety of outcomes stemming from the 2015 *Obergefell* ruling including changes in federal and state tax regulations that ended tax penalties levied upon same-sex married couples who utilize dependent spousal coverage (Kates et al., 2017). In terms of military and veteran benefits, the *Obergefell* decision led to the Department of Veterans Affairs recognizing all same-sex marriages and extending benefits to all same-sex spouses of veterans, including health coverage, survivor compensation, and burial benefits (Kates et al., 2017). Similarly, federal, state, and local employees and contract employees are all eligible for same-sex spousal coverage (Kates et al., 2017).

In terms of private employers, the *Obergefell* decision does not require such employers to offer same-sex spousal coverage; however, an April 2017 federal appeals court ruling (*Zarda vs. Altitude Express, Inc.*) has extended Title VII of the Civil Rights Act's anti-discrimination protections in employment discrimination to sexual orientation (Kates et al., 2017). This ruling, although technically applying only to the states of Illinois, Minnesota, and Wisconsin, has implications for same-sex spousal coverage nationwide in that employers who offer health benefits to only opposite-sex spouses but not to same-sex spouses would likely be in violation of Title VII's anti-discrimination provision (Fensholt, 2017). The *Obergefell* decision is in line with the Equal Employment Opportunity Commission's (EEOC) regulation which found Title VII's prohibition on sex discrimination to extend to sexual orientation (Fensholt, 2017). Further, the EEOC found that private and public sector employees may bring potential Title VII same-sex spousal discrimination cases for its review (Kates et al., 2017). Employers who provide only opposite-sex spousal coverage may also be in violation of state non-discrimination laws (Kates et al., 2017). Discrimination in private health insurance based on sexual orientation and gender identity (SOGI) is prohibited in twelve states (California, Colorado, Delaware, Hawaii, Illinois, Maine, Minnesota, Nevada, New York, Oregon, Rhode Island, Vermont, and West Virginia) as well as the District of Columbia (Kates et al., 2017).

The *Obergefell* decision did clarify that private group health plans may extend some benefits to married same-sex couples offered under the Department of Labor's Employment Retirement Income Security Act of 1974 which sets minimum standards for pension and health plans (Kates et al., 2017). Specifically, with *Obergefell*'s recognition of same-sex couples nationwide, private group health plans may extend both the Consolidated Omnibus Budget Reconciliation Act (COBRA), the law offering employees and their families a temporary extension of group health coverage after a job loss or other qualifying events, as well as special enrollments rights for newly-married spouses, to same-sex married couples (Kates et al., 2017).

The Kaiser Family Foundation provides an overview of the access to employer-sponsored health coverage for same-sex spouses and domestic partners based on a telephone survey of 2137 randomly selected non-federal public and private employers with three or more workers (Dawson, Kates, & Rae, 2017). Survey results, based on a 33% response rate, revealed that overall in 2017 approximately 57% of firms offering health insurance coverage to opposite-sex spouses also provided same-sex spousal coverage while 11% did not provide such benefits (Dawson et al., 2017). Results showed that among firms that offer opposite-sex spousal coverage, 88% of large firms (those with 200 or more employees) were more likely to also offer this coverage to same-sex spouses as compared to 56% of smaller firms (Dawson et al., 2017). In terms of the largest employers (those with more than 1000 workers), 92% of them provided health insurance benefits to same-sex spouses as contrasted with 56% of the smallest employers (those with 3–199 workers) (Dawson et al., 2017). Most of the employees in the United States work at larger firms (200 or more employees) and 71% of such firms offer same-sex spousal health insurance benefits as compared to 97% of the largest firms (those with 1000 or more workers) (Dawson et al., 2017).

In terms of domestic partner (unmarried couples) benefits, some questions had arisen about whether or not the *Obergefell* decision recognizing same-sex marriage would decrease the number of employers offering domestic partner benefits (Dawson et al., 2017). Survey data comparing domestic partner benefits before and after the *Obergefell* decision indicate no statistically significant difference between the percentage of employers offering same-sex domestic partner health coverage in 2017 as compared to 2012 (Dawson et al., 2017). Further, 52% of large firms who provided same-sex spousal benefits also provided same-sex domestic partner benefits (Dawson et al., 2017).

In addition to examining the impact of recent court rulings on the access to health care and insurance within the LGBT community as a whole, research from the 2013 National Health Interview Survey specifically examined health care service utilization and health care access by self-reported sexual orientation. Results indicated that for some measures, including access to care, bisexuals have less access to care as compared to heterosexuals, while lesbian and gay people have access comparable to heterosexuals (Ward, Dahlhamer, Galinsky, & Joestl, 2014) Further, the data revealed that while the uninsured rate did not differ by sexual orientation, bisexual adults reported having a usual place to go for medical care less often and going without medical care due to cost more frequently than lesbian or gay people (Ward et al., 2014). As is common with most state and national health surveys, the National Health Interview Study did not include questions regarding gender identity, thus leaving the possibility of differences in health care access among transgender individuals an open question (Kates et al., 2017).

In terms of coverage, Baker, Cray, and Gates (2013) explore changes in access to both Medicare and Medicaid for LGBT persons. Medicare is a federal program providing health coverage for those persons aged 65 or older or under 65 if they have a disability, regardless of income. Medicaid is a combined state and federal program providing health coverage for low income families and individuals as well as other groups such as pregnant women and those with disabilities. Baker et al. (2013) estimated that the expansion of Medicaid (which made Medicaid available to adults with no children and based eligibility on income) by states who chose to expand made it possible for 390,000 LGBT people to qualify for Medicaid and for approximately 1.12 million uninsured LGBT people to receive federal subsidies to defray the costs of coverage in insurance marketplaces. Due to the legalization of same-sex marriages nationwide, some Medicare benefits that had previously been available only to opposite-sex married couples (e.g., free Medicare Part A hospital premiums, spouses receiving care at the same skilled nursing facility) were extended for the first time to same-sex married couples (Kates et al., 2017).

Two additional areas of expansion in access to health care have resulted from the legalization of same-sex marriages—the Affordable Health Care Act (ACA) and the Children's Health Insurance Program (CHIP). The Affordable Care Act (ACA or "Obamacare") is a signature piece of legislation signed into law in 2010 by President Barack Obama as a major restructuring of the U.S. health care system with the overall goal of reducing the amount of uncompensated care incurred by the average U.S. family by requiring everyone to have health insurance or pay a tax penalty. The Children's Health Insurance Plan (CHIP), offered by each state in cooperation with Medicaid programs, provides affordable health coverage to children living in families whose income is above the eligibility for Medicaid. The eligibility for assistance in the ACA health insurance marketplaces and for coverage under Medicaid and CHIP must now take into account same-sex marriages (Kates et al., 2017).

One development that may reverse some of the gains in the expansion of health care coverage to lower and middle income LGBT individuals is U.S. President Donald Trump and his administration's recent decision to end reimbursements to insurers for reducing the deductibles and co-pays of lower-income ACA enrollees (Luhby, 2017). Under the ACA, insurers are required to continue the discounts although they will not be reimbursed by the federal government. This reduction in federal funding was anticipated by some carriers who adjusted in several ways—either by announcing substantial rate increases for 2018, contemplating the raising of rates in the near future, or withdrawing altogether from the health care exchanges (Luhby, 2017). Enrollees, including LGBT individuals, will continue to receive the subsidies and will not pay much more for their health care in the exchanges, but they may be forced to change plans to keep their rates steady and those who earn too much to qualify for the subsidies may face much higher rates (Luhby, 2017). Given these changes, although insurers must continue providing cost-sharing discounts under the ACA, the Trump administration's decision to end the reimbursements could halt some of the increases in access to care that were starting to accrue to lower and middle income LGBT individuals under the ACA (Luhby, 2017).

ACA Nondiscrimination Protections

Recent policy changes stemming from the ACA have expanded health insurance coverage for LGBT individuals and their families while also providing protections based on gender identity and sexual orientation (USD-HHS, 2015). For example, in 2015, the Centers for Medicaid and Medicare (CMS) issued guidance clarifying that preventive services under the ACA are available for all patients, regardless of gender identity, sex assigned at birth, or recorded birth (USDHHS, 2015). Such guidance combats some of the discrimination that transgender individuals have suffered in the health care system related to the fact that the majority of states will not allow the recorded sex at birth to be changed. Some transgender individuals have then reported problems with providers refusing to provide certain health-related services that do not "match" the gender of the person's birth certificate (Grant et al., 2011).

The ACAs' nondiscrimination protections also included a prohibition against denying health insurance due to a preexisting medical condition, including HIV, mental illness, and transgender-related health services which disproportionately affected LGBT individuals (Kates et al., 2017). More specifically, Section 1557 of the ACA prohibits certain entities (e.g., insurers and health care providers) who receive federal payments through the Department of Health and Human Services (DHHS) from denying health care or health coverage based on sex, pregnancy, gender identity, and sex stereotyping (Kates et al., 2017). The 2013 Urban Institute's Health Reform Monitoring Survey demonstrated that the percentage of under-insured LGB adults decreased significantly between 2013 and 2015 (just before the first open enrollment period of the ACA and just after the close of the second open enrollment period) from 21.7 to 11.1%, representing a larger reduction than that reported by heterosexual adults (Karpman, Skopec, & Long, 2015).

The ACA addresses several other discriminatory practices in health care. Under Section 1557 of the ACA, insurance companies must consider transition-related care for transgender individuals and cannot automatically exclude a specific procedure or therapy that it covers for non-transgender individuals (National Center for Transgender Equality, 2017). For example, if an insurance company covers breast reconstruction for cancer treatment, postmenopausal hormone replacement, or genital surgery repairs after accidents, it cannot deny these treatments for gender dysphoria, a DSM-5 recognized diagnosis for transgender individuals discussed in Chapter 2 of this volume (e.g., National Center for Transgender Equality, 2017; Parekh, 2016).

Due to a recent decision by a federal trial court in August 2017, portions of the ACA Section 1557 that prohibit discrimination on the basis of gender identity and termination of pregnancy have been suspended ("ACA Issues Persist," 2017). The challenge to this portion of Section 1557 of the ACA asserts that these nondiscrimination rules exceed the authority of the DHHS and infringe upon the exercise of religion ("ACA Issues Persist," 2017). While offering no timeframe for its review, the DHHS has requested that the court stay the proceedings while DHHS completes a review of these rules, resulting in a lack of enforcement of these rules nationwide ("ACA Issues Persist," 2017).

In what is becoming a familiar shift, the Trump administration has made changes in DHHS and the Office of Civil Rights (OCR) that may erode several of the ACA's nondiscrimination protections (McGraw, 2018). For example, in May 2017, President Trump signed an executive order related to free speech and religious liberty focused on enforcing existing federal protections for religious freedom and withdrawing the ACA's requirement that employer-sponsored health insurance cover contraception (McGraw, 2018). In October 2017, the Trump administration officially allowed employers to cite religious or moral objections to justify employers' discontinuation of coverage for birth control (McGraw, 2018). In January 2018 the Trump administration announced the establishment of a new division within the DHHS focused on conscience and religious freedom (McGraw, 2018). This new division is supported by faith-based and religious freedom groups who have urged the Trump administration to strictly enforce anti-abortion conscience laws including the 1973 Church amendment requiring federally funded health care facilities to allow health care providers to refuse to perform abortions, sterilization, or other procedures based on religious or moral grounds; the 1996 Coats-Snow amendment extending those protections to medical students and residents; and the 2004 Weldon amendment extending the conscience exemptions (or the refusal to provide care based on religious objections) to a broader range of so-called health entities (Posner, 2018).

The OCR, charged with enforcing anti-discrimination laws, health privacy laws, and conscience laws, is now operated by Trump appointees whose priority is the enforcement of conscience protection laws and religious freedom as opposed to the protection of women's reproduction choices and health care access for transgender people (Posner, 2018). President Trump appointed Roger Severino as director of the (OCR), which is the office charged with enforcing anti-discrimination laws (Posner, 2018). Mr. Severino, formerly headed the Devos Center for Religion and Civil Society at the conservative Heritage Foundation (Posner, 2018). While serving in his role at the Heritage Foundation, Severino criticized the Obama administration's regulation that offers protection to transgender people as a threat to the religious conscience of some for health care providers (Posner, 2018). Shortly after Severino's appointment as director of the OCR, 12 Democratic U.S. senators sent a letter to then secretary of Health and Human Services Tom Price expressing their concern over Severino's history of statements that were unsupportive of LGBT individuals and women's access to health care services (Posner, 2018). Mr. Severino has hired several staff members into the OCR who have previously demonstrated in their work at Christian rights organizations their support for religious protections for individuals who oppose abortion and LBTQ rights (Posner, 2018). As an example, Mandi Ancalle, who now serves as a contract worker for the OCR, is considered a highly-experienced activist with detailed knowledge of the desires of the Christian right's policy goals for the Trump administration, including reviving former President George W. Bush's conscience rule which exempted health care workers from treating women, LGBTQ individuals, and others based on religious objections (Posner, 2018).

To provide perspective on the new focus on conscience violations, Mr. Severino announced at the January 18, 2018 ceremony celebrating the creation of the new Conscience and Religious Freedom Division at OCR that while the Obama administration had only received 10 complaints of conscience violations, the Trump administration had already received 34 (Posner, 2018). Such a steep increase in complaints is most likely due to the deliberate strategy of Christian rights advocacy groups taking advantage of Mr. Severino's focus on the enforcement of conscience laws (Posner, 2018). For example, the Family Research Council, a Christian rights advocacy group, sent a communication to its constituents on January 9, 2018 urging them to file conscience violation complaints with the OCR and offering a tutorial on how to do so (Posner, 2018). The regulations of the new Conscience Division extend beyond the Weldon, Church, and Coats-Snow amendments in their scope and reach, pledging to provide conscience and religious freedom enforcement and technical assistant to federal staff, health care providers, religious organizations, nonprofits, and state and local governments (Posner, 2018).

Susan Berke Fogel, the director of the National Health Law Program, a reproductive rights advocacy group, criticizes the new regulations as an attack on women and LGBT health, citing that the regulations seem to allow anyone to refuse to provide health care for any reason which may well undermine people's health and dignity (Posner, 2018). Fogel points out that the new Conscience Division's decisions regarding conscience violations will most likely be litigated in court; however, she cautions that successful litigation will probably increase such complaints while unsuccessful litigation will serve as evidence that Congress should pass more vigorous conscience laws beyond Church and Weldon (Posner, 2018). Former House Speaker Paul Ryan had signaled his approval of increasing conscience protections as shown by of his support of a bill, the Conscience Protection Act, introduced in 2016 and again in 2017, that would allow health care providers to sue for damages, including from a government provider (Posner, 2018). This bill extends the remedies of filing a complaint with OCR or seeking a court injunction to placing conscience complaints on the same legal level as those in protected classes, who may sue over discrimination for damages and attorney's fees (Posner, 2018).

As of May 2, 2019, the Department of Health and Human Services (HHS) issued its final rules governing the religious rights of health care providers and religious institutions. These rules, which represent an expansion of existing protections, allow health care workers or any workers even tangentially connected to medical procedures and who have a religious or conscience objection to the procedure (e.g., birth control, abortion, sterilization, insemination) to refuse to provide such services all together or to certain individuals such as LGBT persons (Kodjak, 2019). To affirm the shift in focus of the OCR from ensuring equal access to health care services provided by HHS to protecting religious freedom, the DHHS changed its mission statement to clearly affirm its priority of protecting religious beliefs and "moral convictions" of individuals and institutions (Kodjak, 2019).

EXPANDED DATA COLLECTION

Changes in data collection and monitoring of health disparities is another major component of the ACA designed to recognize and include LGBT populations (Kates et al., 2017). The ACA requires national health care surveys to include SOGI questions in the near future, providing for the opportunity to conduct analyses related to SOGI (Kates et al., 2017). At the national level, as of 2013, the National Health Interview Survey includes a question on sexual orientation while at the state level, the Center for Disease Control and Prevention has approved SOGI questions for inclusion on the Behavioral Risk Factor Surveillance System surveys (Kates et al., 2017). In terms of individual clinicians, some groups have urged health care providers to collect patient data regarding SOGI to better inform patients' needs (Kates et al., 2017). These efforts have met with some resistance from clinicians who express uncertainty and a lack of knowledge regarding the appropriate methods for collecting potentially sensitive information (Kates et al., 2017). Best practices in soliciting SOGI information include offering patients the reasons for collecting the information, ensuring confidentiality, providing an opt-out option, and posing several questions to more accurately assess SOGI (Kates et al., 2017). Advocates further advocate that electronic medical records serve as the repository for this data (Kates et al., 2017). A 2016 decision by the National Institutes of Health to designate sexual and gender minorities as a health disparity population further support the collection of SOGI information at all levels of health care (Kates et al., 2017).

While the addition of questionnaire items related to SOGI is a positive step toward a further understanding of health disparities and access to health care among these populations, several researchers who focus on LGBTQ communities are advocating for a transparent examination of terms, definitions, and possible sources of error in such research (e.g., Cimpian, 2017; Mayo, 2017). Mayo (2017) asserts that LGBTQ issues are approached differently depending on the discipline, potentially leading to different interpretations of outcomes. For example, not only does the terminology designating sexual and gender minorities vary within education and humanities research, but also the concept of quantitative methods and fixed-time designations of SOGI within fields such as education and public health are often in sharp contrast with qualitative methods and deliberately fluid and nontemporal designations of SOGI within the fields such as the humanities (Mayo, 2017). Mayo (2017) further asserts that SOGI data must also take into account and query intersection categories including age, race, class, and ethnicity. Including an emphasis on intersectionality has traditionally been more common in the humanities' study of LGBTQ-related issues potentially leading to a more complex yet richer understanding of context and contingency (Mayo, 2017). Mayo (2017) argues for the importance of both approaches, in that qualitative research focusing on complexity and instability may help inform the conceptual frameworks of quantitative research. Similarly, humanities-based queer studies may bolster their arguments with empirical data from disciplines such as public health (Mayo, 2017).

Cimpian (2017) echoes some of the same concerns as Mayo (2017) in terms of the need to account for a continuum of sexuality that recognizes instability, intersectionality, and complexity among sexual minorities. Cimpian (2017) is further concerned with measurement errors that may misclassify sexual minorities, and in particular sexual minority youths who are asked to identify on questionnaires as lesbian, gay, bisexual queer, or questioning. Cimpian (2017) does not include gender minorities (e.g., transgender, intersex, agender, gender-queer) in his examination of measurement error as he asserts that the research regarding gender minorities in general and classification errors related to gender minorities in particular is less well-developed. According to Cimpian (2017), the potential for misclassification of sexual minority youth gathered through population-based self-administered questionnaires can lead to errors and incorrect impressions about health disparities in these communities.

Cimpian (2017) delineates seven sources of error including fluidity, mischievousness, inclusivity, nondisclosure, misunderstanding of terminology, random reporting, and thresholds for categorization. Depending on the source of error in questionnaires, inaccurate data may over or underestimate both the population of sexual minorities as well as health disparities among this community (Cimpian, 2017). Cimpian (2017) and several other researchers (e.g., Diamond, 2008; Diamond, Bonner, & Dickenson, 2015) have argued that sexual orientation can be quite fluid, flexible, and situational with greater variation than can be captured by a cross-sectional survey administered at one point in time. Cimpian (2017) illustrates the impact of fluidity error in the following example wherein an individual reports same-sex only attraction at one time point but then reports only opposite-sex attraction at another time point. This reporting pattern results in the likelihood that this respondent may not be included among the sexual minority population at the second time point. The impact of such a fluidity error on health disparity estimates is unclear, cannot be predicted a priori, and depends upon the values of the outcomes measured at each time point (Cimpian, 2017). Cimpian (2017) points out several ways to decrease fluidity error including cross-sectional research that queries past experiences in addition to current experiences and longitudinal research that assesses sexual orientation over time without the risk of recall errors. Additionally, questionnaire items that include categories that are less rigid and more developmental such as "transition to LGB attraction" (Needham, 2012) or "heteroflexible" (Fish & Pasley, 2015) may decrease fluidity error.

The next source of error discussed is that of mischievous responding (e.g., Cimpian, 2017; Robinson-Cimpian, 2014; Savin-Williams & Joyner, 2014) in which youth respond with extreme answers viewed as humorous, out of the ordinary, or stigmatizing. Such responses typically over estimate both the population of sexual minority youth and health disparities, as their untruthful answers apply to sexual orientation as well as outcome measures (Cimpian, 2017). One caveat to this source of error, is that mischievous responding is just as possible among non-heterosexual youth or sexual minority youth as it is among heterosexual youth (Cimpian, 2017). Thus, mischievous reporting of membership in a very small minority group (e.g., sexual minority youth) may create substantially biased estimates of health disparities whereas mischievous reporting of membership in a very large group (e.g., heterosexual youth) may have less impact on estimates of health disparities (Cimpian, 2017). The research that has addressed ways to mitigate the impact of mischievous responding all rely on the gathering of additional data, either from parents (e.g., RanjiFan et al., 2006) or from the respondents regarding truthfulness of responses or items unrelated to sexual minority status such as extreme height and weight (e.g., Cornell, Klein, Konold, & Huang, 2012; Robinson-Cimpian, 2014).

Cimpian (2017) refers to the third source of measurement error as inclusivity of dimensions which describes the inconsistent use of various dimensions (e.g., identity, romantic and sexual attraction, and behavior) to categorize sexual orientation. Some critiques of earlier research investigating sexual minority adolescents assert that the focus on sexual orientation identity versus items related to attraction and behavior may have underestimated the prevalence of sexual minority youth, given that, developmentally, adolescents may have a less clear sense of their sexual identity relative to attraction (e.g., Savin-Williams, 2001). Including questions about all dimensions of sexual orientation may identify distinct categories that are related to specific outcomes and disparities (e.g., Fish & Pasley, 2015). Cimpian (2017) recommends a broad approach to measuring sexual orientation that includes all three dimensions, as some youth who do not identify as a sexual minority but who may experience romantic and/or sexual attraction could still report experiences of stigma and bias.

The fourth source of error, nondisclosure of actual group status, may lead to an underestimation of sexual minority youth; however, it is unclear whether or not the outcomes or disparities differ for youth who disclose their sexual orientation versus those who do not (Cimpian, 2017). Several options for reducing this source of measurement include ensuring respondents that the research is confidential, and perhaps anonymous, offering self-administered questionnaires, and embedding sexual minority status among a list of nonsensitive items, referred to as the veiled response technique (e.g., Badgett & Goldberg, 2009; Cimpian, 2017). Misunderstanding the survey items is a fifth source of error, affecting many identification statuses including sexual minority, race/ethnicity, and social class (Cimpian, 2017). It is unclear as to how the misunderstanding of survey items impacts the reporting of disparities; furthermore, it is difficult to measure a respondent's level of misunderstanding (Cimpian, 2017). Some prior research has attempted to reduce misunderstanding by using a cognitive processing method, commonly referred to as "think aloud" (Austin, Conron, Patel, & Feedner, 2007). Respondents who are similar to the population of those who will ultimately complete the questionnaire are asked to read and respond to the survey items while verbalizing their thought process, allowing the researchers to refine survey items to increase accurate understanding of the final survey instrument (Cimpian, 2017). Finally, some researchers have used technology that embeds definitions in computer-administered questionnaires to clarify survey items (Andrews, Nonnecke, & Preece, 2003).

Random error is a sixth source of measurement error, resulting from respondents answering survey items in a random way. The impact of random responses is variable, possibly inflating estimates of sexual minority status and decreasing estimates of health disparities (Cimpian, 2017). Reducing survey fatigue (e.g., by moving survey items pertaining to sexual orientation and other demographics earlier in the survey) is one possible mechanism of reducing the impact of random error (Cimpian, 2017). Attempting to mitigate survey fatigue does not address, however, the possibility of biased random reporting of health disparities, as such outcome measures are likely to appear later in the survey (Cimpian, 2017). A final source of error is the issue of researchers choosing the thresholds or cut-off points for the categorization of sexual minority status (Cimpian, 2017). As sexuality has been viewed on a continuum (e.g., exclusively heterosexual to exclusively homosexual) by many researchers since the 1940s (e.g., Kinsey, Pomeroy, & Martin, 1948), the problem of reducing this continuum to a categorical measure has created several forms of error (Cimpian, 2017). For example, researchers' choice of where to place the threshold of heterosexual versus homosexual can decease the likelihood of replicating findings in other studies that may define thresholds differently; furthermore, if researchers' thresholds define some non-sexual minority individuals as sexual minorities, then the results will overestimate the sexual minority population and likely underestimate health disparities (Cimpian, 2017). The reverse would be in effect if researchers' thresholds define some sexual minority individuals as non-sexual minorities, as results will underestimate the sexual minority population and likely overestimate health disparities (Cimpian, 2017). Cimpian (2017) concludes his investigation of measurement error in research concerning sexual minority youth with the hopes that future research will more accurately measure sexuality on a continuous spectrum and separate the "latent" or underlying construct of sexual orientation from the aforementioned sources of classification error.

ATTEMPTS TO REPEAL THE ACA: IMPACT ON LGBT HEALTH

The ACA's provisions that expanded the health care access of all Americans, added nondiscrimination protections, and expanded data collection would have been diminished if the attempt to repeal and replace the ACA in 2017 had been successful (GovTrack.US, *H.R. 1628: American Health Care Act [AHCA]* of 2017). The American Health Care Act of 2017 (AHCA) was championed by a group of United States House of Representative and Senate Republicans as a way to replace the ACA through budget reconciliation which allows Congress to pass a bill with a simple majority in the Senate rather than the 60 votes needed to block a filibuster (GovTrack.US, 2017). Passing a bill in this manner with a simple majority in the Senate requires the bill to only make changes that would impact the federal budget as opposed to changes such as the ACA's ban on insurance companies denying coverage to people with preexisting health conditions (GovTrack.US, 2017). The AHCA sought to retain some components of the ACA including the health care exchanges administered by the states and the federal government which sold individual and small business health insurance plans; the requirement that dependents may continue to be covered by their parents' plan until age 26; the federal government's payment of subsidies for premiums based on income; and a revised version of the individual mandate which would impose a penalty for individuals who do not obtain health insurance (The Henry J. Kaiser Family Foundation, 2017). The AHCA would have repealed several features of the ACA including the expansion of Medicaid eligibility to low income individuals who are not disabled or parents of dependent children; the expansion of Medicaid coverage of mental health and addiction services; the elimination of fines for large employers who do not offer health insurance coverage; small business tax credits; and limits on the health insurance premiums paid by older individuals as opposed to younger individuals (The Henry J. Kaiser Family Foundation, 2017).

Several provisions of the AHCA were projected to have a specific and negative impact on LGBT individual's access to health care (The Fenway Institute, 2017). By 2020, the AHCA's stipulation that Medicaid eligibility be contingent on income, disability, or parental status, would require people living with HIV who seek coverage from Medicaid for health insurance and life-saving HIV medication to meet the definition of disabled—that their disease has progressed to AIDS (The Fenway Institute, 2017). Fear of not being able to re-enroll in Medicaid in case of a job loss might deter individuals with HIV from seeking a higher paying job with private insurance (The Fenway Institute, 2017). The AHCA's revised version of the individual mandate, which would replace the ACA's flat yearly penalty for lack of coverage with a 30% insurance surcharge for individuals who have a lapse in coverage of more than 63 days, would force individuals with HIV who lose their coverage and are unable to replace it within the required timeframe to pay the 30% surcharge (The Fenway Institute, 2017). The AHCA's prohibition of Medicaid reimbursements for Planned Parenthood's reproductive health, maternal health, and child health services could disproportionately and negatively impact the LGBT community, and more specifically Black and Latino men who have sex with men and transgender women of color, who are burdened by disproportionately higher rates of HIV, other sexually transmitted infections, and unwanted pregnancies (The Fenway Institute, 2017).

On May 4, 2017, the United States House of Representatives voted in favor of passing the AHCA and repealing the Patient Protection and ACA with a vote of 217 in favor and 213 opposed (Kaplan & Pear, 2017). The House's narrow passage of the bill revealed stark disagreements within the Republican party regarding essential health benefits, protections for those with preexisting conditions, and higher insurance rates for older versus younger enrollees (Doran, 2017). In response to the passage of the House's version of the AHCA, the Senate developed several amendments or bills, including the Health Care Freedom Act also known as "skinny repeal" of the ACA (Klein, 2017). The Health Care Freedom Act would have left the ACA's Medicaid expansion intact, but would have repealed the individual mandate to have health coverage and the requirement of large employers to cover their employers, resulting in an estimated 15 million Americans without health insurance and premium increases of 20%; however, none of the amendments received enough votes to pass, leading to a 49–51 defeat of the bill in the Senate (Klein, 2017).

In September 2017, Republicans made one last attempt to repeal Obamacare via the Graham-Cassidy plan which would have provided funds to states to operate their own health care programs while reducing Medicaid funding as well as ending both subsidies to help individuals purchase health insurance policies and the reimbursements provided to insurance companies offering price reductions on copayments and deductibles to low income individuals (Kodjak, 2017). The Graham-Cassidy plan failed to gain enough support to put the bill to a vote on the Senate floor, with several Republicans refusing to support the bill due to its attempts to decrease

Medicaid funding and to weaken protections for people with preexisting conditions (Cornwell, 2017). After seven years, the Republican effort to repeal Obamacare failed (Cornwell, 2017).

While the ACA is currently the law of the land and continues to provide health insurance for an estimated 20 million Americans, including low income, ethnic minority, and LGBT individuals, on December 14, 2018, Judge Reed O'Conner, a federal district court judge in Texas, responded to a lawsuit brought by Republican attorneys general from 20 states challenging the constitutionality of the ACA's individual mandate (Hadar, 2018). Judge O'Connor ruled that because a recent Trump administration tax reform bill set the individual mandate's tax to zero, then Congress could no longer constitutionally impose a tax or penalty on those individuals who did not obtain health insurance (Hadar, 2018). Judge O'Connor ruled that without the individual mandate, the rest of the ACA should not stand (Hadar, 2018). As the judge did not issue an injunction, the ACA continues during the appeal process which will likely land at the U.S. Supreme Court (Hadar, 2018).

Summary

This chapter focused on culturally competent health care, access to health insurance, and the Affordable Care Act's impact on LGBT health and well-being. Butler et al.'s (2016) review of attempts to provide culturally competent LGBT health care training concluded with a call for a mainstream approach to delivering culturally competent care to LGBT individuals, ensuring that patients have the choice of where to obtain care that is not driven by stigma or lack of skill. Next, the chapter explained recent legal and policy changes that have led to expanded access to health insurance for LGBT individuals, including the legalization of same-sex marriage and the expansion of many coverage and anti-discriminatory provisions of the ACA. The chapter also discussed several attempts to erode the ACA's provisions that expanded the health care access of all Americans, added nondiscrimination protections, and expanded data collection. In sum, the access to health care for LGBT persons faces renewed challenges under the Trump administration. It is likely that the U.S. Supreme Court will again weigh in on the overall legality of the ACA with possible negative consequences and impacts on health disparities experienced by marginalized populations such as the LGBT community. Chapter 4 of this volume will discuss the history and evolution of HIV/AIDS within the LGBT community as well as some promising avenues for prevention and intervention.

REFERENCES

Andrews, D., Nonnecke, B., & Preece, J. (2003). Electronic survey methodology: A case study in reaching hard-to-involve internet users. *International Journal of Human-Computer Interaction, 16,* 185–210.

Austin, S., Conron, K., Patel, A., & Feedner, N. (2007). Making sense of sexual orientation measures: Findings from a cognitive processing study with adolescents on health survey questions. *Journal of LGBT Health Research, 3,* 55–65.

Badgett, M., & Goldberg, N. (2009). *Best practices for asking questions about sexual orientation on surveys.* Los Angeles, CA: UCLA, The Williams Institute. Retrieved from https://escholarship.org/uc/item/706057d5.

Baker, K., Cray, A., & Gates, G. (2013). *Infographic: How new coverage options affect LGBT communities.* Washington, DC: Center for American Progress. Retrieved from https://www.americanprogress.org/issues/lgbt/news/2013/09/12/74029/infographic-how-new-coverage-options-affect-lgbt-communities/.

Bowen, D., Powers, D., & Greenlee, H. (2006). Effects of breast cancer risk counseling for sexual minority women. *Health Care Women International, 27*(1), 59–74.

Butler, M., McGreedy, E., Schwer, N., Burgess, D., Call, K., Przedworski, J., ... Kane, R. (2016). *Improving cultural competence to reduce health disparities: Lesbian, gay, bisexual, and transgender populations.* Agency for Healthcare Research and Quality (US). Retrieved from https://www.ncbi.nlm.nih.gov/books/NBK361118/.

Cimpian, J. (2017). Classification errors and bias regarding research on sexual minority youth. *American Educational Research Association, 46*(9), 517–529.

Cornell, D., Klein, J., Konold, T., & Huang, F. (2012). Effects of validity screening items on adolescent survey data. *Psychological Assessment, 24,* 21–35.

Cornwell, S. (2017, September 26). Republican attempt to Obamacare fails. *Reuters News Agency* [Web log post]. Retrieved from https://www.reuters.com/article/us-usa-healthcare/republicans-fail-again-to-kill-off-obamacare-in-senate-idUSKCN1C00BT.

Dawson, L., Kates, J., & Rae, M. (2017, September). *Access to employer-sponsored health coverage for same-sex spouses: 2017 Update.* The Henry J. Kaiser Family Foundation. Retrieved from https://www.kff.org/disparities-policy/issue-brief/access-to-employer-sponsored-health-coverage-for-same-sex-spouses-2017-update/.

Diamond, L. (2008). *Sexual fluidity: Understanding women's love and desire.* Cambridge, MA: Harvard University Press.

Diamond, L., Bonner, S., & Dickenson, J. (2015). The development of sexuality. In R. M. Lerned (Ed.), *Handbook of child psychology and developmental science* (pp. 888–931). New York, NY: Wiley.

Doran, W. (2017, May 4). Does new version of the AHCA protect coverage for pre-existing conditions? *Politifact North Carolina* [Web log post]. Retrieved from http://www.politifact.com/north-carolina/statements/2017/may/04/robert-pittenger/does-new-version-ahca-protect-coverage-pre-existin/.

Fensholt, E. (2017, April 27). *Federal court extends Title VII protections to sexual orientation: Implications for same-sex spouse coverage, domestic partners, and transgender rights.* Lockton Benefits Blog [Web log post]. Retrieved from http://locktonbenefitsblog.com/federal-court-extends-title-vii-protections-to-sexual-orientation-implications-for-same-sex-spouse-coverage-domestic-partners-and-transgender-rights/.

Fish, J., & Pasley, K. (2015). Sexual (minority) trajectories, mental health, and alcohol use: A longitudinal study of youth as they transition to adulthood. *Journal of Youth and Adolescence, 44,* 1508–1527.

GovTrack.US, Civic Impulse, LLC. (2017). *H.R. 1628: American Health Care Act of 2017.* Retrieved from https://www.govtrack.us/congress/bills/115/hr1628.

Grant, J., Mottet, L., Tanis, J., Harrison, H., Herman, J., & Keisling, M. (2011). *Injustice at every turn: A report of the national transgender discrimination survey.* Washington, DC: National Center for Transgender Equality and National Gay and Lesbian Task Force. Retrieved from http://www.thetaskforce.org/static_html/downloads/reports/reports/ntds_full.pdf.

Hadar, R. (2018, December 16). Senator Susan Collins: Obamacare court decision 'far too sweeping,' health care law 'should be maintained'. *ABC News.* Retrieved from https://abcnews.go.com/Politics/sen-susan-collins-obamacare-court-decision-sweeping-law/story?id=59839457.

Kaplan, T., & Pear, R. (2017, May 4). House passes measure to repeal and replace the Affordable Care Act. *The New York Times* [Web log post]. Retrieved from https://www.nytimes.com/2017/05/04/us/politics/health-care-bill-vote.html.

Karpman, M., Skopec, L., & Long, S. (2015, April). *QuickTake: Uninsurance rate nearly halved for lesbian, gay, and bisexual adults since mid-2013.* Urban Institute Health Policy Center. Retrieved from http://hrms.urban.org/quicktakes/Uninsurance-Rate-Nearly-Halved-for-Lesbian-Gay-and-Bisexual-Adults-since-Mid-2013.html.

Kates, J., Ranji, U., Beamesderfer, A., Salganicoff, A., & Dawson, L. (2017, August). *Health and access to care and coverage for lesbian, gay, bisexual, and transgender individuals in the U.S.* The Henry J. Kaiser Family Foundation. Retrieved from https://www.kff.org/disparities-policy/issue-brief/health-

and-access-to-care-and-coverage-for-lesbian-gay-bisexual-and-transgender-individuals-in-the-u-s/.

Kinsey, A., Pomeroy, W., & Martin, C. (1948). *Sexual behavior in the human male.* Oxford, England: Saunders.

Klein, E. (2017, July 28). The GOP's massive health care failures, explained. *Vox* [Web log post]. Retrieved from https://www.vox.com/health-care/2017/7/28/16055284/gop-massive-health-care-failures-explained.

Kodjak, A. (2017, September 19). Latest GOP effort to replace Obamacare could end health care for millions. *NPR Health News* [Web log post]. Retrieved from https://www.npr.org/sections/health-shots/2017/09/19/552044236/latest-gop-effort-to-replace-obamacare-could-end-health-care-for-millions.

Kodjak, A. (2019, May 2). *New Trump rule protects health care workers who refuse care for religious reasons* [Web log post]. Retrieved from https://www.npr.org/sections/health-shots/2019/05/02/688260025/new-trump-rule-protects-health-care-workers-who-refuse-care-for-religious-reason.

Luhby, T. (2017, October 13). *What's in Trump's health care executive orders?* [Web log post]. Retrieved from https://money.cnn.com/2017/10/12/news/economy/trump-health-care-executive-order/index.html.

Mayo, C. (2017). Queer and trans youth, relational subjectivity, and uncertain possibilities: Challenging research in complicated contexts. *American Educational Research Association, 46*(9), 530–538.

McGraw, M. (2018, January 18). *Trump administration announces new 'conscience and religious freedom' division at HHS* [Web log post]. Retrieved from http://abcnews.go.com/Politics/trump-administration-announce-conscience-religious-freedom-division-hhs/story?id=52434480.

National Center for Transgender Equality. (2017, June). *What are my healthcare rights?* Retrieved from https://transequality.org/know-your-rights/healthcare.

Needham, B. (2012). Sexual attraction and trajectories of mental health and substance use during the transition from adolescence to adulthood. *Journal of Youth and Adolescence, 41,* 179–190.

O'Rourke, P. J. (n.d.). *Quotes.* BrainyQuote.com. Retrieved from https://www.brainyquote.com/quotes/p_j_orourke_617600.

Parekh, R. (2016, February). *What is gender dysphoria?* American Psychiatric Association Expert Q&A. Retrieved from https://www.psychiatry.org/patients-families/gender-dysphoria/what-is-gender-dysphoria.

Posner, S. (2018, January). *One doctor is risking Illinois' federal funding* [Web log post]. Retrieved from https://www.theinvestigativefund.org/investigation/2018/01/28/one-doctor-risking-illinois-federal-funding/.

RanjiFan, X., Miller, B., Park, K., Winward, B., Christensen, M., Grotevant, H., & Tai, R. (2006). An exploratory study about inaccuracy and invalidity in adolescent self-report surveys. *Field Methods, 18,* 223–244.

Robinson-Cimpian, J. (2014). Inaccurate estimation of disparities due to mis-chievous responders: Several suggestions to assess conclusions. *Educational Researcher, 43,* 171–185.

Savin-Williams, R. (2001). A critique of research on sexual-minority youths. *Journal of Research on Adolescence, 24,* 5–13.

Savin-Williams, R., & Joyner, K. (2014). The dubious assessment of gay, les-bian, and bisexual adolescents of add health. *Archives of Sexual Behavior, 43,* 1027–1030.

Soergel, A. (2015). *9 Need-to-know quotes from the* Obergefell v. Hodges *opinions* [Web log post]. Retrieved from https://www.usnews.com/news/articles/2015/06/26/9-need-to-know-quotes-from-the-obergefell-v-hodges-opinions.

The Fenway Institute, Fenway Health Newsroom, Health Care, Health Policy, HIV/AIDS, LGBT Health. (2017, March). *The American Health Care Act would harm LGBT people, people living with HIV, and Black and Latino Americans, according to Fenway Institute analysis.* Retrieved from http://fenwayhealth.org/the-american-health-care-act-would-harm-lgbt-people-people-living-with-hiv-and-black-and-latino-americans-according-to-fenway-institute-analysis/.

The Henry J. Kaiser Family Foundation. (2017, May). *Summary of the American Health Care Act.* Retrieved from http://files.kff.org/attachment/Proposals-to-Replace-the-Affordable-Care-Act-Summary-of-the-American-Health-Care-Act.

U.S. Department of Health and Human Services. (2015). *Advancing LGBT health and well-being* (LGBT issues coordinating committee 2015 annual report). Retrieved from https://www.hhs.gov/sites/default/files/dhhs-lgbt-2015-annual-report.pdf.

Ward, B., Dahlhamer, J., Galinsky, A., & Joestl, S. (2014). *Sexual orientation and health among U.S. adults: National Health Interview Survey* (National Health Statistics Report No. 77). Retrieved from https://www.cdc.gov/nchs/data/nhsr/nhsr077.pdf.

CHAPTER 4

HIV/AIDS

This chapter will discuss disparities in sexually transmitted infections, including the human immunodeficiency virus (HIV), that exist among some of the most stigmatized members of the LGBT community.

> Because of the lack of education on AIDS, discrimination, fear, panic, and lies surrounded me. (Ryan White, hemophiliac who died from AIDS in 1990 at the age of 19)

These life-threatening disparities illustrate how silence, bias, and isolation that were also present in the pre and immediate Stonewall era can lead to unequal treatment, victimization, and poor health outcomes. Furthermore, such health disparities have devastating consequences for men who have sex with men (MSM) and transgender women in particular with MSM accounting for approximately 2% of the population but nearly 70% (26,200) of new HIV infections as of 2014 (U.S. DHHS, 2018). Further, as of 2015 more than 600,000 gay and bisexual men were living with HIV in the United States and were estimated to account for 55% (10,047) of people who received an AIDS diagnosis (U.S. DHHS, 2018). Disparities within this population are apparent, as racial minorities are overrepresented in those gay and bisexual men with an AIDS diagnosis—39% African American, 31% White, and 24% Hispanic/Latino (U.S. DHHS, 2018). As 1 in 6 or approximately 17% of gay and bisexual men living with HIV are unaware of their

© The Author(s) 2020
S. R. Notaro, *Marginality and Global LGBT Communities*,
Neighborhoods, Communities, and Urban Marginality,
https://doi.org/10.1007/978-3-030-22415-8_4

infection, they are less likely to seek drug therapy and to engage in behaviors that would prevent transmitting HIV to partners (U.S. DHHS, 2018). Gay and bisexual men also report higher rates of other sexually transmitted infections including syphilis, gonorrhea, and chlamydia. Moreover, men who have sex with men (MSM) are more likely to exhibit antimicrobial resistant strains of gonorrhea, resulting in decreased effectiveness of drugs designed to fight infection (U.S. DHHS, 2017).

History of HIV/AIDS

Before examining the current state of the transmission, prevention, and intervention of HIV infections, and ways in which an understanding of the Stonewall resistance (discussed in Chapter 1 of this volume) might prove empowering, it is important to trace the history of HIV/AIDS. In the 1970s, after experiencing an uplifting sense of belonging spurred by Stonewall riots, the LGBT community began to openly explore sexuality, enjoying the same sexual freedoms as heterosexuals (Bausum, 2015). And then, in 1981, the symptoms of AIDS (Acquired Immunodeficiency Syndrome) were first identified—skin lesions, pneumonia, night sweats, throat infections—that did not respond to treatment. All of those affected, mostly young men who had been healthy prior to these symptoms, died, often within months (Bausum, 2015). As the crisis was identified with homosexual men, staunch political conservatives such as Patrick J. Buchanan declared that AIDS was God's will and served as a punishment for immoral behavior:

> The poor homosexuals. They have declared war upon nature, and now nature is exacting an awful retribution. (Patrick Buchanan, 1983, *New York Post*)

Some other conservative politicians urged that persons infected with AIDS should be branded and quarantined (Bausum, 2015). During the presidency of Ronald Reagan, the AIDS crisis was largely ignored, with President Reagan finally mentioning it publicly for the first time near the end of his term in 1987 (Bausum, 2015). By the end of 1987 more than 50,000 cases of AIDS, mostly among gay men, had been diagnosed, resulting in extremely high mortality (Bausum, 2015). As in the pre-Stonewall era, silence and stigma were rampant as the U.S. government failed to provide funding or support for this devastating new disease (Bausum, 2015). Beliefs among some gay men that their lifestyles were under attack while receiving no support from the government created a deadly environment associated with more infections and mortality (Bausum, 2015).

Just when it seemed that the momentum from the Stonewall resistance was permanently squelched by the dire AIDS crisis, a new era of activism formed to demand federal funding and political action to combat AIDS. In 1987, the AIDS Quilt was first displayed with panels honoring almost 50,000 Americans who had died of AIDS (Bausum, 2015). During the same year, gay persons and straight supporters formed ACT UP or the AIDS Coalition to Unleash Power, which helped to unite gay men and lesbians in the fight against AIDS (Bausum, 2015). The tactics and strategies employed by ACT UP harkened back to those of earlier gay rights groups that had emerged in the immediate months and years after the Stonewall riots—zaps, theater, and civil disobedience (Bausum, 2015). ACT UP targeted several key institutions who could do more for the AIDS crisis including the Food and Drug Administration and the National Institutes of Health. Notably, the White House, under George H.W. Bush's presidency, was the target of a 1992 protest in which ashes of AIDS victims were tossed on the White House lawn (Bausum, 2015).

AIDS continued to ravage not only the gay male community, but also persons who injected drugs (PWID) and those who underwent drug transfusions. This dire situation changed, however, when President Bill Clinton provided hundreds of millions of federal dollars for AIDS research (Bausum, 2015). Three years into his first term, the National Institutes of Health formulated a powerful and effective antiretroviral "cocktail" that prevented the progression of AIDS. Although not a cure, this discovery ended the death sentence for those who could access the cocktail. AIDS deaths in the United States reached a peak of nearly 50,000 in 1995 but then declined. Additionally, the new funding for awareness and prevention greatly decreased the number of new infections.

In response to evidence that the HIV/AIDS epidemic was especially critical in sub-Saharan Africa and low and middle income communities, President George W. Bush created the President's Emergency Plan for AIDS Relief (PEPFAR) in 2004 (Peng, 2015). Funding for antiretroviral treatment (ART) was the main focus of PEPFAR. Evidence from the Joint United Nations Programme on HIV/AIDS (UNAIDS) demonstrated that, from 1995 to 2013, antiretroviral drugs provided by PEPFAR and other agencies such as the Global Fund to Fight AIDS, Tuberculosis, and Malaria have averted an estimated 7.6 million AIDS-related deaths globally, including 4.8 million deaths in sub-Saharan Africa (UNAIDS, 2014).

In 2010 President Barack Obama launched the first National HIV/AIDS strategy and updated it in 2015 ("Fact Sheet," 2015). The four goals of the initiative remain the same—to reduce the number of new HIV infections, to increase access to health care and improve health outcomes for people living with HIV, to reduce HIV-related disparities and health inequities, and to achieve a more coordinated national response ("Fact Sheet," 2015).

Although considerable progress has been made in the AIDS epidemic, including marked reductions in new HIV infections and AIDS-related deaths, Table 4.1 provides evidence that HIV remains a significant global public health problem (UNAIDS, 2017). According to 2017 global estimates from UNAIDS, 36.9 million people were living with HIV, 1.8 million people were newly infected with HIV, and 940,000 persons died from AIDS-related deaths (UNAIDS, 2017). In terms of the United States, 2017 estimates found that 1.1 million people were living with HIV, 38, 739 people were newly infected with HIV, and 15, 807 persons died from AIDS (CDC, 2019).

While earlier diagnosis and treatment would prevent HIV transmission, as of 2017, 59% of the 36.9 million people living with HIV were receiving

Table 4.1   2017 estimates of HIV/AIDS worldwide and in the United States

Worldwide	United States
36.9 million living with HIV	1.1 million living with HIV
1.8 million new HIV infections	38,739 new HIV infections
940,000 AIDS-related deaths	15,807 AIDS-related deaths

Note Author created using information adapted from UNAIDS (2017). *UNAIDS Fact Sheet, World AIDS Day 2018.* Joint United Nations Programme on HIV/AIDS. UNAIDS Data 2017. Retrieved from https://www.unaids.org/sites/default/files/media_asset/UNAIDS_FactSheet_en.pdf

Author created using information adapted from Centers for Disease Control and Prevention. *Estimated HIV incidence and prevalence in the United States, 2010–2016.* HIV Surveillance Supplemental Report 2019, 24 (1). Published February 2019. Retrieved from https://www.cdc.gov/hiv/pdf/library/reports/surveillance/cdc-hiv-surveillance-supplemental-report-vol-24-1.pdf

ART (UNAIDS, 2017). The United Nations has adopted a new target that by 2020, 90% of all people living with HIV will know their status, 90% of those diagnosed will have sustained access to ART, and 90% of those on ART will be virally suppressed (UNAIDS, 2014). Achieving this goal requires coordinated and effective strategies at the urban, rural, regional, and national levels (Granich et al., 2015).

As mentioned earlier in this chapter, recent data demonstrates that men who have sex with men (MSM), many of whom identify as gay, bisexual, and transgender, are the group most at risk for new HIV infections in the United States and globally (U.S. DHHS, 2018; Vermund, 2014). Even more specific models examining age and racial/ethnic differences within MSM suggest that the highest rates of continued transmission in the United States and globally exist among young African American and Latino MSM (Vermund, 2014). In Africa estimates suggest that transmission would likely continue among the most at risk populations even if incidence were to decrease in the general population. These vulnerable groups include men who have sex with men, persons who inject drugs (PWID), female sex workers, and migrant men employed by the trucking and mining industries who often have multiple and concurrent partners (Vermund, 2014). Similar high transmission among MSM is found in Asia, South America, the Caribbean, and Europe (Vermund, 2014).

These trends are alarming in many ways including data indicating that nearly 75% of young men of color who have sex with men (YMCSM) in the United States are not reached by current prevention efforts (Finlayson, 2011; Patel, Masyukova, Sutton, & Horvath, 2016). Patel et al. (2016) suggest that traditional intervention efforts may be less likely to reach this population because these individuals may be less likely to label themselves as gay or bisexual and/or may be unlikely to visit or access LGBT or HIV agencies and services.

These findings also place into context the evidence of global declines in AIDS-related deaths which peaked worldwide in 2004 and have since declined by more than 51% (UNAIDS, 2017). In 2017, 940,000 persons died from AIDS-related illnesses worldwide, compared to 1.4 million in 2010 and 1.9 million in 2004 (UNAIDS, 2017). While such declines are a positive sign in the fight against HIV, the progress is robust only where prevention strategies have been widely implemented and embraced by the affected population (Vermund, 2014). While prevention strategies have increased significantly over time, they rely on behavior change and uptake by affected populations (Vermund, 2014). The most widely employed behaviorally based prevention strategies (e.g., male condoms, antiretroviral drugs to kill the virus near the time of exposure or at early infection and to prevent the transmission of the virus from mother to infant, male circumcision, and needle exchange), all face potentially daunting barriers to success—awareness, availability, acceptability, affordability, and adherence (Vermund, 2014). It is important to emphasize that these approaches must be understood in the context of the social determinants of health such as external and societal biases that impact access to and quality of health care for those most vulnerable to HIV/AIDS.

HIV Transmission and Risky Sexual Behaviors

Understanding what may produce behavior change, and what may impede it, are critical factors in the transmission of HIV. Diaz, Ayala, and Bein (2004) tested a multivariate mediation model of predictors of sexually risky behaviors among a sample of gay (including MSM) Latino men in three large U.S. cities. The first component of the mediation model tested whether social oppression (including homophobia, racism, and poverty) was positively associated with higher levels of participation in sexually risky behaviors (e.g., failure to consistently use condoms) by producing high levels of psychological distress. The second component of the model examined whether individuals who experience higher levels of social oppression and psychological distress are more likely to participate in "difficult" sexual situations (e.g., having sex to relieve depression and loneliness; sex under the influence of drugs). The third component of the model hypothesized that participation in difficult sexual situations mediates the impact of social oppression and psychological distress on sexual risk behavior.

Results indicated that a substantial number of Latino gay men in the United States reported social oppression related to being poor, Latino, and gay, multiple instances of verbal and physical abuse during childhood, and discrimination in adulthood related to their sexual orientation and ethnicity. Racial discrimination was experienced within the gay community as participants reported being objectified as sexually exotic in mostly white gay communities (Diaz et al., 2004). Participants also reported high levels of financial distress in the last twelve months, which was strongly and positively related to psychological distress in the last 6 months.

Diaz et al. (2004) found support for their mediational model which illuminates the continued ethnic disparities that exist in HIV/AIDS prevalence and incidence among MSM. First, social oppression related to race/ethnicity, class, and sexual orientation was strongly and positively correlated with sexual behaviors that led to higher levels of risk for HIV transmission. Second, social oppression and psychological distress predicted participation in risky sexual behaviors. Third, social oppression affected sexual risk by increasing the likelihood that individuals would participate in situations that make it difficult to practice safer sex. For example, men who experienced more discrimination and psychological distress were more likely to engage in sex under the influence of drugs or alcohol or to use sex as a way of alleviating anxiety and stress. Participating in difficult sexual situations then mediated the impact of social oppression on risky sexual behavior. Models that emphasize the impact of contextual, external, and situational factors shed light on why MSM, and particularly those of color, continue to bear such a heavy HIV burden. Prior work by Diaz and Ayala (2001) demonstrated that social isolation and low self-esteem among Latino gay men can be alleviated by resiliency and strength-based approaches (e.g., family acceptance of sexual orientation, community involvement and activism in support of gay and Latino rights).

These findings demonstrating that community involvement and activism can create a sense of empowerment and enhance self-esteem among Latino gay men resonate strongly with testimonials from gay men and women who participated in, witnessed, and learned about the Stonewall Inn riots (Carter, 2004). To further bolster prevention efforts, we must understand how to most effectively decrease the continued social isolation, discrimination, and bias that can foster risky sexual behaviors, less adherence to other prevention strategies, as well as less access to high-quality, culturally competent health care.

THE MINORITY STRESS MODEL

As introduced in Chapter 1 of this volume, the minority stress model (e.g., Meyer, 2003) offers a framework for understanding and examining the impact of bias, discrimination, homophobia, and marginality on the unequal and poor health outcomes of lesbian, gay, bisexual, and transgender individuals. The model explores the variability within sexual minority communities by explicitly investigating the intersectional and overlapping identifies within the LGBTQ community—e.g., LGBTQ individuals of color who hold unified identities as racial/ethnic minorities as well as sexual minorities. Research has demonstrated that, at least in the United

States, LGBT individuals of color have a long and rich history of involvement in the "mainstream" gay rights movement (e.g., Stonewall), as well as within LGBT communities of color (Meyer, 2010). These communities of support may serve as protective factors or buffers against homophobia, harassment, and discrimination and in turn, lower the risk of health disparities (Meyer, 2010).

Jeffries, Marks, Lauby, Murrill, and Millett (2013) investigated the premise of the minority stress model in their examination of the impact of homophobic events on the odds of black MSM engaging in risky sexual behaviors (e.g., unprotected anal intercourse) and on whether social integration factors (e.g., social support, closeness with family and friends, attachment to black gay and religious communities, MSM social network size) ameliorated these associations. Jeffries et al. (2013) identified homophobia as one possible societal factor that may increase HIV risk infection among MSM given prior evidence that HIV disparities within this sub-population are not fully explained by individual-level risk behaviors. For example, Black MSM often report less HIV risk behaviors (e.g., drug use, unprotected sex) than non-black MSM (Feldman, 2010; Millet, Flores, Peterson, & Bakeman, 2007). Jeffries et al. (2013) hypothesized that black MSM who had been diagnosed with HIV infection as well as those who had not been diagnosed and who had experienced homophobia (hostility solely based on their sexual orientation) would have increased odds of participating in unprotected anal intercourse (UAI). Jeffries et al. (2013) tested their hypothesis by analyzing data from the Brothers y Hermanos cross-sectional study that investigated correlates of HIV risk behavior and HIV infection among 1154 black MSM residing in New York City and Philadelphia.

Participants were recruited from community-based organizations and other venues frequented by black MSMs using respondent-driven sampling whereby program staff initially recruited core subjects who then each recruited additional participants (Jeffries et al., 2013). Each participant completed an audio computer-assisted self-interview (ACASI) and, with the exception of those who reported that they had been previously diagnosed with HIV, received a rapid oral fluid HIV antibody test (Jeffries et al., 2013). The ACASI assessed demographic, behavioral, and psychosocial variables including UAI, five perceived homophobic events and six social integration constructs. Participants were asked to report events that occurred because of perceptions that they were homosexual or not masculine enough. The five negative, homophobic events were categorized into none; low (respondent had to act more manly than usual to be accepted or felt uncomfortable among heterosexuals at least once); medium (respondents had been treated rudely, made fun of, or called names at least once); and high (respondents were hit or beaten, at least once, irrespective of other homophobic experiences) (Jeffries et al., 2013). Results indicated that the prevalence of each type of homophobic event were similar for respondents who were previously and not previously diagnosed with HIV. Over the past 12 months, approximately 9–13% were beaten, 34–39% were treated rudely, and 36–41% felt uncomfortable among heterosexual black people (Jeffries et al., 2013).

Jeffries et al. (2013) assessed six social integration concepts including social support, closeness with family members, closeness with gay and heterosexual friends, attachment to the black and religious communities, and size of MSM social network (Jeffries et al., 2013). Approximately 17% of the respondents who were not previously diagnosed with HIV tested positive for the virus via a rapid oral fluid antibody test and a confirming Western blot blood test and were subsequently referred to medical treatment facilities for follow-up care (Jeffries et al., 2013). MSM who were not previously diagnosed with HIV infection and who reported a medium level of homophobic events were significantly more likely to engage in UAI as compared to MSM who reported no homophobic events. In comparison, MSM who were previously diagnosed with HIV infection and who reported low, medium, or high levels of homophobic events were significantly more likely to engage in UAI as compared to MSM who reported no homophobic events.

The correlations between the severity of homophobic experiences and UAI for both groups of MSM were not buffered by participants' social support, closeness with family or friends, or attachment to black gay and religious communities, or MSM social network size (Jeffries et al., 2013). Jeffries et al. (2013) postulate that the fact that all levels of homophobic events were associated positively and significantly with UAI among MSM previously diagnosed with HIV, but not among those with no diagnosis, may result from the psychological trauma of managing HIV stigma. Indeed, prior research has demonstrated that homophobic experiences negatively affect levels of self-esteem, anxiety, depression, and internalized homophobia among MSM which may then influence MSMs to seek comfort and intimacy through unprotected anal intercourse (e.g., Diaz, Ayala,

Bein, Henne, & Marin, 2001; Stokes & Peterson, 1998). The authors caution that their results, including no evidence that social integration buffers or dampens the association between homophobic experiences and unprotected anal intercourse, should be interpreted with caution and not generalized beyond this cross-sectional, non-randomized, sample of black MSM living in two U.S. cities (Jeffries et al., 2013). The authors suggest partnerships with communities, academic units, and government agencies as possible interventions that may reduce the experience of homophobic events that target black MSM and potentially result in increased risk for HIV infection (Jeffries et al., 2013).

Balaji, Bowles, Hess, Smith, and Paz-Bailey (2017) build on the work of Jeffries et al. (2013) by examining the relationship between sexual minority stigma or "enacted stigma" and sexually risky behaviors in a nationally representative sample. Balaji et al. (2017) hypothesize that enacted stigma related to sexual minority status may mediate the relationship between the individual and HIV risky sexual behaviors (Balaji et al., 2017). To examine their hypothesis, the authors analyzed survey data from 9819 MSM from the 2011 national HIV Behavioral Surveillance System. The mean age of the sample was 34.6 years with 40% identifying as non-Hispanic White, 27% as non-Hispanic Black, 25% as Hispanic, and 7% as other or multiple race groups. In terms of education, income, and health insurance, 94% completed at least high school, one third reported earning less than $20,000 annually, and 30% had no health insurance (Balaji et al., 2017). Regarding sexual orientation and HIV infection status, 81% identified as gay or homosexual, 93% had disclosed their sexual orientation to at least one person, and 14% self-reported being HIV-positive. All respondents, regardless of self-reported HIV infection status, were offered anonymous HIV testing.

Enacted stigma was conceptualized with three variables including verbal harassment (being called names), discrimination (receiving poorer services in businesses, restaurants, schools, at work, in health care setting,), and physical assault (being physically attacked). During the past 12 months, 59% of respondents reported no enacted stigma while 32% reported verbal harassment, 23% reported discrimination, and 8% reported physical assault. Results of multivariable analyses indicated that younger age, identification as gay/bisexual, and disclosure of sexual identity were associated with a greater risk of experiencing enacted stigma (Balaji et al., 2017). Balaji et al. (2017) posit that asking subjects whether or not they experienced stigma due to others knowing about their homosexuality instead of others knowing that they were HIV positive may have led to their unexpected finding of no association between self-reported HIV status and enacted stigma. Those respondents who reported enacted stigma related to sexual minority status in the past 12 months were more likely to report unprotected anal intercourse at last sex with a HIV discordant (when one partner is infected with HIV and the other is not) male and past 12 month unprotected anal intercourse with a male partner; four or more male sex partners; and exchange sex (e.g., sex in exchange for money or drugs). Thus, Balaji et al. (2017) provide evidence consistent with prior research that experiencing stigma related to sexual minority status may put these individuals at risk for acquiring and transmitting HIV.

Balaji et al. (2017) call for future research that explores whether MSM who experience enacted stigma feel less empowered, have lower self-efficacy, and have internalized feelings of shame and guilt that negatively impact their agency to protect themselves with condoms during anal intercourse (Balaji et al., 2017). Further, they emphasize that individual experiences of enacted stigma are associated with numerous forms of societal stigma present in communities, institutions, and laws that also negatively impact HIV risk behaviors (Balaji et al., 2017). For example, a 2014 study found that U.S. states with laws that criminalize various aspects of HIV such as nondisclosure of HIV status to sexual partners have a higher incidence and prevalence rate of HIV infection, possibly stemming from the increased stigma associated with the criminalization of HIV (National Alliance of State and Territorial AIDS Directors and National Coalition of STD Directors, 2014).

Balaji et al. (2017) acknowledge several limitations of their analyses including the fact that their sample of 20 U.S. cities with high prevalence of AIDS may not be representative of all MSM. Further, no rural MSM were included, despite the evidence that sexual minority stigma may be experienced to a larger extent in rural as compared to urban cities (Balaji et al., 2017). Additional limitations include self-reported data, a lack of sampling weights to account for complex sampling methods, possible inaccurate attributions of stigma to sexual minority status, and data being collected in 2011 prior to nationwide recognition of same-sex marriage, which could have decreased stigma for MSM (Balaji et al., 2017). The authors further acknowledge that their analyses did not include possible mediating factors including mental health, stress, internalized homophobia, or social support that might mitigate the impact of enacted stigma on

HIV risk behaviors (Balaji et al., 2017). Balaji et al. (2017) stress that any HIV prevention efforts must function synergistically in biomedical, behavioral, and structural domains while addressing the intersections of racial, ethnic, socioeconomic, and sexual identities among MSM.

Social Media and HIV/AIDS Risk

To more fully understand the impact of social media use on the sexual risk behaviors among urban, low income, young men of color who have sex with men (YMCSM) and young transgender women, Patel et al. (2016) conducted a formative study in New York City with a convenience sample of 102 individuals. Participants were recruited from community-based organizations serving LGBT youth, bars frequented by minority gay self-identified youth, and one dance competition. Demographic information revealed that over 90% of respondents were under 30 years of age; mostly Hispanic or Black (85.3%); male (80.4%); self-identified as gay or bisexual (85.2%); had seen a doctor in the previous 12 months (85.2%), and used condoms at last sexual intercourse (87.3%). In terms of HIV and sexually transmitted infections (STIs), approximately 15% reported a STI in the prior 12 months and 11% reported a positive HIV status. The majority of respondents (67.6%) reported accessing the Internet and social media via cell phones or other mobile devices. All of the individuals had at least one social media profile while the vast majority (83.3%) had multiple profiles and accessed the Internet and social media sites multiple times per day (87.3%). In terms of sexual risk behavior and social media use, the majority of respondents (56.7%) used social media to seek sexual partners while approximately 20% used it to exchange sex for money and clothes or drugs (10%).

Several limitations of Patel et al.'s (2016) study, including its cross-sectional design and small convenience sample, preclude broader generalizations of the findings; however, the overall results demonstrated that among their sample, social media access and use were universal and frequently used to engage in risky sexual behaviors. Further, the type of sites used for finding sexual partners varied (e.g., general sites versus more specific sexual networking sites) and such variations in social media platforms were sometimes associated with "exchange" sex. These findings point to the need to tailor prevention efforts using social media in targeted and specific ways to address the different areas of risk (Patel et al., 2016).

This sample also self-reported high prevalence of HIV and STIs; however, high levels of self-reported condom use at last sexual encounter, ever being tested for HIV, and having seen a doctor in the last 12 months, are encouraging signs suggesting that the positive health behaviors occurring among this vulnerable population could be increased through effective use of social media platforms (Patel et al., 2016). This possibility is bolstered in that social media platforms are in line with Vermund's (2014) assertion that effective prevention strategies must have high awareness, availability, acceptability, affordability, and adherence. Patel et al. (2016) further argue for the use of social media in reaching this vulnerable population in that online social networks can disseminate information "virally," bolster social support, and change norms.

Garett, Smith, Chiu, and Young (2016) investigated HIV/AIDS stigma among a sample of Latino and African American MSM who resided in Los Angeles, California and who reported using social media or social networking sites. Garett et al. (2016) focused on HIV stigma and minority MSM given prior evidence that HIV/AIDS stigma is a major negative influence in the prevention of HIV infection. HIV/AIDS stigma has been associated with a lower likelihood of disclosing HIV/AIDS status, a higher likelihood of engaging in high-risk sexual behaviors, and decreased access to HIV care (e.g., Brooks, Etzel, Hinojos, Henry, and Periez, 2005). Additionally, the investigation of the use of social media among this population is warranted given prior evidence that while 58% of the general population reported accessing social networking sites, 80% of LGBT adults reported such use (Pew Research Center, 2013). Garett et al. (2016) surveyed 112 respondents who were recruited from online websites, venues frequented by gay men, and respondent referrals who met the criteria for their study (e.g., African American and Latino males; English-speaking; registered Facebook users; at least 18 years old; engaged in sex with men in the past 12 months). The respondents completed a questionnaire to measure several items including HIV/AIDS stigma as well as type and frequency of use of social, sexual, and/or general social networking sites (Garett et al., 2016).

The mean age of respondents was 22 with most participants identifying as homosexual (76%) and Latino (60%) or African American (30%). 75% of respondents reported spending one or more hours per day in social networking sites in the past three months. The mean HIV/AIDS stigma composite score for the entire sample was 22.2, with a range of 15–45. Approximately 4% of respondents reported a positive HIV status while another 13%

reported that they were unaware of their status. T tests revealed no significant difference between stigma scores for HIV-negative and HIV-positive respondents. The HIV/AIDS stigma composite score was positively and significantly associated with increased time spent on social networking sites (Garett et al., 2016). The low HIV/AIDS stigma composite score is surprising in this sample of minority MSM, as prior research has indicated high stigma levels among this population (e.g., Brooks et al., 2005). The authors point out that given some differences between minority MSM and minority communities in regard to HIV stigma, future research should explore differences in stigma between minority MSM who use social networking sites and minority MSM who do not use social networking sites (Garett et al., 2016). Several limitations of this study limit the generalizability of the findings and preclude any claims of causation, including the cross-sectional design; small sample size; the individual-level measurement of HIV/AIDS stigma as opposed to broader community, policy, and institutional stigma; and the possibility that assessing Internet use with time intervals as opposed to open-ended questions may have skewed the responses (Garett et al., 2016).

HIV Prevention and Intervention in the United States

In the United States, HIV/AIDS prevention/intervention efforts include community-based participatory research programs (CBPR), community-based organizations, biomedical approaches, and informational campaigns (U.S. DHHS, 2018). The less common and more complicated approach, CBPR, involves the community as equal copartners (rather than subjects or respondents) in the design, execution, and evaluation of interventions (Rhodes et al., 2014). CBPR involves a partnership between outside experts including university-based scientists and researchers and lay community members and representatives from community-based organizations (Rhodes et al., 2013). This approach involves action and change at multiple intersections, including at the individual, group, community, policy, and societal levels (Rhodes et al., 2013). Building such partnerships between the community and scientists may produce interventions and programs that are more relevant and culturally appropriate, more precise in terms of measurement, analysis and interpretation of results, more likely to be adopted, sustained, and disseminated, and more likely to attract robust participation rates (Rhodes et al., 2013). Finally, the process of CBPR has the potential to strengthen the community's sense of its problem-solving capacity and engagement in research to make changes in the community (Rhodes et al., 2013).

Rhodes et al. (2013) developed the HOLA (*Hombres Ofreciendo Liderazgo Y Ayuda* or Men Offering Leadership and Help) as a response to Latino MSM who requested an HIV prevention intervention during the initial implementation of the CBPR intervention, HoMBReS (*Hombres Manteniendo Bienstar y Relaciones Saludables* or Men Maintaining Well-Being and Healthy Relationships). While the original intervention, HoMBRES, focused on HIV prevention for heterosexual Spanish-speaking Latino men, the adapted intervention, HOLA, focused on Spanish-speaking, less acculturated, Latino MSM (Rhodes et al., 2013). To ensure that the partnership met the needs and priorities of the community, the researchers employed an 11 step process to develop the HOLA intervention (Rhodes et al., 2013). The academic researchers established a subgroup of their new intervention team that included Latino MSM, representatives from local community-based organizations, and local business owners (Rhodes et al., 2013). As an initial step, the researchers reviewed published and unpublished reports and briefs on the sexual health of Latinos residing in the United States and on sexual health interventions for Latino MSM in the United States Next a needs assessment was conducted by interviewing 21 Latino MSM, aged 18 to 45 years old and administering a questionnaire to a respondent-driven sample of 190 Latino MSM. Results of these ethnographic interviews and the survey indicated several priorities among Latino MSM including the need for accurate information about HIV and STD transmission, prevention, and treatment, and the negative impact of internalized homophobia and traditional associations of masculinity and manhood with risky sexual behaviors.

The researchers finalized the intervention priorities and goals through close consultation with community forums, each attended by local Latino MSM and community-based organization representatives. The intervention priorities focused on increasing awareness of the prevalence of HIV and STD infections as well as on transmission and symptoms; disseminating information on access to and eligibility for health care services including HIV/STD testing; enhancing skills in correct condom use; decreasing risky health behaviors; changing norms of masculinity, maleness, and sexuality that may compromise health; and building advocacy and supportive relationships to empower the community (Rhodes et al., 2013). The HOLA researchers trained community members to serve as lay health advisors or navigators (*navegantes*) to build on the social support structures already in place in the community including the help that Latino MSM were providing to each other in terms of transportation, housing, and jobs (Rhodes et al., 2013). Utilizing Latino MSM instead of non-Latino MSM to deliver the intervention was conceptualized as a more effective way to minimize the stigma related to immigration and same-sex orientation within the Latino community. The intervention team designed training modules for the navigators using both social cognitive theory (Bandura, 1986) and empowerment education (Freire, 1973) to frame their intervention and understand the processes involved in changing knowledge, attitudes, and behaviors (Rhodes et al., 2013). The intervention materials included wallet-sized cards that reinforced the navigators' support model of "pay attention, ask questions, offer advice, and together organize next steps" (Rhodes et al., 2013). The navigators utilized additional materials including role-playing scripts, data collection forms, and DVDs to illustrate self-efficacy and communication skills surrounding condom use, HIV testing, and living with HIV (Rhodes et al., 2013).

The navigators executed the HOLA intervention in one-on-one sessions and group discussions, meeting monthly to debrief, share successes and challenges, and provide social support to one another. Rhodes et al. (2014) describe the challenges in the HOLA intervention as common to most CBPR efforts. First, it can be difficult to define who represents the community and to ensure that a variety of voices and viewpoints are represented in the intervention planning, implementation, and evaluation efforts. Next, the community's desire to exercise some flexibility in adjusting the research agenda to accommodate for changing priorities and needs can conflict with the need to secure and maintain funding from agencies with proscribed funding-criteria. On a related note, intense competition among community-based organizations for HIV prevention funds can negatively impact CBPR collaborations. Another challenge that surfaced in the HOLA project was the focus of community-based organizations on tasks, processes, and the maintenance of partnerships versus the attention toward outcomes that is the traditional standard for researchers and scientists. Finally, changes in leadership and staffing among CBPR partners that are often associated with decreases in skills and capacity can lead to gaps in the ability to achieve the interventions' goals. Given these challenges, all CBPR members must be fully committed and accept the realities of this approach, recognizing that although the process can be more difficult and time-consuming than a traditional researcher-driven project, the results can be more authentic, effective, and sustainable (Rhodes et al., 2014).

Currently, there are few effective HIV programs targeting MSM and Latino MSM in particular (Rhodes et al., 2013). The HOLA intervention helped to fill that gap with a CBPR approach designed for immigrant Spanish-speaking Latino MSM, most of whom recently arrived in the United States who had not participated in HIV prevention programs in their countries of origin. Given that the burden of HIV among Latino MSM continues to rise, HOLA's structure that built upon the foundation of existing community strengths, natural helpers, and social support is especially crucial and potentially impactful in the efforts to assist Latino MSM in their fight against HIV/AIDS. HOLA developed skills among the navigators and other community partners including public speaking, leadership, and mobilization of resources that will help the community at large build capacity to surmount other health challenges (Rhodes et al., 2013).

Given the growth in studies examining the use of social media and technology by Latino MSM (e.g., Meadowbrooke, Veinot, Loveluck, Hickok, & Bauermeister, 2014), researchers analyzed baseline survey data from 167 respondents who participated in the HOLA intervention cited above to examine differences between Latino MSM and transgender persons living in the U.S. south who used sexual and social networking websites and applications (apps) and those who did not (Sun, Reboussin, Mann, Garcia, & Rhodes, 2016). Increasingly, websites and global positioning system or GPS-based mobile applications target MSM with some (e.g., Grindr) claiming to have five million male users in nearly 200 countries (Sun et al., 2016). These platforms enable users to identify other MSM by displaying profiles and photographs organized by geographic distance to the user and subsequently to arrange in-person meetings (Sun et al., 2016). As users may be interested in locating friends and social support, as well as sexual partners, the researchers assert that social networking platforms can be viewed as positive and affirming (Sun et al., 2016).

On average the respondents were 30 years old having lived in the United States for approximately 10 years with three quarters reporting Mexico as their country of origin (Sun et al., 2016). Approximately 28% of respondents reported using social or sexual networking websites or applications to find sexual partners at least once per month while 70% of the sample using the Internet daily and 85% owned a cellular telephone (Sun et al., 2016). Multivariate analyses demonstrated that respondents who reported using social or sexual websites or applications at least monthly were more likely to be younger and to report more male sex partners in the past 6 months and a history of STD diagnosis and illegal drug use other than marijuana in the past 6 months (Sun et al., 2016). Sun et al. (2016) caution that due to several limitations of their study (e.g., cross-sectional design, small non-probability sample), their findings do not support the premise that the increase in number of male sex partners and rates of STD diagnosis are caused by the use of social and sexual networking websites and applications (Sun et al., 2016). Despite this lack of causality, given the vulnerability of young minority MSM to HIV infection and the increasing popularity of social and sexual networking sites among this community, more research is needed to explore the efficacy of social media-based HIV interventions as well as future and more advanced networking technology in this population (Sun et al., 2016).

CENTERS FOR DISEASE CONTROL AND PREVENTION

The United States Department of Health and Human Services' Centers for Disease Control and Prevention (CDC) is one of the main federal agencies involved in the efforts to decrease the spread of HIV in the United States. The CDC's approach to prevention and intervention is three-pronged, including the funding of community-based organizations (CBOs), antiretroviral drugs, and information campaigns and partnerships (U.S. DHHS, 2018). Within the CDC, the National Center for HIV/AIDS, Viral Hepatitis, STD, and TB Prevention follow the National HIV/AIDS Strategy, launched in 2010 during the Obama administration to address HIV in the United States (U.S. DHHS, 2014). This national strategy specifies three goals designed to diagnose HIV early, provide effective care, and decrease transmission. The goals include increasing the number of HIV-positive persons who know their status to 90%; increasing the proportion of newly diagnosed persons who are linked to care within three months to 85%; and increasing the proportion of HIV-diagnosed individuals with suppressed viral loads with an emphasis on the most vulnerable communities of African Americans, Latinos, and gay and bisexual men of all races (U.S. DHHS, 2014).

To evaluate the progress toward achieving these national goals and inform resource allocation for HIV prevention efforts, the CDC monitors the national HIV Care Continuum, which was launched in 2013 under the Obama administration (U.S. DHHS, 2014). Specifically, the

HIV care continuum details the steps from the time a person is diagnosed with HIV through successful treatment of HIV with medications (U.S. DHHS, 2014). The ultimate goal of the Continuum is to achieve viral suppression to the point where the HIV virus is present in very low amounts or undetectable (U.S. DHHS, 2014). This approach is designed to help people with HIV live longer and reduce the likelihood of transmitting HIV to others. Careful monitoring of those infected with HIV enables the CDC to make progress in its goal of achieving viral suppression. The CDC monitors the proportion of people with HIV who are in different stages of infection, including those who have been diagnosed, linked to care with a health care provider within three months of learning their status, received medical care for HIV infection, prescribed antiretroviral drugs, and virally suppressed to a very low level of HIV in the blood. The HIV Continuum can sometimes move in different directions, as is the case when a virally suppressed individual stops taking antiretroviral drugs (U.S. DHHS, 2014).

To monitor the HIV Continuum, the CDC uses two surveillance systems that provide complimentary information. The National HIV Surveillance System (NHSS) provides data (including race/ethnicity, route of transmissions, age) from every U.S. state and territory and the District of Columbia on people who are diagnosed or who have died with HIV (U.S. DHHS, 2014). The Medical Monitoring Project (MMP) provides information (e.g., outcomes of treatment, number receiving care, number prescribed antiretroviral therapy, and number of those who are virally suppressed) from a weighted sample of people in U.S. states, cities, and Puerto Rico who are living with HIV and who have been diagnosed (U.S. DHHS, 2014). The MMP data can be examined by race/ethnicity and sexual orientation (e.g., young black MSM). The federal, state, and local government track the movement along the HIV Care Continuum to identify areas of need and a blueprint to improve outcomes.

The CDC spearheads many efforts to improve outcomes along the HIV Care Continuum, including the funding of community-based organizations (CBOs). In 2017, the CDC provided approximately $11 million per year for five years to 30 CBOs to provide HIV testing to young gay and bisexual men of color and young transgender persons of color to decrease numbers of undiagnosed HIV infections and increase linkages to care and prevention services (U.S. DHHS, 2018). In 2015 the CDC began funding Project PrIDE (PreP, Data2Care, Implementation, Data, Evaluation), a multipronged intervention program that targets MSM and transgender persons by attempting to reduce the number of new infections and increase access to care for those persons living with HIV. The main components of Project PrIDE (e.g., PrEP and Data2Care) are three-year demonstration projects that support 12 health departments in distributing PrEP, an antiretroviral drug that can be taken by an HIV negative person before potential exposure to HIV to reduce risk of infection, and in expanding or enhancing the linkage, retention, and reengagement in HIV care (U.S. DHHS, 2015). A final and complimentary component of the CDC's efforts to decrease HIV infection is through national information campaigns and partnerships that provide culturally appropriate messages about HIV testing, prevention, and engagement in care to gay and bisexual men (U.S. DHHS, 2015).

HIV PREVENTION AND INTERVENTION GLOBALLY

The international response to the HIV/AIDS epidemic has generated recommendations for the design and implementation of HIV programs at the country level (Silva-Santisteban, Eng, Iglesia, Falistocco, & Mazin, 2016). One group that has put forth recommendations includes the Investment Framework for the Global Response to HIV—developed by a group representing a variety of organizations including UNAIDS, World Health Organization (WHO), PEPFAR, the World Bank, and the Global Fund. The recommendations include evidence-based interventions for prevention, treatment, and support for people with HIV/AIDS in general. At the individual level, recommendations emphasize condom distribution along with voluntary testing and counseling. At the societal level, recommendations focus on enacting laws to protect vulnerable populations, and to reduce stigma and poverty while increasing access to education and jobs (Silva-Santisteban et al., 2016). In 2016 the WHO published updated guidelines for HIV prevention and care for key populations, including the dissemination of pre-exposure antiretroviral drugs (e.g., PrEP) as well as early antiretroviral treatment following HIV diagnosis (e.g., PEP), increased access to testing, and strengthening protective laws (WHO, 2016).

Latin America

In Latin America (the continent of South America in addition to Mexico, Central America, and the islands of the Caribbean whose inhabitants speak a Romance language) and the Caribbean (Cuba, Dominican Republic, Haiti, Guadeloupe, Martinique, Puerto Rico, Saint-Barthelemy, Saint-Martin), nearly 2 million people are estimated to be living with HIV with men who have sex with men, transgender women, and sex workers at highest risk (UNAIDS, 2017). Data specific to transgender women as a subpopulation of MSM is often missing from global examinations of the HIV response (Baral et al., 2013). Baral et al. (2013) conducted a meta-analysis using data from the United States, six Asia-Pacific countries, five Latin American countries, and three European countries that estimated that transgender women were nearly 50 times more likely to become infected with HIV than the general adult population of reproductive age. Given that, globally, some of the highest HIV prevalence rates are found in transgender women in Latin America (e.g., 18–48%), Silva-Santisteban et al. (2016) conducted a review of HIV prevention efforts in 17 Latin American countries that monitor HIV rates of transgender women separately from MSM. Silva-Santisteban et al. (2016) were interested in examining the multitude of intersectional factors (e.g., individual, interpersonal, and structural) that contribute to the vulnerability of transgender women's risk for HIV infection in Latin America. At the individual level, some of the most impactful risk factors include unprotected receptive anal sex, substance use, high numbers of sexual partners, and a high number of sex workers (Silva-Santisteban et al., 2016). At the interpersonal level, low levels of condom negotiation skills with partners and sex work-clients and high-risk partner pools are significant risk factors for transgender women, while structural factors include social exclusion, violence, discrimination, bias, poverty, limited employment, and a lack of legal recognition of gender identity (Silva-Santisteban et al., 2016).

The UNAIDS Fast Track Strategy has been adapted by Latin American countries with the goal of ending AIDS as a public health threat by 2030 by achieving "90-90-90" targets such that 90% of people living with AIDS know their HIV status, 90% of people diagnosed with HIV are receiving treatment, and 90% of people on treatment have achieved viral suppression (Silva-Santisteban et al., 2016). The National Strategic Plans (NPSs) comprise the outlines by which governments track and report their progress toward achieving the "90-90-90" targets within the Global AIDS Response Progress Reporting or GARPR (Silva-Santisteban et al., 2016). GARPR maintains the official documents that track the progress of national goals to reduce HIV infection and transmission—a process that requires the coordination of stakeholders to assess HIV prevalence and incidence, as well as the social context and identification of the most vulnerable populations, strategies and protocols for the allocation of resources (Silva-Santisteban et al., 2016).

Silva-Santisteban et al.'s (2016) review assessed the ways in which 17 Latin American countries design and implement prevention programs for transgender women and the extent and impact of these programs, along with the ways in which these responses support international recommendations on HIV prevention efforts among vulnerable populations. Their review included several South American countries (e.g., Argentina, Bolivia, Brazil, Chile, Colombia, Ecuador, Paraguay, Peru, Uruguay, and Venezuela) as well as the Central American countries of Costa Rica, El Salvador, Guatemala, Honduras, Nicaragua, Panama, and Mexico (Silva-Santisteban et al., 2016). Their review focused on several areas including legal rights of transgender people, design and implementation of programs, access to and coverage of prevention services, use of new technologies, alignment with international recommendations, community participation, and best practices. Prior to the desk review of documents that were submitted within GARPR, along with public reports, health surveys, and needs assessment, Silva-Santisteban et al. (2016) conducted 12 key informant interviews with representatives of United Nations (U.N.) agencies (e.g., UNAIDS, Pan American Health Organization) and a focus group with transgender women to guide their document review. The 12 key informant interviews, which were conducted via telephone, required the respondents to identify key HIV prevention strategies for transgender women in Latin American countries.

Silva-Santisteban et al. (2016) analyzed the data by country and by the main elements of the intervention approach. The first element reviewed included protective laws and social environments for transgender women. Of the 17 south and central American countries reviewed, only Argentina, Uruguay, and Mexico have passed gender identity laws allowing transgender persons to change their legal identity by altering their name and sex on identity documents. In Columbia and Panama, judicial processes have been established to facilitate the change in legal identity. The data revealed that of the 10 South American countries reviewed, all (with the exception of Peru and Paraguay) have passed laws prohibiting discrimination on the basis of sexual orientation and gender identity. As for Central America, its laws are considered conservative in terms of LGBT populations. For example, Costa Rica, Guatemala, Peru, and Mexico have identified certain groups as opposing laws that protect LGBT rights and programs aimed at providing sexual education, condom distribution, and intravenous drug use harm reduction strategies to LGBT populations (Silva-Santisteban et al., 2016). Although every Latin American country in this review identified transgender women as a key population in their HIV progress reports, only four countries (Argentina, Brazil, Mexico, and Uruguay) have put into place interventions targeting transgender women and thus recognizing their specific health needs as distinct from MSM. The other countries include transgender women with MSM in terms of data analysis, intervention design and implementation.

The most common HIV prevention strategies include information and education; condom distribution; diagnosis and treatment of sexually transmitted infections (STIs); voluntary HIV counseling and testing; and peer education. Most prevention services focus on STI and HIV diagnosis, treatment and counseling and are provided in primary care facilities including general hospitals (Silva-Santisteban et al., 2016). A few countries also offer outreach efforts including education and testing at social and sex work locations while several of the largest clinics in Mexico also provide antiretroviral treatment along with oral and mental health. The key informant interviews with transgender women revealed that Bolivia, El Salvador, and Panama do not distribute enough condoms to meet the demand of the population, especially given the prevalence of sex work among poor, transgender women. Based on the review of progress reports, Silva-Santisteban et al. (2016) estimate that in the majority of Latin American countries, less than 50% of MSM and transgender women have been tested for HIV in the last 12 months, resulting in a gap in the HIV Continuum of Care. The use of antiretroviral HIV drugs before exposure (e.g., PrEP) and post-exposure (e.g., PEP) is not yet widespread in Latin American countries, as this practice is currently implemented by only three countries (e.g., Brazil, Argentina, Mexico).

In the conclusion of their review, Silva-Santisteban et al. (2016) note a lack of prevention services that move beyond individual-level risk reduction (e.g., condom use, HIV testing and counseling) and a disease control approach to a more comprehensive rights-based perspective that address the social determinants of the HIV epidemic. Most of the HIV prevention efforts in Latin American countries are hampered by limited community involvement, a weak public health system, limited human resources, poor integration of referral and treatment services, and a high level of discrimination against and mistrust among transgender women. Additionally, Silva-Santisteban et al. (2016) identified inconsistencies in the strategies outlined in some countries' planning documents and the actual prevention efforts that were implemented. Ecuador is a prime example of this situation in that its NSP or HIV planning document emphasized a human rights approach to HIV prevention along with an acknowledgment of health as a right and the continued marginalization of transgender women. Despite this rights-based approach detailed in Ecuador's NSP, the actual implementation of prevention efforts focused on individual risk amelioration including condom distribution and HIV testing. The countries identified as most thoroughly executing a comprehensive rights-based approach targeting transgender women that is consistent with its NSP or national HIV strategy include Argentina, Brazil, Mexico, and Uruguay (Silva-Santisteban et al., 2016).

Both Argentina and Uruguay address HIV and other related health issues of the LGBT population through a social inclusion and rights-based model bolstered by the implementation of employment and poverty-reduction programs. Brazil and Mexico prioritize HIV treatment for vulnerable populations including transgender women and intravenous drug users, regardless of viral load or CD4 count. Brazil is credited with the most comprehensive use of PEP, the post-exposure antiretroviral drug, and with the assessment of PrEP, the pre-exposure antiretroviral drug, as an integrated public health strategy. Silva-Santisteban et al. (2016) summarize their review by emphasizing that despite the recognition of transgender women as a key population for HIV in official strategic plans and progress reports, very few of the intervention programs focus specifically on this population. Further, HIV prevention is predominantly aimed at reducing individual risk through testing and condom distribution, rather than employing a rights-based and disease control combination. Data collected on the response to HIV mostly categorize MSM and transgender women together, thereby impeding the planning, implementation, and monitoring of approaches specifically targeted toward transgender women; furthermore, the extreme paucity of data concerning transgender men results in a gap in the understanding of the impact of HIV on this subgroup. Final recommendations include adopting a multipronged approach based on human rights; considering social determinants such as discrimination, stigma, unemployment, and poverty; strengthening of public health and community systems with adequate human resources for testing, retesting, and treatment; and integrating transgender-specific health needs in the HIV care continuum (Silva-Santisteban et al., 2016).

Africa

The HIV epidemic as well as the progress in HIV intervention and prevention varies by region within the continent of Africa, with the highest prevalence of HIV existing in East and Southern Africa (e.g., Botswana, Kenya, Lesotho, Malawi, South Africa, Swaziland, Tanzania, Uganda, Zambia, and Zimbabwe) (UNAIDS, 2017). This region accounts for only 6.2% of the global population but over half of the total number of people living with HIV (19.4 million) (UNAIDS, 2017). Table 4.2 demonstrates the state of the HIV epidemic in West and Central Africa (e.g., Benin, Burkina Faso, Cameroon, Central African Republic, Chad, Congo-Brazzaville, Cote d'Ivoire, Gabon, Guinea, Mali, Mauritania, Niger, Senegal, Togo, The Gambia, Ghana, Liberia, Nigeria, Sierra Leone, Cabo Verde, Guinea-Bissau, Sao Tome & Principe, & Equatorial Guinea) as compared to East and Southern Africa as well as the challenges faced throughout the region in providing antiretroviral treatment (UNAIDS, 2017).

In terms of HIV intervention in East and Southern Africa, some countries including South Africa and Kenya have recently increased the political and financial resources for prevention, treatment, and care, while most other countries in the region rely heavily on external donations to fund their HIV response (UNAIDS, 2017). The most impacted populations within East and Southern Africa are men who have sex with men or MSM, transgender people, young women, sex workers, prisoners, and people who

Table 4.2 2016 regional HIV and AIDS data for Africa

	West and Central Africa	East and Southern Africa
	6.1 million people living with HIV	19.4 million people living with HIV
	2% adult HIV prevalence	7% adult HIV prevalence
	370,000 new HIV infections	790,000 new HIV infections
	310,000 AIDS-related deaths	420,000 AIDS-related deaths
	36% adults on antiretroviral treatment	61% adults on antiretroviral treatment
	22% children on antiretroviral treatment	51% children on antiretroviral treatment

Note Author created using information adapted from UNAIDS (2017). Joint United Nations Programme on HIV/AIDS. UNAIDS Data 2017. Retrieved from http://www.unaids.org/en/resources/documents/2017/2017_data_book

inject drugs or PWID (UNAIDS, 2017). Positive developments include data demonstrating that the UNAIDS targets of 90-90-90, described previously in this chapter, are well within sight, given that in 2016, 76% of people living with HIV were aware of their status, 79% were in treatment, and 83% of those receiving treatment were virally suppressed (UNAIDS, 2017).

Barriers to HIV care and prevention include historical cultural, structural, and legal barriers including stigma, discrimination, and bias which disproportionately and negatively impact HIV risk among key populations. For example, in 2016 HIV prevalence among young women (aged 15–24) in the region was twice that of young men (3.4% versus 1.6%) (UNAIDS, 2017). High levels of sex work, young women marrying much older men, lack of educational opportunities, and intimate partner violence all contribute to an increased HIV risk for young women (UNAIDS, 2016). In 2013 regional ministers of health and education in Eastern and Southern Africa began in earnest to fund programs designed to address many of these barriers with a focus on keeping young girls in school, providing sex education and targeted reproductive services, reducing sexual violence and female genital mutilation, and increasing political power (UNAIDS, 2016). One example of a successful intervention is the DREAMS intervention project designed to reduce HIV infections among adolescent girls and young women by 40% in Kenya, Lesotho, Malawi, Mozambique, South Africa, Swaziland, Tanzania, Uganda, Zambia, and Zimbabwe (USAID, 2016). Intervention components focus on decreasing social isolation, discrimination, stigma, and gender-based violence while increasing access to education and economic opportunities (USAID, 2016). Results of the intervention are forthcoming, but preliminary data reveal that more than 1 million adolescent girls and young women received services associated with DREAMS in 2016 (PEPFAR, 2017).

Attempts to reduce HIV transmission among people who inject intravenous drugs (PWID) in East and Southern Africa are expanding but currently exist on a small scale. The most prevalent "harm reduction" strategies for PWID include needle and syringe programs, education on safe injecting practices, and opioid substitution therapy. Kenya serves as a best practice nation in this region for their implementation of harm reduction strategies as Kenya has provided such services since 2012 resulting in a marked increase in reports of using a clean syringe at last injection among PWID from 2012 to 2015 (51.6% compared to 90%) (Hyde, 2016).

Overall, many challenges to HIV intervention and prevention remain entrenched in East and Southern Africa which act as barriers to achieving the UNAIDS 90-90-90 targets. At the individual and interpersonal level, the use of both PrEP and PEP must be scaled up, along with sex and reproductive education, voluntary medical male circumcision, condom and lubricant distribution, and harm reduction for PWID. At a structural level, funding must increase for community-based clinics and health services, as well as programs targeting HIV-related stigma, discrimination, and bias which disproportionately affects the populations most vulnerable to HIV— MSM, sex workers, transgender people, and PWID.

Although HIV prevalence is lower in West and Central Africa in comparison to East and Southern Africa (see Table 4.2), less than half of those living with HIV in West and Central Africa are aware of their HIV status, resulting in a very low uptake of antiretroviral drug treatment (UNAIDS, 2017). This lack of treatment is the most impactful influence on this region being home to the most AIDS-related deaths globally (UNAIDS, 2017). In terms of specific key populations impacted by HIV, four out of ten children aged 0–14 who die of AIDS once lived in this region (UNAIDS, 2017). Women are also a key population disproportionately impacted by HIV in this region, with adolescent girls and young women aged 15–24 more likely to acquire HIV than their male counterparts of the same age (UNAIDS, 2016). Many of the same factors impact the HIV epidemic for children and women in this region, including the failure to diagnose and administer antiretroviral therapy to pregnant women and to the estimated 540,000 children living with HIV in this region, as well as high levels of underaged child and forced marriage, domestic violence, and rape (UNAIDS, 2017). One example of a successful HIV intervention targeting young women is MTV Shuga, a campaign that delivers original content focused on HIV and sexual and reproductive health messaging (MTV Staying Alive, 2017). Originating in Kenya in 2009, MTV Shuga has now been shown in Nigeria and several other countries in the region (MTV Staying Alive, 2017). A 2016 study funded by the World Bank in Nigeria revealed a 35% increase in HIV testing for Nigerian youth who reported watching MTV Shuga for up to six months and over half for those who watched the series for longer periods of time (The World Bank, 2016).

In addition to children and young women, key affected populations in this region include sex workers, PWID, and men who have sex with men, all of whom are negatively impacted by stigma, discrimination, and legal barriers such as the criminalization of sex work, drug use, and same-sex relations that prevent access to HIV counseling, therapy and treatment (UNAIDS, 2017). For example, Northern Nigeria and Mauritania impose the death penalty for MSM while homosexuality is also illegal in Cameroon, Gambia, Ghana, Guinea, Senegal, Sierra Leone, and Togo (Amnesty International, 2017). Overall, the response to the HIV epidemic in West and Central Africa requires enhanced and sustainable local and international funding, as well as a more integrated public health system to effectively implement voluntary medical male circumcision, harm reduction for PWID, and antiretroviral treatment (both PrEP which is not yet available in this region and PEP) (UNAIDS, 2017).

Asia and the Pacific

The HIV epidemic, as well as the progress in HIV intervention and prevention, in Asia and the Pacific varies greatly within the region and by country. Asia and the Pacific is generally considered to include countries near the Western Pacific Ocean and typically includes East Asia, South Asia, Southeast Asia, and Oceania. The region as a whole accounts for the second highest HIV prevalence in the world with 5.1 million people living with HIV, while India has the third largest HIV epidemic in the world with 2.1 million people living with HIV (UNAIDS, 2017). Table 4.3 demonstrates

Table 4.3 2016 regional HIV and AIDS data for Asia and the Pacific and India

Asia and the Pacific	India
5.1 million people living with HIV	2.1 million people living with HIV
0.2% adult HIV prevalence	0.3% adult HIV prevalence
270,000 new HIV infections	80,000 new HIV infections
170,000 AIDS-related deaths	62,000 AIDS-related deaths
47% adults on antiretroviral treatment	50% adults on antiretroviral treatment
40% children on antiretroviral treatment	33% children on antiretroviral treatment

Note Author created using information adapted from UNAIDS (2017). Joint United Nations Programme on HIV/AIDS. UNAIDS Data 2017. Retrieved from http://www.unaids.org/en/resources/documents/2017/2017_data_book

the state of the HIV epidemic in Asia and the Pacific as a whole as well compared with India, as well as the challenges faced throughout the region in providing antiretroviral treatment (UNAIDS, 2017).

In terms of HIV intervention in Asia and the Pacific, some countries have made significant progress in the HIV epidemic, with some prevention programs estimated to have decreased new HIV infections by 13% since 2013 (UNAIDS, 2017). Despite these positive developments, late diagnosis of HIV is a major concern across the region. Similarly to Africa, in Asia and the Pacific, the populations most impacted by HIV are men who have sex with men or MSM, transgender people, sex workers, prisoners, and people who inject drugs or PWID (UNAIDS, 2017). MSM residing in urban areas (e.g., Bangkok, Thailand, Yangon, and Yogyakarta) are particularly affected by HIV with prevalence rates ranging from 20 to 29% overall and incidence or new infections especially high among young MSM aged 18–21 as compared with MSM over the age of 30 (UNAIDS, 2017). The rate of new infections among young MSM in this region (including high income countries such as Australia) is even more alarming given survey results indicating that young MSM have less access to HIV prevention and testing services and engage in less condom use as compared to older MSM (UNAIDS, 2017). Often referred to as a subpopulation of MSM, transgender women in some urban areas (e.g., Delhi, Mumbai, and Phnom Penh) have been found to have a higher HIV prevalence as compared with MSM (Asia Pacific Coalition on Male Sexual Health, 2013). The extreme isolation and discrimination faced by transgender people as well as a lack of legal recognition of transgender identity and rights throughout Asia and the Pacific are barriers to accessing HIV prevention and services and formulating effective policies and programs for this key population (Asia Pacific Coalition on Male Sexual Health, 2013).

In terms of injection drug use, over one third of people throughout the globe who inject drugs (PWID) reside in Asia and the Pacific where HIV prevalence and incidence among this population varies among countries. For example, in 2015 20–65% of new adult HIV infections were found among PWID in the three countries of Vietnam, Pakistan, and Myanmar (UNAIDS, 2017). Several factors drive the high HIV prevalence among PWID in this region including high incarceration rates combined with limited harm reduction in the form of opioid substitution therapy and needle exchange programs within prisons (UNAIDS, 2017). Outside of the prison environment, harm reduction programs for PWID vary considerably among countries with Malaysia leading the way by increasing its needle and syringe program sites from 297 in 2012 to 729 in 2013, and thereby contributing to the finding of 93% of PWID in Malaysia reporting having used a clean needle at their last injection (UNAIDS, 2017). To increase the proportion of PWID who know their HIV status and who access antiretroviral treatment, Vietnam has taken the lead by enhancing the coordination of opioid substitution therapy along with HIV counseling and testing resulting in larger numbers of PWID who reside in Vietnam accessing and remaining in care as compared to those PWID who do not receive these comprehensive services (Harm Reduction International, 2014).

Overall, Asia and the Pacific will need to drastically increase HIV services and treatment to obtain the 2020 UNAIDS 90-90-90 target that 90% of all people living with HIV will know their status, 90% of all those diagnosed with AIDS will receive antiretroviral therapy (ART), and 90% of all people receiving ART will have viral suppression (UNAIDS, 2017). Variations in funding and national responses to the HIV epidemic are demonstrated in 2016 data revealing the access to ART in Thailand (69%) as compared to Pakistan (5.9%) (UNAIDS, 2017). The most entrenched barriers to scaling up access to HIV treatment and counseling throughout the region include stigma, discrimination, and legal barriers (UNAIDS, 2017). For example, 11 countries in the region including Malaysia and Papua New Guinea impose HIV restriction laws regarding entry, stay, travel, and residence of people living with HIV while same-sex activities are criminalized in 18 countries including Pakistan, Bangladesh, and Malaysia (Global Commission on HIV and the Law, 2013). Although some progress has been made (e.g., India and Pakistan have formally recognized transgender as a "third" gender since 2009 and 2010), stigma and discrimination faced by people living with HIV throughout Asia and the Pacific are deeply entrenched and ubiquitous. A final necessary improvement is increased national funding for the HIV response, beyond the global expenditures of countries including the United States. While a few countries including Thailand, China, and Malaysia fund 90–99% of their HIV responses, most of the remaining countries in the region need to drastically increase their internal spending on the fight against HIV (UNAIDS, 2017).

SUMMARY

This chapter delineated long-standing and entrenched barriers to HIV care and prevention including historical cultural, structural, and legal systems that have fueled the stigma, discrimination, and bias faced by key populations who are disproportionately impacted by HIV. These challenges to HIV intervention and prevention in the United States and globally make the goal of achieving the UNAIDS 90-90-90 targets by 2020 unlikely. At the individual and interpersonal level, the use of antiretroviral medications including both PrEP and PEP must be scaled up, along with sex and reproductive education, voluntary medical male circumcision, condom and lubricant distribution, and harm reduction for PWID. At a structural level, domestic and global funding must increase for community-based clinics and health services, as well as integrated, comprehensive programs targeting HIV-related stigma, discrimination, and societal and legal bias which disproportionately affect the populations most vulnerable to HIV—MSM, sex workers, transgender people, and PWID.

Promising areas of intervention and prevention include social media and other rapidly developing technological approaches to HIV/AIDS prevention among young men of color MSM and transgender women. Future research examining the impact of social media along with the Stonewall legacy's historical and empowerment-based message of resistance could prove impactful in the search for effective HIV/AIDS interventions. One aspect of intervention research could explore whether or not today's populations who are most vulnerable to HIV (e.g., of young minority MSM and transgender women) could be inspired and learn lessons from those who came before them in the Stonewall movement and who share a common experience of discrimination, bias, victimization, poverty, and racism. Understanding how to infuse this message into social media interventions could lead to promising and effective new ways to decrease the numbers of new HIV infections impacting these communities.

Despite these challenges, historically LGBT communities also possess a great deal of resilience, support, and strengths based on sub-communities and cultural currency that may be harnessed to bolster effective HIV interventions. Research should examine whether prevention efforts that honor and build upon the legacy of the Stonewall resistance that was discussed in Chapter 1 of this volume. The Stonewall Inn riots saw the most vulnerable members of the LGBT community join together to demand equal treatment, respect, and dignity—a strategy that might be effective in stemming the disparities in HIV among MSM and transgender women. While the aftermath of this rallying cry led to gains in civil and political rights that still pay dividends decades after the Stonewall riots, the new challenge is to explore whether harnessing this history, relaying it to those most at risk in the LGBT community, and infusing it in multipronged prevention strategies is an effective and feasible prevention strategy.

Going forward, those impacted the most by HIV/AIDS, young minority MSM and transgender women, must receive reinforcement that HIV is not related to a moral deficiency—as some ultraconservative politicians claimed when AIDS was first discovered—but rather the risk of HIV is influenced by situations, personal interactions, and social determinants or external societal factors that perpetuate HIV among their community (Adams, 2012; Diaz et al., 2004; Friedman, Cooper, & Osborne, 2009; Hallfors, Iritani, Miller, & Bauer, 2007). Research should explore whether fostering a sense of community among those most vulnerable to HIV based on a connection to past Stonewall activism could lead individuals to make life-saving choices and to demand changes in the structural and external societal factors that perpetuate HIV/AIDs in their communities, including access to high-quality health care and culturally competent providers.

References

Adams, P. (2012). Beyond individual-level sexual risk behaviors: HIV/AIDS and racial health disparities. In S. R. Notaro (Ed.), *Health disparities among underserved populations: Implications for research, policy, and praxis* (pp. 227–240). Bingley, UK: Emerald Group Publishing.

Amnesty International. (2017). *LGBTI rights: Mapping anti-gay laws in Africa*. Retrieved from https://www.amnesty.org.uk/lgbti-lgbt-gay-human-rights-law-africa-uganda-kenya-nigeria-cameroon.

Asia Pacific Coalition on Male Sexual Health (APCOM). (2013). *Overlooked, ignored, forgotten: HIV and basic rights of transgender people in Asia and the Pacific*. Retrieved from http://apcom.org/sites/default/files/PolicyBrief-TG%289%29.pdf.

Balaji, A., Bowles, K., Hess, K., Smith, J., & Paz-Bailey, (2017). Association between enacted stigma and HIV-related risk behavior among MSM, National HIV Behavioral Surveillance System, 2011. *AIDS Behavior, 21,* 227–237.

Bandura, A. (1986). *Social foundations of thought and action: A social cognitive theory.* Englewood Cliffs, NJ: Prentice Hall.

Baral, S., Poteat, T., Stromdahl, S., Wirtz, A., Guadamuz, T., & Beyrer, C. (2013). Worldwide burden of HIV in transgender women: A systematic review and meta-analysis. *Lancet, 13*(3), 214–222.

Bausum, A. (2015). *Stonewall: Breaking out in the fight for gay rights.* New York, NY: Speak.

Brooks, R., Etzel, M., Hinojos, E., Henry, C., & Perez, M. (2005). Preventing HIV among Latino and African American gay and bisexual men in a context of

HIV-related stigma, discrimination, and homophobia: Perspectives of providers. *AIDS Patient Care and STDS, 19*(11), 737–744.

Buchanan, P. (1983, May 24). AIDS disease: It's nature striking back. *New York Post*.

Carter, D. (2004). *Stonewall: The riots that sparked the gay revolution*. New York, NY: St. Martin's Griffin.

Diaz, R., & Ayala, G. (2001). *Social discrimination and health: The case of Latino gay men and HIV risk*. New York: Policy Institute of the National Gay and Lesbian Task Force.

Diaz, R., Ayala, G., & Bein, E. (2004). Sexual risks as an outcome of social oppression: Data from a probability sample of Latino gay men in three U.S. cities. *Cultural Diversity and Ethnic Minority Psychology, 10*(3), 255–267.

Diaz, R., Ayala, G., Bein, E., Henne, J., & Marin, B. (2001). The impact of homophobia, poverty, and racism on the mental health of gay and bisexual Latino men: Findings from 3 U.S. cities. *American Journal of Public Health, 91*, 927–932.

Fact Sheet: The National HIV/AIDS Strategy: Updated to 2020. (2015, July 30). *The White House, Office of the Press Secretary*. Retrieved from https://www.whitehouse.gov/the-press-office/2015/07/30/fact-sheet-national-hivaids-strategy-updated-2020.

Feldman, M. (2010). A critical literature review to identify possible causes of higher rates of HIV infection among young Black and Latino men who have sex with men. *Journal of the National Medical Association, 102*, 1206–1221.

Finlayson, T., Le, B., Smith, A., Bowles, K., Cribbin, M., Miles, I., … DiNenno, E. (2011). HIV risk, prevention, and testing behaviors among men who have sex with men—National HIV behavioral surveillance system, 21 US cities, United States, 2008. *Morbidity and Mortality Weekly Report, 60*, 1–34.

Freire, P. (1973). *Education for critical consciousness*. New York, NY: Seabury Press.

Friedman, S., Cooper, H., & Osborne, A. (2009). Structural and social contexts of HIV risks among Black Americans. *American Journal of Public Health, 99*(6), 1002–1008.

Garett, R., Smith, J., Chiu, J., & Young, S. (2016). HIV/AIDS stigma among a sample of primarily African-American and Latino men who have sex with men social media users. *AIDS Care, 28*(6), 731–735.

Global Commission on HIV and the Law. (2013). *LGBTI people in Asia continue to face stigma and discrimination*. Retrieved from https://hivlawcommission.org/2013/12/18/lgbti-people-in-asia-continue-to-face-stigma-and-discrimination/.

Granich, R., Gupta, S., Hersch, B., Williams, B., Montaner, J., Young, B., & Zuniga, J. (2015). Trends in AIDS death, new infections and ART coverage in the top 30 countries with the highest AIDS mortality burden; 1990–2013. *PLos One, 10*(7), 1–16. https://doi.org/10.1371/journal.pone.0131353.

Hallfors, D., Iritani, B., Miller, W., & Bauer, D. (2007). Sexual and drug behavior patterns and HIV and STD racial disparities: The need for new directions. *American Journal of Public Health, 97*(1), 125–132.

Harm Reduction International. (2014). *Global state of harm reduction.* Retrieved from https://www.hri.global/contents/1524.

Hyde, L. (2016). *Achievements and challenges in introducing a harm reduction programme in Kenya: A case study.* Community Action on Harm Reduction, Alliance for Public Health. Regional Technical Support Hub for Eastern Europe and Central Asia. Retrieved from http://www.cahrproject.org/wp-content/uploads/2016/04/kenya-report.pdf.

Jeffries, W., Marks, G., Lauby, J., Murrill, C., & Millett, G. (2013). Homophobia is associated with sexual behavior that increases risk of acquiring and transmitting HIV infection among Black men who have sex with men. *AIDS Behavior, 17,* 1442–1453.

Meadowbrooke, C., Veinot, T., Loveluck, J., Hickok, A., & Bauermeister, J. (2014). Information behavior and HIV testing intentions among young men at risk for HIV/AIDS. *Journal of the Association for Information Science and Technology, 65,* 609–620.

Meyer, I. (2003). Prejudice, social stress, and mental health in lesbian, gay, and bisexual populations: Conceptual issues and research evidence. *Psychological Bulletin, 129,* 674–697.

Meyer, I. (2010). Identity, stress, and resilience in lesbians, gay men, and bisexuals of color. *Counseling Psychologist, 38*(3), 1–9.

Millet, G., Flores, A., Peterson, J., & Bakeman, R. (2007). Explaining disparities in HIV infection among black and white men who have sex with men: A meta-analysis of HIV risk behaviors. *AIDS, 21,* 2083–2091.

MTV Staying Alive. (2017). *What is MTV Shuga?* Retrieved from https://www.mtvstayingalive.org/about-us/.

National Alliance of State and Territorial AIDS Directors (NASTAD) and National Coalition of STD Directors (NCSD). (2014). *Addressing stigma: A blueprint for HIV/STD prevention and care outcomes for Black and Latino gay men.* Retrieved from https://www.nastad.org/resource/stigma-toolkit-addressing-stigma-blueprint-improving-hivstd-prevention-and-care-outcomes.

Patel, V., Masyukova, M., Sutton, D., & Horvath, K. (2016). Social media use and HIV-related risk behaviors in young Black and Latino Gay and Bi Men and transgender individuals in New York city: Implications for online interventions. *Journal of Urban Health: Bulletin of New York Academy of Medicine, 93*(2), 388–399. https://doi.org/10.1007/s11524-016-0025-1.

PEPFAR. (2017). *Annual report to Congress.* Retrieved from https://www.pepfar.gov/documents/organization/267809.pdf.

Peng, L. (2015, July 10). Changing how AIDS funding is used. *National Journal.* Retrieved from https://www.nationaljournal.com/s/24437?mref=magazine-landing.

Pew Research Center. (2013). *A survey of LGBT Americans-Attitudes, experiences, and values in changing times.* Retrieved from http://www.pewsocialtrends.org/files/2013/06/SDT_LGBT-Americans_06-2013.pdf.

Rhodes, S., Daniel, J., Alonzo, J., Duck, S., Garcia, M., Down, M., ... Marsiglia, F. (2013). A systematic community-based participatory approach to refining an evidence-based community-level intervention: The HOLA intervention for Latino men who have sex with men. *Health Promotion Practice, 14*(4), 607–616.

Rhodes, S., Mann, L., Alonzo, J., Downs, M., Abraham, C., Miller, C., ... Reboussin, B. (2014). CBPR to prevent HIV within racial/ethnic, sexual, and gender minority communities: Successes with long-term sustainability. In S. D. Rhodes (Ed.), *Innovations in HIV prevention research and practice through community engagement* (pp. 135–160). New York, NY: Springer.

Silva-Santisteban, A., Eng, S., de la Iglesia, G., Falistocco, C., & Mazin, R. (2016). HIV prevention among transgender women in Latin America: Implementation, gaps, and challenges. *Journal of Interpersonal AIDS Society, 19*(Suppl. 2), 1–10.

Stokes, J., & Peterson, J. (1998). Homophobia, self-esteem, and risk for HIV among African American men who have sex with men. *AIDS Education Prevention, 10,* 278–292.

Sun, C., Reboussin, B., Mann, L., Garcia, M., & Rhodes, S. (2016). The HIV risk profiles of Latino sexual minorities and transgender persons who use websites or apps designed for social and sexual networking. *Health Education and Behavior, 43*(1), 86–93.

The World Bank. (2016). *Experimental evaluation of MTV Shuga: Changing social norms and behaviors with entertainment education.* Retrieved from http://pubdocs.worldbank.org/en/438421467236362785/Entertainment-Edu-workshop-Flyer-6-3-16.pdf.

UNAIDS. (2013). Joint United Nations Programme on HIV/AIDS. *UNAIDS report on the global AIDS epidemic 2013.* Geneva, Switzerland. Retrieved from http://www.unaids.org/sites/default/files/media_asset/UNAIDS_Global_Report_2013_en_1.pdf.

UNAIDS. (2014). Joint United Nations Programme on HIV/AIDS. *90-90-90 An ambitious treatment target to help end the AIDS epidemic.* Geneva, Switzerland. Retrieved from http://www.unaids.org/en/resources/documents/2017/90-90-90.

UNAIDS. (2016). *Joint United Nations Programme on HIV/AIDS* (Prevention gap report). Retrieved from http://www.unaids.org/sites/default/files/media_asset/2016-prevention-gap-report_en.pdf.

UNAIDS. (2017). *Joint United Nations Programme on HIV/AIDS.* UNAIDS Fact Sheet, World AIDS Day 2018. Joint United Nations Programme on HIV/AIDS. UNAIDS Data 2017. Retrieved from https://www.unaids.org/sites/default/files/media_asset/UNAIDS_FactSheet_en.pdf.

United States Department of Health and Human Services, Centers for Disease Control and Prevention. (2014). *Understanding the HIV care continuum*. Retrieved from https://www.cdc.gov/hiv/pdf/DHAP_Continuum.pdf.

United States Department of Health and Human Services, Centers for Disease Control and Prevention. (2015). *Project PrIDE: PrEP, Implementation, Data2Care, Evaluation*. Retrieved from https://www.cdc.gov/hiv/research/demonstration/projectpride.html.

United States Department of Health and Human Services, Centers for Disease Control and Prevention. (2017). *STDs in men who have sex with men*. Retrieved from https://www.cdc.gov/std/stats16/msm.htm.

United States Department of Health and Human Services, Centers for Disease Control and Prevention. (2018). *HIV among gay and bisexual men*. Retrieved from https://www.cdc.gov/hiv/group/msm/index.html.

United States Department of Health and Human Services, Centers for Disease Control and Prevention. (2019). *Estimated HIV incidence and prevalence in the United States, 2010–2016* (HIV Surveillance Supplemental Report). Retrieved from https://www.cdc.gov/hiv/pdf/library/reports/surveillance/cdc-hiv-surveillance-supplemental-report-vol-24-1.pdf.

United States Department of Health and Human Services, National Institutes of Health, Office of Disease Prevention and Health Promotion. (2014). *Lesbian, gay, bisexual, and transgender health*. Retrieved from https://www.healthypeople.gov/2020/topics-objectives/topic/lesbian-gay-bisexual-and-transgender-health.

USAID. (2016). United States Agency for International Development. *Dreams: Partnership to reduce HIV/AIDS in adolescent girls and young women*. Retrieved from https://www.usaid.gov/what-we-do/global-health/hiv-and-aids/technical-areas/dreams.

Vermund, S. (2014). Global HIV epidemiology: A guide for strategies in prevention and care. *Current HIV/AIDS Report, 11*, 93–98. https://doi.org/10.1007/s11904-014-0208-x.

White, Ryan. (n.d.). *Ryan White Quotes*. BrainyQuote.com. Retrieved from https://www.brainyquote.com/quotes/ryan_white_300685.

World Health Organization. (2016). *Consolidated guidelines on HIV prevention, diagnosis, treatment and care for key populations*. Retrieved from http://apps.who.int/iris/bitstream/handle/10665/246200/9789241511124-annexes-eng.pdf;jsessionid=83110BBA6901C11E08A092238D41733A?sequence=5.

CHAPTER 5

Substance Use and Abuse

DISCRIMINATION AND SUBSTANCE ABUSE AMONG THE LGBT COMMUNITY IN THE UNITED STATES

This chapter will discuss the impact of discrimination and bias on the substance use and abuse of the LGBT community.

> Jeremy and I are 34. In our lifetime, the gay community has made more progress on legal and social acceptance than any other demographic group in history. As recently as my own adolescence, gay marriage was a distant aspiration, something newspapers still put in scare quotes. Now, it's been enshrined in law by the Supreme Court. Public support for gay marriage has climbed from 27 percent in 1996 to 61 percent in 2016. In pop culture, we've gone from "Cruising" to "Queer Eye" to "Moonlight." Gay characters these days are so commonplace they're even allowed to have flaws. Still, even as we celebrate the scale and speed of this change, the rates of depression, loneliness and substance abuse in the gay community remain stuck in the same place they've been for decades. (Michael Hobbes, 2017, *Together Alone: The Epidemic of Gay Loneliness.* Highline)

Prior research has demonstrated that substance use (e.g., alcohol, other drugs, and smoking) are serious public health concerns for the general population in the United States (e.g., Substance Abuse and Mental Health Services Administration [SAMHSA], 2012). Additionally, the rates of substance use disorder diagnoses among LGBT and MSM (men who have sex

© The Author(s) 2020
S. R. Notaro, *Marginality and Global LGBT Communities,*
Neighborhoods, Communities, and Urban Marginality,
https://doi.org/10.1007/978-3-030-22415-8_5

with men, who may or may not identify as bisexual or homosexual) individuals are disproportionately high as compared with heterosexual individuals (e.g., Parsons, Grov, & Golub, 2012). These elevated rates of substance use disorders combined with higher rates of HIV and some STIs (sexually transmitted infections) among those who identify as lesbian, gay, bisexual, and MSM suggests that substance use and problems related to such use are more highly correlated with HIV or STIs among LGBT individuals as compared with heterosexuals (e.g., Parsons et al., 2012; Wray, Pantalone, Kahler, Monti, & Mayer, 2016).

Importantly, this chapter will provide data to further shed light on the lived experience of individuals such as "Kristina," a transgender woman seeking treatment for substance abuse whose challenges were exacerbated by discrimination, isolation, and lack of family support. Kristina supported her drug habit by working as a prostitute and selling drugs before she began performing in transgender clubs.

My 12-Step group has been my life support system. No one in my family has spoken to me for over 15 years, since I came out as queer. The members of my group are my family, my friends, my lifeline. Going to meetings isn't just how I stay sober, it's how I stay connected to people who care. Straight folks, even gay folks, don't really understand how cut off we are in the trans community. (Kristina, personal interview, Desert Hope, American Addiction Centers, 2019)

ALCOHOL ABUSE IN THE UNITED STATES

Previous studies have shown that MSM living with HIV report higher rates of binge drinking (five or more drinks at one time period) as compared to women and men who have sex only with women (e.g., Vellozzi et al., 2009). Skeer et al. (2012) found that 20% of HIV-positive MSM in their sample reported binge drinking at least once per week. Wray et al. (2016) point out that binge drinking can have alarming and serious health consequences for people living with HIV (e.g., higher risk for liver toxicity, poor response to antiretroviral therapy, increased cognitive difficulties). To date, there is a lack of research focused on determining the contributing factors of heavy alcohol drinking among MSM (Wray et al., 2016). Prior studies examining discrimination and the minority stress model have demonstrated that MSM of color living with HIV who experience racial discrimination are more likely to have lower CD4 counts (the number of white blood cells in a cubic millimeter of blood that fight infection) and to have a detectable HIV viral load and less likely to adhere to antiretroviral therapy (e.g., Bogart, Landrine, Galvan, Wagner, & Klein, 2013).

Past research exploring motivations for heavy drinking among the LGBT community have found that drinking heavily to cope with or avoid negative emotions stemming from discrimination may play a role in these negative health behaviors (e.g., Hatzenbuehler, Corbin, & Fromme, 2011). Additional motivating factors for heavy drinking among LGBT individuals include drinking to have more fun, to enhance positive emotions, and to enhance sexual experiences (e.g., Wray et al., 2016). There is a dearth of research which explores both direct and indirect mechanisms by which these various motives for heavy drinking impact the likelihood of experiencing alcohol-related problems, especially among MSM with HIV who often report multiple forms of discrimination related to their sexual orientation and HIV status (Wray et al., 2016). To expand upon prior research, in two analogous studies, Wray et al. (2016) examined direct and indirect relationships among discrimination based on sexual orientation and HIV status, heavy drinking, alcohol-related problems, and reasons to drink. The motivations to drink included coping (e.g., "To forget your worries"); enhancement (e.g., "Because you like the feeling"); social facilitation (e.g., "To be sociable"), and sexual (e.g., "To be more confident in approaching sex partners"). In Study One, which focused on MSM, HIV-negative individuals recruited in the northeast via online social media advertisements, flyers, and contact at LGBT events, alcohol use was assessed in the past thirty days with three items related to frequency and quantity of drinking while alcohol-related problems (e.g., getting in trouble at work because of drinking) in the past six months were assessed with 13 yes/no items from the Short Michigan Alcoholism Screening Test (SMAST). A total of 171 participants (mean age = 27.2, 86% white; 12% Black or African American; 17% Hispanic or Latino) completed linked online surveys.

Wray et al. (2016) hypothesized that drinking to cope would be positively associated with problems with drinking while other motives for drinking would indirectly impact problems with drinking through alcohol use. Results of the path models in Study One indicated that MSM, HIV-negative individuals who reported more perceived discrimination based on sexual orientation also drank more heavily for several reasons including to cope with negative emotions, to enhance mood, and to facilitate sex. Only alcohol use and coping motives were directly and positively associated with alcohol-related problems. There was a significant and indirect effect of perceived discrimination on alcohol problems through coping motives; however, perceived discrimination did not significantly and indirectly impact alcohol problems through drinking to enhance mood. Drinking to enhance mood was positively associated with alcohol use, which in turn, was positively associated with alcohol-related problems. Study One revealed that heavy-drinking MSM who are HIV negative and who also experience more discrimination and who drink to cope with negative emotions were directly at risk for alcohol-related problems over and above their alcohol use compared to those individuals who drank for other reasons including to enhance their mood or to facilitate sex (Wray et al., 2016). For HIV-negative MSM who drank heavily, drinking to enhance positive emotions are associated with higher levels of alcohol use, which in turn leads to more alcohol problems, regardless of discrimination (Wray et al., 2016).

Study Two focused on heavy-drinking MSM HIV-positive individuals enrolled in a randomized controlled trial to test an intervention for heavy drinking. A total of 185 participants (mean age = 42.2, 73% white; 22% Black or African American; 17% Hispanic or Latino) were recruited from an urban community health center in the northeast that provides sexual and gender minority health services. The measures for discrimination, drinking motives, and sexual motives for drinking were identical to those in Study One; however, the measures of alcohol use and alcohol problems differed. Study Two used a technique to help cue the memory of drinking on each day over the past 30 days and a different measure of alcohol problems, the Short Inventory of Problems or the SIP which assesses 15 negative consequences of alcohol use over 3 months (Wray et al., 2016). The survey data was collected via trained interviewers or through audio computer assisted self-interview technology (ACASI).

In Study Two, 50% of participants experienced discrimination based on HIV-status (e.g., ignored by potential sexual partners) while 65% experienced discrimination based on HIV status or sexual orientation (Wray et al., 2016). The results of Study Two were consistent with Study One in that reporting more discrimination based on HIV status or sexual orientation was significantly and directly associated with drinking to cope with negative emotions, which was then positively and significantly related to alcohol problems. Results of both studies demonstrated that MSM individuals, whether HIV positive or HIV negative, who reported more discrimination also reported drinking more frequently for sexual reasons; however, in Study Two, more discrimination was not associated with drinking to enhance positive mood as it was in Study One. Social motives were also directly and negatively associated with alcohol problems, but not alcohol use, among MSM living with HIV in Study Two, whereas social motives were not associated with drinking or problems in Study One. While these results could suggest that HIV-positive MSM who drink for social reasons are at lower risk for alcohol problems, Wray et al. (2016) urge caution in the interpretation of these findings given the high probability of multi-collinearity and the association between social and enhancement motives. These strong associations among these two variables may have led to the result of HIV-positive MSM who drink for social reasons being at lower risk for alcohol related problems. Additionally, the authors present evidence of multicollinearity in the results of a stepwise regression analysis showing that social motives were positively associated with alcohol use unless enhancement motives were included in the model.

Study Two also found that for HIV-positive MSM, frequent drinking for sexual reasons were associated with heavier drinking and in turn, alcohol-related problems. These findings for HIV-positive MSM differ from those for HIV-negative MSM in Study One. MSM HIV-positive individuals may feel that drinking excessively may lessen their inhibitions about being rejected by potential sexual partners. Additionally, the difference in results could be attributed to age and alcohol use factors in that participants in Study Two were substantially older and drank more heavily than participants in Study One.

Overall, taken together, Study One and Study Two demonstrated that discrimination based on sexual orientation and HIV status is a risk factor for alcohol problems among MSM who are both HIV negative and HIV positive. Drinking to cope with negative emotions was a mediating factor between discrimination and alcohol problems in both studies. No other motivating factor acted as a mediator in the relationship between discrimination and alcohol problems. Interventions may need to focus on discrimination as a major factor in heavy drinking among MSM as well as more effective coping strategies. Given that across both studies drinking to have a better time socially was associated with more alcohol problems through heavier patterns of use, interventions should also target the motivating factor of drinking to have a good time. For HIV-positive MSM who drink heavily, interventions may need to specifically address the motivation of drinking to increase confidence in approaching sexual partners by building skills related to approaching sexual partners without excessive drinking.

Wray et al. (2016) acknowledge several limitations of their work. First, the small sample size of minority MSM prevented the exploration of these relationships within racial minorities. Second, Wray et al. (2016) the authors of the study did not use the same measures of alcohol use or alcohol problems in Study One and Study Two. Third, there were substantially different ages in Study Two (mean age = 42.2) versus Study One (mean age = 27.8) and drinking (number of binge drinking days in the past 30 days = 7.6 in Sudy Two versus 3.3 in Study One). These differences in measurement, age, and heavy drinking could account for the observed differences in the associations across studies. These findings of HIV-positive MSM being on average older and heavier drinkers than HIV negative MSM are consistent with some prior research reporting similar differences in age and drinking patterns in these populations (e.g., Skeer et al., 2012). Fourth, these samples consisted mostly of heavy drinking MSM, so the results may not be generalizable to MSM who drink more moderately. On a related note, Study Two participants were willing to participate in a drinking intervention which may further limit the generalizability of the findings. Finally, the results are cross-sectional and thus cannot provide evidence for causality in the relationships among discrimination, drinking motives, alcohol use, and alcohol problems. Wray et al. (2016) advocate for longitudinal studies to examine discrimination experienced in adolescence and young adulthood in MSM populations with both positive and negative HIV status as predictors of later reasons to drink and associated drinking problems.

SMOKING IN THE UNITED STATES

Related to alcohol use is a concern about disparate smoking behaviors among LGBT individuals, especially given the Center for Disease Control and Prevention's assertion that smoking remains one of the most preventable causes of early death in the United States (United States Department of Health and Human Services, 2014). Results have shown that the smoking prevalence among LGBT individuals or "sexual minorities" is approximately twice that of heterosexual individuals (e.g., Balsam, Beadnell, & Riggs, 2012; Gruskin, Greenwood, Matevia, Pollack, & Bye, 2007); however, less research has focused on the smoking prevalence of gender minorities including individuals identifying as transgender and on possible effects of transgender-based discrimination on smoking behaviors (Gamarel et al., 2016). Indeed, prior research has examined associations between discrimination and smoking among LGBT communities in a minority stress framework but little research has focused on transgender women (gender minorities) in terms of the impact of minority stress on smoking behavior and cessation attempts (Gamarel et al., 2016).

Research is also needed that examines the barriers to smoking cessation among transgender women because this population experiences a high prevalence of other negative health outcomes including depression, substance use, and HIV risk (e.g., Gamarel, Reisner, Laurenceau, Nemoto, & Operario, 2014; Hotton, Garofalo, Kuhns, & Johnson, 2013). Some limited data on smoking prevalence among transgender women in California found that transgender women smoked at twice the rate of other Californians (Bye, Gruskin, Greenwood, Albright, & Krotki, 2005). Additionally, smoking while also ingesting cross-sex hormones (e.g., estrogen in a male body) can increase the risk of heart disease and smoking may slow down the recovery from surgery that some transgender women choose (e.g., Mueck & Seeger, 2005; Silverstein, 1992).

In a minority stress framework, discrimination based on transgender status can exacerbate and increase the risk of smoking, as smoking may serve as a mechanism to cope with the discrimination that manifests in name-calling and violence experienced by some transgender individuals (e.g., Hendricks & Testa, 2012). More research is needed to test the relationships among discrimination, gender-identity bias, and smoking in transgender women. To that end, Gamarel et al. (2016) conducted a study to examine the association between discrimination and smoking patterns in transgender women and to identify barriers to smoking cessation in transgender women who smoked. The study included two urban locations—San Francisco, CA, and Oakland, CA and focused recruitment efforts on venues known to attract transgender women including community-based organizations, bars, and nightclubs. All participants were at least 18 years of age, self-identified as transgender women (pre- or post-operative), provided informed consent, and were compensated with $50.00 as well as safe-sex kits and brochures with resources listing local community-based organizations specializing in transgender needs.

The cross-sectional study administered a one-time survey via ACASI to 241 transgender women between August 2004 and July 2006. Self-reported data included age, race, socioeconomic status, HIV status (positive, negative, unknown), hormone use, and engagement in sex work. Depression was measured via the Center for Epidemiological Studies or the CES-D while discrimination was measured with an 11 item scale that included the frequency of harmful experiences related to being transgender or transitioning to become a woman. A sample question asked respondents to rate on a 5-point Likert scale "How often were you made fun of for being transgender" with responses ranging from never to almost daily. The transgender discrimination scores ranged from 11 to 45 (M = 26.63, SD = 7.83), where higher scores indicate greater levels of discrimination. Participants who indicated ever smoking were further asked to report the number of cigarettes smoked per day resulting in the categories of current smokers, no smoking history, and not current smoker. Respondents were also asked about smoking cessation attempts resulting in the three categories of successful cessation, unsuccessful attempt, and never attempted.

The demographics demonstrated that the respondents' ages ranged from 18 to 65 years (M = 36.52, SD = 10.5) with all respondents identifying as either African American (n = 123, 51%) or White (n = 118, 49%). The majority of participants reported less than a high school education (n = 161, 66.8%) and annual incomes of less than $1000 per month (n = 154, 63.9%). The majority of participants self-reported a HIV-positive serostatus as well as engagement in sex work in the past 6 months (n = 124, 51.9%), and lifetime use of hormones (n = 169, 70.1%). In terms of smoking, the vast majority of respondents reported having smoked in their lifetime (n = 174, 72%) with about 40% smoking a pack or more per day, 26% smoking 10–19 cigarettes a day, 25% smoking 1–9 cigarettes per day, and 9% smoking a few cigarettes per week. The average age of smoking initiation was 14.77 (SD = 5.16) while 82% of lifetime smokers (n = 119) indicated a previous attempt to quit.

In terms of racial/ethnicity differences, white respondents were significantly less likely to report never smoking and were four times more likely to report current smoking as compared to African American respondents. In terms of other substance use, participants who reported alcohol use were significantly more likely to report daily and intermittent smoking as compared to those who reported no alcohol use in the past thirty days. Those who reported daily smoking had significantly higher discrimination scores as compared to those who never smoked. Participants who reported an HIV seropositive status were 49% less likely to be current smokers as compared to participants who reported an HIV negative or unknown status. Higher levels of transgender-based discrimination were positively associated with an increase in the odds of being a current smoker and with unsuccessful attempts to quit smoking when compared to those who had successfully quit smoking. Further, higher levels of discrimination were associated with greater odds of reporting no attempt to quit as compared to those who reported a successful or unsuccessful attempt to quit smoking.

Gamarel et al. (2016) used logistic regression to examine the relationship between study variables, smoking, and smoking cessation attempts in current smokers versus non-smokers. Given the small number of intermittent smokers, the smoking categories of intermittent and daily smokers were collapsed into current smokers.

In the sample, over 69% reported being a current smoker. Smokers reported a significantly higher frequency of discrimination experiences as compared to transgender women who did not currently smoke. These findings are similar to those in sexual minority (LGB) populations in the United States (McCabe, Boyd, Hughes, & d'Arcy, 2003). Whereas over 60% of the sample had attempted to quit smoking at some point in their lives, only 17% reported successful cessation. Higher discrimination was associated with unsuccessful cessation attempts or never having tried to quit smoking. Given these findings, interventions should target discrimination as a barrier to smoking cessation in transgender women who smoke. This study also found that alcohol use was a barrier to smoking cessation in that drinking alcohol in the past 30 days was associated with an increased odds ratio of never attempting to quit smoking as compared to unsuccessful attempts.

Complex racial differences emerged in that white transgender women who lived in San Francisco were more likely to report current, daily, or prior smoking as compared with African American women who lived in Oakland. Further white women were more likely to have attempted to stop smoking as compared to Black women in the study. Gamarel et al. (2016) theorize that these racial differences may be related to geographical resource differences in that San Francisco (where the majority of the white respondents resided) may have more resources related to smoking cessation programs than Oakland, CA where the majority of African American respondents lived.

Gamarel et al. (2016) identified several limitations of their study. First, their sample was one of convenience with no random selection and focused on a high-risk population of sex workers. Gamarel et al. (2016) point out that this limitation is common among gender minority research because of the lack of inclusion of gender minorities in representative population surveys. A second limitation is related to the geographical differences between the tolerance for gender minorities in San Francisco versus Oakland in that gender-based discrimination may not be as prevalent in San Francisco in comparison to Oakland, CA or other parts of the country. Next, the self-report which could lead to social desirability bias and the cross-sectional design cannot support temporal or causal claims. In terms of measurement, the study did not capture the dates of quit attempts or the numbers of quit attempts, so comparisons between those respondents who attempted to quit recently or who had several quit attempts to those who attempted to quit in the past were not possible. As alcohol was assessed with a single item measure and did not account for frequency or quantity, it was not possible to assess whether different levels of alcohol consumption were related to smoking cessation. Gamarel et al. (2016) advocate for future research within a more heterogeneous sample of gender minorities to inform smoking cessation interventions through the further exploration of differences in race, ethnicity, socioeconomic status, sexual identity, and discrimination.

PRESCRIPTION DRUG MISUSE AND ILLICIT DRUG USE AMONG YOUNG MSM IN THE UNITED STATES

In addition to illicit drug use, research focusing on substance use among young adults has demonstrated that 31.4% of young adults aged 18–29 report prescription drug misuse at least once in their lifetime (SAMHSA, 2010). Recent research has focused on the prescription drug misuse of young MSMs or young men who have sex with men (e.g., Kecojevic, Wong, Corliss, & Lankenau, 2015). According to SAMHSA (2010), prescription drug misuse is defined as the use of opioids, tranquilizes, and stimulants when not prescribed by a doctor or when taken only for the effect caused. Given prior research that found a greater likelihood of high-risk behaviors including substance use and prescription drug misuse among young men who have sex with men (YMSM) who also reported maltreatment or abuse during childhood, Kecojevic et al. (2015) hypothesized that experiences of stress, discrimination, bias, and stigma could increase the risk of prescription drug misuse and illicit drug use among YMSM. The authors sought to understand whether or not the further stress of racism placed minority YMSM at an even greater risk of adopting negative coping behaviors including prescription drug misuse. Kecojevic et al. (2015) examined the association between childhood abuse, minority stress (including homophobia, discrimination, bias, and racism) and mental health distress. They also investigated whether or not perceptions of general stress are associated with these psychosocial stressors and mental health concerns. The authors hypothesized that YMSM who self-reported high levels of childhood abuse and minority stress would report increased levels of mental health distress and general stress which would in turn lead to a greater likelihood of prescription drug misuse and illicit drug use.

This cross-sectional study collected data from 2012 to 2013 in a sample of 18–29 year-old men who reported misusing a prescription drug (e.g., opioid, tranquilizer, stimulant) in the prior 6 months; engaging in sex with a male partner in the prior 6 months; speaking English; and living in Philadelphia, PA (Kecojevic et al., 2015). The authors employed a variety of strategies to locate 18–29 year old males who met the study criteria including targeted and "chain-referral" sampling, recruitment from parks, streets, gay bars and clubs, and community-based organizations. A total of 191 participants provided verbal informed consent and completed face-to-face interviews lasting approximately one hour administered via portable computers (Kecojevic et al., 2015). The participants received $25.00 in compensation as well as resources including HIV testing information. Demographic information collected included age, race (e.g., White or non-White), and sexual orientation (e.g., bisexual, heterosexual, other).

The frequency of several forms of childhood abuse (e.g., emotional, physical, sexual) was assessed via a Childhood Trauma Questionnaire (Bernstein et al., 1994). Measures of discrimination in the form of lifetime experiences with homophobia and racism were adopted from Diaz, Ayala, Bein, Jenne, and Marin (2001) and Wong, Schrager, Holloway, Meyer, and Kipke (2014). Racism (e.g., lifetime experiences of verbal and physical threats and attacks, police harassment due to race or ethnicity) was measured via a 4 item Likert composite scale ranging from never to many times. Homophobia was measured with a 4 item Likert composite scale ranging from never to many times regarding lifetime experiences of verbal and physical threats and attacks, police harassment, friends and family teasing other gay people, and needing to move to avoid harassment based on sexual orientation. Social racism and homophobia were measured with a composite 4 item scale ranging from strongly disagree to strongly agree assessing the extent to which the respondent felt uncomfortable in "gay" spaces or online and whether they were rejected as a potential sexual partner due to their race/ethnicity. Internalized homophobia (e.g., the extent to which participants disliked themselves for their sexual attraction to men, wished they were not sexually attracted to men, felt guilty for having sex with men, and felt stress or conflict from having sex with men) was measured with the short version of Ross and Rosser's (1996) 4 item Likert scale ranging from strongly disagree to strongly agree. Psychological distress (e.g., depression, anxiety, somatization or perceptions of bodily dysfunction) experienced in the prior week was measured with the Brief Symptom Inventory (BSI-18) (Derogatis, 2000). General stress appraisal (e.g., frequency of feeling upset because of an unexpected event) was measured via the 10 item Perceived Stress Scale (PSS) (Cohen, Kamarck, & Mermelstein, 1983), with responses ranging from never to very often.

Misuse of prescription drugs was assessed with a question asking respondents whether or not they had misused (pills taken that were not prescribed or taken just for the feeling) any of the three most commonly abused prescription drugs (e.g., tranquilizers, opioids, and stimulants) in the past 6 months as well as the amount of pills taken in the past 6 months. Respondents were asked the same questions concerning illicit drugs including ecstasy, heroin, cocaine, crack, and crystal methamphetamine.

The demographic analyses revealed an average age of 23.7 (SD = 3.3) with one-third of the sample identifying as White ($n = 64$) and two thirds as non-White ($n = 71$). Nearly 60% ($n = 109$) of respondents identified as gay or homosexual while approximately 42% identified as bisexual, heterosexual, or other. Childhood abuse (e.g., emotional, physical, and sexual) was reported at levels considered above standardized thresholds. Depression, anxiety, somatization, and perceived general stress were reported at higher levels than in previous research with YMSM populations (Kecojevic et al., 2015).

While some participants infrequently misused prescription drugs, some subjects misused prescription drugs frequently, especially opioids (78%) and tranquilizers (80%), with stimulants misused to a lesser extent (52%). Reports of childhood abuse and discrimination were positively and significantly correlated with each other and with mental health distress and general stress. Higher levels of childhood abuse were significantly and positively correlated with a higher prevalence of substance use as compared to those who did not report child sexual abuse. Specifically, of the three forms of child abuse included in this study, reports of physical child abuse were significantly and positively correlated with heavy misuse of opioids. Opioid misuse could serve as a coping mechanism for the pain and anxiety resulting from childhood physical abuse (e.g., Dube et al., 2003; Kecojevic et al., 2015). These findings are also consistent with prior research demonstrating that social discrimination can be associated with discomfort with one's sexual identity as well as psychosocial stress which may in turn increase the risk of substance use disorders (e.g., McCabe, Bostwick, Hughes, West, & Boyd, 2010).

Higher levels of social discrimination were positively and significantly related to increased stimulant use whereas reports of racism were positively correlated with increased levels of opioid and tranquilizer misuse.

Experiences of somatization or distress from perceptions of bodily dysfunction were significantly and positively associated with increased stimulant misuse and with illicit drug use. The authors hypothesize that their finding of the association of self-reported depressive symptoms with higher stimulant misuse, but less opioid misuse, is in line with the effect of stimulants as a mood enhancer. Taken together, these findings suggest that YMSM may rely on different types of drugs to achieve, enhance, or avoid specific effects (Kecojevic et al., 2015). In terms of age effects, older YMSM were more likely to misuse opioids as compared to other ages, leading Kecojevic et al. (2015) to hypothesize that older YMSM have easier access to opioids. Bisexual, heterosexual, and "other" YMSM were at higher risk for misuse of all three class of prescription drugs as compared to gay and homosexual YMSM. Kecojevic et al. (2015) hypothesize that individuals who do not self-identify as gay, but who have sex with men, may experience a conflict between their sexual actions and their sexual identities, possibly leading to drug misuse as a coping mechanism (Kecojevic et al., 2015). Racial minority YMSM were less likely to misuse tranquilizers and stimulants or illicit drugs as compared to White YMSM.

Overall, the study findings support prior research (e.g., Wong et al., 2014) that demonstrated correlations between stress and substance use in YMSM. YMSM who expressed childhood abuse, discrimination, or mental health distress may experience a greater risk for prescription drug misuse as a way to cope with or alleviate negative feelings (Kecojevic et al., 2015). This study found no differential effects of risk factors between subtypes of prescription drug misuse. Kecojevic et al. (2015) call for more research examining prescription drug misuse within this population including longitudinal studies designed to explore causal paths and more qualitative studies to identify additional risk factors including sensation-seeking and impulsivity. The findings of the current study suggest that health providers should take into account the full mental health and psychosocial history of patients, recognizing childhood abuse in all of its forms as potential risk factors for substance abuse and prescription drug misuse in YMSM. Further, clinicians working with YMSM should consider substance abuse treatment that incorporates strategies for coping with negative life experiences.

Kecojevic et al. (2015) identified several limitations of their study including the self-report data that could be impacted by social desirability and recall bias, especially in terms of respondents accurately recalling the number of pills taken in the prior 6 months. The cross-sectional design of the study precludes the formation of causal inferences and the sample may not generalize to YMSM who do not engage in substance abuse or who reside in locations other than Philadelphia. Finally, no adjustments were made for potential peer influences on respondents' social networks.

COMORBIDITY OF MENTAL HEALTH AND SUBSTANCE USE DISORDERS

While substance use disorders and prescription drug misuse among sexual minorities including individuals who identify as transgender women and MSM pose serious public health concerns, comorbidity or co-occurrence of mental health disorders may precede substance abuse problems and may complicate and negatively impact substance abuse treatment (e.g., Grella, Hser, Joshi, & Rounds-Bryant, 2001). Further, lesbian, gay, and bisexual individuals report provider and institutional discrimination and bias as substantial barriers to accessing mental, physical, and substance use treatment (e.g., Buchmueller & Carpenter, 2010). Fluente, Livington, Roley, and Sorensen (2015) investigated whether mental and physical health needs and treatment utilization of LGB individuals differ from heterosexuals seeking substance abuse treatment in one publicly funded health system in the County of San Francisco. Data was collected from all substance abuse treatment facilities in the County that received any government funding. Treatment records of residential, detoxification, and outpatient services received from 2007 to 2009 resulted in 107,470 total treatment episodes experienced by 13,211 individuals with an average age of 38.10 years (SD = 13.48).

In this sample, gay and bisexual men were more likely to report white ethnicity and higher levels of education. Analyses revealed that sexual orientation is predictive of mental and physical health status as individuals identifying as LGB reported higher rates of prior mental health diagnoses and a higher likelihood of taking psychiatric medications at the time of treatment for substance use (Fluente et al., 2015). Specifically, lesbian and bisexual women had two times greater odds of prior mental health diagnoses as compared to heterosexual women whereas gay and bisexual men had 3.5–4 times greater odds of prior mental health diagnoses as compared to heterosexual men. Further, gay and bisexual men and bisexual women were more likely to report current treatment for psychiatric disorders at the time of admission for substance use treatment as compared to heterosexual individuals. These findings demonstrate comorbidity of psychiatric and substance abuse disorders among the LGB individuals in this sample, suggesting the need for continuity and coordination of health care (Fluente et al., 2015).

Fluente et al. (2015) discuss several implications for health care service and delivery that emerged from this study. First, they point to a need for additional screening and coordination of care for LGB individuals given the experience of comorbidity of mental and substance use disorders reported in their sample. Fluente et al. (2015) encourage providers to first seek training in working with LGB populations and then to inquire about sexual orientation respectfully during office visits as a way to aid in risk assessment and screening of mental, physical, and substance abuse concerns and to ensure the coordination of psychiatric medications being taken at the time of substance use treatment. The integration and coordination of care for LGB individuals in the electronic health record presents several advantages including the prevention of LGB clients from repeatedly disclosing their sexual orientation to new providers, decreasing drug interactions, and increasing treatment compliance (Fluente et al., 2015). Fluente et al. (2015) acknowledge several limitations including the cross-sectional design which included only one urban area of San Francisco, California. Also, while the minority stress model (e.g., Meyer, 2003) was supported, its effects may have been attenuated due to the progressive social and cultural milieu of the sample. Finally, this self-report data may not generalize to LGB individuals in general as it may only be relevant to LGB individuals seeking treatment for substance use.

Impact of Sexual Orientation and Gender Influences on Alcohol Use Globally

Hughes, Wilsnack, and Kantor (2016) identify a lack of funding for research focusing on sexual minorities, with the exception of HIV/AIDS, in both the United States and globally. This issue extends to studies of alcohol use among sexual minorities and sexual minority women in particular as evidenced by a review of studies funded by the National Institute of Health between 1989 and 2011 (Coulter, Kenst, Bowen, & Scout, 2014). Coulter et al.'s (2014) review determined that excluding HIV/AIDS, only .1% of all NIH-funded studies focused on sexual minorities and of those studies, only 13.5% focused on sexual minority women; moreover, only 13% of all funded sexual minority studies focused on alcohol use.

Available research estimates that alcohol use varies according to country with global estimates ranging from a low of 3% for women and 37% for men in the Indian state of Karnataka to a high of 94% for women and 97% for men in Denmark (e.g., Wilsnack, Wilsnack, Kristjanson, Vogeltanz-Holm, & Gmel, 2009). In the United States and globally, rates of alcohol use are typically higher for men as compared with women (e.g., SAMHSA, 2013; Wilsnack et al., 2009). Furthermore, data from the global Gender, Alcohol, and Culture: An International Study (GENACIS), demonstrated that men are more likely than women to drink frequently (e.g., drinking on 5 or more days per week) and to drink more heavily and women as compared to men were more likely to be classified as never drinkers or former drinkers (e.g., Wilsnack et al., 2009).

Turning to data focusing on sexual minorities and gender influences on alcohol use identifies an interesting gender paradox (Hughes et al., 2016). In studies in both the United States and globally, sexual minority women (e.g., those women identifying as lesbian or bisexual) reported significantly higher levels of high-risk drinking as compared to heterosexual women whereas sexual minority men reported higher levels high-risk drinking as compared to heterosexual men, but to a much lesser extent or not at all (e.g., Bloomfield, Wicki, Wilsnack, Hughes, & Gmel, 2011; McCabe, Hughes, Bostwick, West, & Boyd, 2009; Talley, Hughes, Aranda, Birkett, & Marshal, 2014; Van Griensven et al., 2004). Hughes et al. (2016) refer to these findings as a gender paradox given that heterosexual men on average drink more than heterosexual women whereas the reverse is true among sexual minority men and women.

While Hughes et al. (2016) acknowledge that minority stress (e.g., internalized homophobia, discrimination, bias) experienced by many sexual minorities is associated with an increased risk of problem drinking among this population, they point out that the rejection of traditional gender roles would indeed predict larger increases in drinking among sexual minority women than in sexual minority men (e.g., Meyer, 2003). Furthermore, Hughes et al. (2016) assert that sexual and gender influences have distinct differences whereby sexual differences encompass biological variations between male and female bodies that on average result in females reaching higher blood alcohol levels more quickly than men, given the same amount of alcohol consumption (e.g., Holmila & Raitasalo, 2005). The impact of gender on alcohol use and misuse is a function of socially constructed views and norms attributed to women and men in a particular society; moreover, gender differences in alcohol use are most pronounced in countries with the largest differences in gender roles (e.g., Hughes et al., 2016; Wilsnack et al., 2009).

Hughes et al. (2016) speculate that countries who conceptualize the male gender as masculine and aggressive may perceive men's consumption of alcohol as a mechanism to demonstrate and amplify these attributes. This hypothesis is supported by research demonstrating that in national U.S. samples, risk-taking is correlated with heavy drinking among men but not among women; moreover, women are more likely to report risk-reduction strategies when drinking (e.g., Iwamoto, Cheng, Lee, Takamatsu, & Gordon, 2011; Nguyen, Walters, Wyatt, & DeJong, 2011). Hughes et al. (2016) point to additional examples of societally-based gender differences in alcohol use including a greater degree of acceptance of males participating in public drinking and drinking to a state of intoxication, which could support male superiority and authority over women. On a contrasting note, the traditional view of women as caretakers of children who also discourage excessive drinking of their male partners are potential factors leading to less drinking among women in these societies (e.g., Holmila & Raitasalo, 2005; Kuntsche, Knibbe, Kuntsche, & Gmel, 2011).

Despite these historical findings, some research exploring birth cohorts and alcohol use globally have identified high rates of heavy drinking among women in younger cohorts in the United States and Europe, suggesting changes in "traditional" societal roles and perceptions of women's drinking (e.g., Keyes, Li, & Hasin, 2011). On a related note, Makela, Tigerstedt, and Mustonen (2012) report findings from a Finnish survey which demonstrated disproportionate increases in drinking amounts and frequency as well as intoxication among women over a forty-year time span as compared to among men.

In addition to the experience of minority stress, research conducted globally has identified several other factors which impact problem drinking among sexual minorities. For example, in a review of data from 12 countries, sexual orientation, gender expression, and gender appearance were associated with peer victimization, which in turn impacted alcohol and other drug use (Collier, van Beuskekom, Bos, & Sandfort, 2013). Societal attitudes and organizational policies are also powerful influences on the health and well-being of sexual minorities. For example, the World Health Organization had debated for many years whether or not to include sexual minority health and discrimination in health care in its agenda (e.g., Daulaire, 2014). Despite strong opposition from some African and Middle Eastern countries, progress has been made in that the Pan American Health Organization (PAHO), the subregion of WHO representing the Americas, passed the first United Nations resolution to address sexual minority health and discrimination in health care (e.g., Daulaire, 2014; Pan American Health Organization [PAHO], 2013).

Given the findings of the impact of gender roles on drinking behavior, Hughes et al. (2016) advocate for prevention and intervention efforts that encourage greater gender role flexibility which may prove beneficial and effective in reducing alcohol use among both heterosexuals and sexual minorities. Clinical interventions focusing specifically on challenges experienced by sexual minorities (e.g., discrimination, victimization, internalized homophobia) may also prove impactful. Their ultimate recommendation involves much more complex and broad interventions that address social determinants of health (e.g., economic resources, workplace acceptance) that often serve as barriers to opportunity and equity in marginalized populations. Finally, Hughes et al. (2016) argue for more research examining and harnessing the power of resilience and protective factors (e.g., community, family) among sexual minorities as compared to disease and deviance as well as a shift away from the view of sexual minorities as one homogenous population.

Prescription Drug Misuse Use Among Adolescents and Sexual Identity

Disparities in substance abuse among sexual minority adolescents represent a global health problem as supported by research demonstrating higher levels of self-reported substance abuse among sexual minority adolescents as compared with their heterosexual peers (e.g., Goldberg, Strutz, Herring, & Halpern, 2013; Homma, Chen, Poon, & Saewyc, 2012; Li et al., 2018). Due to the availability and popularity of prescription drugs among adolescents coupled with the experience of minority stress, recent studies have focused on the misuse of prescription drugs among sexual minority adolescents, with most available data emanating from the United States (e.g., Li et al., 2018; Meyer, 2003). As discussed earlier in this chapter, according to SAMHSA (2010), prescription drug misuse is defined as the use of opioids, tranquilizes, and stimulants when not prescribed by a doctor or when taken only for the effect caused. A 2016 nationally representative study of substance use among 12th grade high school students in the United States found lifetime (18%), annual (12%) and 30-day (5.4%) prevalence of misuse of prescription drugs (Johnston, O'Malley, Miech, Bachman, & Schulenberg, 2017). The growth in the popularity of misusing prescription drugs can be attributed to several factors including the ease of obtaining prescription drugs from family and peers (e.g., McCabe & Boyd, 2005); as well as a false sense of safety in using prescription drugs as compared with illegal drugs (e.g., Fleary, Heffer, & McKyer, 2013).

U.S. studies of adolescent sexual minorities have reported a higher prevalence of the misuse of prescription drugs and earlier initiation of misuse as compared to heterosexual peers (e.g., Corliss, Rosario, Wypij, Frazier, & Austin, 2010; Kecojevic et al., 2012). The fact that the misuse of prescription drugs can lead to dependence and addiction in the same ways as illegal drugs necessitates more research examining the factors which influence the misuse of prescription drugs (e.g., Li et al., 2018; McCabe, West, Morales, Cranford, & Boy, 2007).

There has been sparse research examining the relationship between sexual orientation and prescription drug misuse in Asian countries including China. Furthermore, prior research has not regularly included adolescents who reported their sexual orientation as "unsure," although these adolescents may experience sexual minority stress from bullying and discrimination that can in turn lead to mental health problems (e.g., Birkett, Russell, & Corliss, 2014; Coulter et al., 2016). To better understand the risk factors associated with prescription drug misuse among adolescents who report "unsure" sexual orientation as well as those adolescents who consider themselves sexual minorities or heterosexual, Li et al. (2018) examined prescription drug misuse and sexual orientation in a school-based nationally representative sample in 7 Chinese provinces (Guangdong, Liaoning, Shandong, Hunan, Shanxi, Chongqing, and Guizhou). The analyses were drawn from data collected in the 2015 School-based Chinese Adolescents Health Survey (SCAHS), a large-scale cross-sectional study of health behaviors among 7th to 12th grade Chinese adolescents that has collected data every two years since 2007 (Guo et al., 2015; Li et al., 2018; Wang et al., 2014). The 2015 data collection effort resulted in a response rate of 95.3% and 150,822 self-administered questionnaires completed anonymously. Sexual orientation was measured by asking students about their sexual attractions to the opposite sex, same-sex, both opposite and same-sex, and unsure. Respondents who indicated same-sex or both opposite and same-sex were classified as sexual minorities. Prescription drug misuse was defined as the nonmedical use of prescription drugs (NMUPD)—opioids and sedatives—the two most commonly used prescription drugs among adolescents in China.

Results indicated that 8.8, 4.4, and 2.2% of the students reported lifetime, past-year, and past-month NMUPD, respectively. Compared with heterosexual students (8.2%), sexual minority and unsure students were more likely to report lifetime NMUPD (14.4 and 10.0%, respectively; $\chi^2 =$ 244.34, $P < 0.001$). Sexual minority and unsure adolescents were also more likely to report past-year and past-month use of NMUPD after adjusting for several covariates including social demographics (e.g., sex, age, household socioeconomic status); lifestyle (e.g., parental marital status); interpersonal relationships (e.g., peer relationships); smoking; and alcohol use.

Li et al. (2018) assert that their findings regarding the increased likelihood of NMUPD among sexual minority adolescents and unsure adolescents as compared to their heterosexual counterparts may be explained by chronic and repeated exposure to sexual minority stress (e.g., Meyer, 2003). Li et al.'s assertions are in line with prior research demonstrating that exposure to chronic stress from bullying increases the risk of the initiation and escalation of substance use among adolescents (e.g., Tharp-Taylor, Haviland, & D'Amico, 2009). Further, chronic stress could negatively impact brain reward pathways that increase the vulnerability to substance use (e.g., Frank, Watkins, & Maier, 2011; Saal, Dong, Bonci, & Malenka, 2003). Finally, Li et al. (2018) point out that in their sample, the most common reason cited for NMUPD was to relieve stress.

Based on their findings, Li et al. (2018) recommend several areas for intervention in the misuse of prescription drugs among sexual minority and unsure adolescents. First, anti-bullying and anti-discrimination policies should be created by the Department of Education to reduce the experience of minority stress in the school-setting. Second, families should be encouraged and provided with resources to better support sexual minority adolescents including the appropriate management and control of prescription drugs located within the home. Finally, sexual minority adolescents suffering from drug addiction should be provided with tools and resources including psychological counseling to combat pervasive and chronic sexual minority stress. Li et al. (2018) summarize the strengths of their study as using a large-scale randomized sample that allowed for robust analysis of between group differences and the inclusion of "unsure" adolescents who are not commonly included in studies of sexual minority adolescent mental health. Limitations of the study include the cross-sectional design which precludes causal inferences; the use of sexual attraction to measure sexual orientation as opposed to other indicators such as sexual behaviors; the possible impact of missing data from students who had dropped out of school or were absent on the day of survey administration; and the inclusion of only two types of prescription drugs—opioids and sedatives (Li et al., 2018).

SUMMARY

This chapter explored the association among discrimination and substance use (e.g., alcohol, cigarettes, and prescription drugs) and sexual orientation in the United States and globally. In terms of alcohol use, two studies conducted by Wray et al. (2016) demonstrated that discrimination based on sexual orientation and HIV status is a risk factor for alcohol problems among men who have sex with men (MSM) who are both HIV negative and HIV positive. Possible interventions should explore ways to reduce discrimination experienced by MSM while also equipping them with ways to cope with negative emotions that were shown to mediate the relationship between discrimination and alcohol misuse.

In terms of smoking, this chapter provided an overview of the findings of several studies which demonstrated that lesbian, gay, bisexual, and transgender women smokers reported a significantly higher frequency of discrimination experiences as compared to heterosexual women and transgender women who did not currently smoke (e.g., Gamarel et al., 2016; McCabe et al., 2003). As higher discrimination was also associated with unsuccessful cessation attempts or never having tried to quit smoking, interventions should target discrimination as a barrier to smoking cessation in LGB and transgender women who smoke.

The misuse of prescription drugs among MSM was discussed in a review of Kecojevic et al.'s (2015) study which found that reports of childhood abuse and discrimination were positively and significantly correlated with each other and with mental health distress and general stress. Given these findings, Kecojevic et al. (2015) advocate for additional research examining prescription drug misuse within this population including longitudinal studies designed to explore causal paths and more qualitative studies to identify additional risk factors including sensation-seeking and impulsivity.

In terms of comorbidity or the co-occurrence of mental health disorders, Fluente et al.'s (2015) study was informative as it demonstrated comorbidity of psychiatric and substance abuse disorders among LGB individuals, suggesting interventions that increase continuity and coordination of health care. This chapter next discussed data focusing on sexual minorities and gender influences on alcohol use. Overall, findings suggested that several factors impact problem drinking among sexual minorities, including the experience of minority stress, societal attitudes concerning gender expression and gender appearance, and organizational policies (e.g., Collier et al., 2013). Possible interventions should address the social determinants of health (e.g., economic resources, workplace discrimination) that often impede opportunity for marginalized populations (e.g., Hughes et al., 2016).

Lastly, given the popularity and accessibility of prescription drugs among adolescents coupled with the experience of minority stress, this chapter discussed recent studies that have focused on the misuse of prescription drugs among sexual minority adolescents (e.g., Li et al., 2018; Meyer, 2003). In both the United States and globally, the increased misuse of prescription drugs among adolescents can be attributed to several factors including the ease of obtaining prescription drugs from family and peers (e.g., McCabe & Boyd, 2005), as well as to a false sense of safety in using prescription drugs as compared with illegal drugs (e.g., Fleary et al., 2013). Li et al. (2018) identified possible interventions targeting the reduction of prescription drug misuse among sexual minority adolescents in several arenas that focused on the school setting (e.g., anti-bullying initiatives); the family unit (e.g., increased family support and closer supervision of prescription drugs within the home); and external supports (e.g., psychological counseling).

References

Balsam, K., Beadnell, B., & Riggs, K. (2012). Understanding sexual orientation health disparities in smoking: A population based analysis. *American Journal of Orthopsychiatry, 82*(4), 482–493.

Bernstein, D., Fink, L., Handelman, L., Foote, J., Lovejoy, M., Wenzel, K., … Ruggiero, J. (1994). Initial reliability and validity of a new retrospective measure of child abuse and neglect. *American Journal of Psychiatry, 151*, 1132–1136.

Birkett, M., Russell, S., & Corliss, H. (2014). Sexual orientation disparities in school: The mediational role of indicators of victimization in achievement and truancy because of feeling unsafe. *American Journal of Public Health, 104*, 1124–1128.

Bloomfield, K., Wicki, M., Wilsnack, S., Hughes, T., & Gmel, G. (2011). International differences in alcohol use according to sexual orientation. *Substance Abuse, 32*(4), 210–219.

Bogart, L., Landrine, H., Galvan, F., Wagner, G., & Klein, D. (2013). Perceived discrimination and physical health among HIV positive Black and Latino men who have sex with men. *AIDS Behavior, 17*, 1431–1441.

Buchmueller, T., & Carpenter, S. (2010). Disparities in health insurance coverage, access, and outcomes for individuals in same-sex versus different sex relationships, 2000–2007. *American Journal of Public Health, 100*(3), 489–495.

Bye, L., Gruskin, E., Greenwood, G., Albright, V., Krotki, K. (2005). *California lesbians, gays, bisexuals, and transgender (LGBT) tobacco use survey—2004*. Retrieved from https://www.lgbttobacco.org/files/2004%20-%20Bye%20LGBTTobaccoStudy.pdf.

Cohen, S., Kamarck, T., & Mermelstein, R. (1983). A global measure of perceived stress. *Journal of Health and Social Behavior, 24*, 385–396.

Collier, K., van Beuskekom, G., Bos, H., & Sandfort, T. (2013). Sexual orientation and gender identity/expression related peer victimization in adolescence: A systematic review of associated psychosocial and health outcomes. *Journal of Sex Research, 50*(3–4), 299–317.

Corliss, H., Rosario, M., Wypij, D., Wylie, S., Frazier, A., & Austin, S. (2010). Sexual orientation and drug use in a longitudinal cohort study of U.S. adolescents. *Addictive Behaviors, 35*, 517–521.

Coulter, R., Birkett, M., Corliss, H., Hatzenbuehler, M., Mustanksi, B., & Stall, R. (2016). Associations between LGBTQ-affirmative school climate and adolescent drinking behaviors. *Drug and Alcohol Dependence, 161*, 340–347.

Coulter, R., Kenst, K., Bowen, D., & Scout. (2014). Research funded by the National Institutes of Health on the health of lesbian, gay, bisexual, and transgender populations. *American Journal of Public Health, 104*(2), 105–112.

Daulaire, N. (2014). The importance of LGBT health on a global scale. *LGBT Health, 1*(1), 8–9.

Derogatis, L. (2000). *The Brief Symptom Inventory-18 (BSI-18): Administration, scoring, and procedures manual*. Minneapolis, MN: National Computer Systems.

Desert Hope Treatment Centers. (2019). American Addiction Centers. Retrieved from https://deserthopetreatment.com/drug-abuse/lgbt-community/.

Diaz, R., Ayala, G., Bein, E., Jenne, J., & Marin, B. (2001). The impact of homophobia, poverty, and racism on the mental health of gay and bisexual Latino men: Findings from 3 U.S. cities. *American Journal of Public Health, 91*, 927–932.

Dube, S., Felitti, V., Dong, M., Chapman, D., Giles, W., & Anda, R. (2003). Childhood abuse, neglect, and household dysfunction and the risk of illicit drug use: The adverse childhood experiences study. *Pediatrics, 111*, 564–572.

Fleary, S., Heffer, R., & McKyer, E. (2013). Understanding nonprescription and prescription drug misuse in late adolescence/young adulthood. *Journal of Addiction, 2013*, 1–8.

Fluente, A., Livington, N., Roley, J., & Sorensen, J. (2015). Mental and physical health needs of lesbian, gay, and bisexual clients in substance abuse treatment. *Journal of Substance Abuse Treatment, 58*, 78–83.

Frank, M., Watkins, L., & Maier, S. (2011). Stress and glucocorticoid-induced priming of neuroinflammatory responses: Potential mechanisms of stress-induced vulnerability to drugs of abuse. *Brain, Behavior, and Immunity, 25*(Suppl. 1), S21–S28.

Gamarel, K., Mereish, E., Manning, D., Iwamoto, M., Operario, D., & Nemoto, T. (2016). Minority stress, smoking patterns, and cessation attempts: Findings from a community sample of transgender women in the San Francisco Bay area. *Nicotine & Tobacco Research, 18*(3), 306–313.

Gamarel, K., Reisner, S., Laurenceau, J., Nemoto, T., & Operario, D. (2014). Gender minority stress, mental health, and relationship quality: A dyadic investigation of transgender women and their cisgender male partners. *Journal of Family Psychology, 28*(4), 437–447.

Goldberg, S., Strutz, K., Herring, A., & Halpern, C. (2013). Risk of substance abuse and dependence among young adult sexual minority groups using a multidimensional measure of sexual orientation. *Public Health Reports, 128,* 144–152.

Green, K., & Feinstein, B. (2012). Substance use in lesbian, gay, and bisexual populations: An update on empirial research and implications for treatment. *Psychology of Addictive Behaviors, 26*(2), 265–278.

Grella, C., Hser, Y., Joshi, V., & Rounds-Bryant, J. (2001). Drug treatment outcomes for adolescents with comorbid mental and substance use disorders. *The Journal of Nervous and Mental Disease, 189*(6), 384–392.

Gruskin, E., Greenwood, G., Matevia, M., Pollack, L., & Bye, L. (2007). Disparities in smoking between the lesbian, gay, and bisexual population and the general population in California. *American Journal of Public Health, 97*(8), 1496–1502.

Guo, L., Xu, Y., Deng, J., He, Y., Gao, X., Li, P., … Lu, C. (2015). Non-medical use of prescription pain relievers among high school students in China: A multilevel analysis. *BMJ Open, 5*(7), 1–11. Retrieved from https://www.ncbi.nlm.nih.gov/pmc/articles/PMC4513537/pdf/bmjopen-2014-007569.pdf.

Hatzenbuehler, M., Corbin, W., & Fromme, K. (2011). Discrimination and alcohol-related problems among college students: A prospective examination of mediating effects. *Drug and Alcohol Dependence, 115,* 213–220.

Hendricks, M., & Testa, R. (2012). A conceptual framework for clinical work with transgender and gender nonconforming clients: An adaptation of the minority stress model. *Professional Psychology: Research and Practice, 43*(5), 460–467.

Hobbes, M. (2017, March 2). *Together alone: The epidemic of gay loneliness* [Web log post]. Retrieved from https://highline.huffingtonpost.com/articles/en/gay-loneliness/.

Holmila, M., & Raitasalo, K. (2005). Gender differences in drinking: Why do they still exist? *Addiction, 100*(12), 1763–1769.

Homma, Y., Chen, W., Poon, C., & Saewyc, E. (2012). Substance use and sexual orientation among East and Southeast Asian adolescents in Canada. *Journal of Child Adolescent Substance Abuse, 21,* 32–50.

Hotton, A., Garofalo, R., Kuhns, L., & Johnson, A. (2013). Substance use as a mediator of the relationship between life stress and sexual risk among young transgender women. *AIDS Education Prevention, 25*(1), 62–71.

Hughes, T., Wilsnack, S., & Kantor, L. (2016). The influence of gender and sexual orientation and alcohol use and alcohol-related problems: Toward a global perspective. *Alcohol Research, 38*(1), 121–132.

Iwamoto, D., Cheng, A., Lee, C., Takamatsu, S., & Gordon, D. (2011). "Maning" up and getting drunk: The role of masculine norms, alcohol intoxication and alcohol-related problems among college men. *Addictive Behaviors, 36*(9), 906–911.

Johnston, L., O'Malley, P., Miech, R., Bachman, J., & Schulenberg, J. (2017). *Monitoring the future national survey results on drug use, 1975–2016: Overview, key findings on adolescent drug use.* Ann Arbor: Institute for Social Research, University of Michigan.

Kahler, C., Wray, T., Pantalone, D., Kruis, R., Mastroleo, N., Monti, P., & Mayer, K. (2015). Daily associations between alcohol use and unprotected anal sex among heavy drinking HIV-positive men who have sex with men. *AIDS Behavior, 19*(3), 422–430.

Kecojevic, A., Wong, C., Corliss, H., & Lankenau, S. (2015). Risk factors for high levels of prescription drug misuse and illicit drug use among substance-using young men who have sex with men (YMSM). *Drug and Alcohol Dependence, 150,* 156–163.

Kecojevic, A., Wong, C., Schrager, S., Silva, K., Bloom, J., Iverson, E., & Lankenau, S. (2012). Initiation into prescription drug misuse differences between lesbian, gay, bisexual, transgender, (LGBT) and heterosexual high-risk young adults in Los Angeles and New York. *Addictive Behaviors, 37,* 1289–1293.

Keyes, K., Li, G., & Hasin, D. (2011). Birth cohort effects and gender differences in alcohol epidemiology: A review and synthesis. *Alcoholism: Clinical and Experimental Research, 35*(12), 2101–2112.

Kuntsche, S., Knibbe, R., Kuntsche, E., & Gmel, G. (2011). Housewife or working mum—Each to her own? The relevance of societal factors in the association between social roles and alcohol use among mothers in 16 industrialized countries. *Addiction, 106*(11), 1925–1932.

Li, P., Huang, Y., Guo, L., Wang, W., Xi, C., Lei, Y., … Lu, C. (2018). Sexual attraction and the nonmedical use of opioids and sedative drugs among Chinese adolescents. *Drug and Alcohol Dependence, 183,* 169–175.

Makela, P., Tigerstedt, C., & Mustonen, H. (2012). The Finnish drinking culture: Change and continuity in the past 40 years. *Drug and Alcohol Review, 31*(7), 831–840.

McCabe, S., Bostwick, W., Hughes, T., West, B., & Boyd, C. (2010). The relationship between discrimination and substance use disorders among lesbian, gay, and bisexual adults in the United States. *American Journal of Public Health, 100,* 1946–1952.

McCabe, P., & Boyd, C. (2005). Sources of prescription drugs for illicit use. *Addictive Behavior, 30,* 1342–1350.

McCabe, S., Boyd, C., Hughes, T., & d'Arcy, H. (2003). Sexual identity and substance use among undergraduate students. *Substance Abuse, 24*(2), 77–91.

McCabe, S., Hughes, T., Bostwick, W., West, B., & Boyd, C. (2009). Sexual orientation, substance abuse behaviors and substance dependence in the United States. *Addiction, 104*(8), 1333–1345.

McCabe, S., West, B., Morales, M., Cranford, J., & Boyd, C. (2007). Does early onset of non-medical use of prescription drugs predict subsequent prescription drug abuse and dependence? Results from a national study. *Addiction, 102,* 1920–1930.

Meyer, H. (2003). Prejudice, social stress, and mental health in lesbian, gay, and bisexual populations: Conceptual issues and research evidence. *Psychological Bulletin, 129*(5), 674–697.

Mueck, A., & Seeger, H. (2005). Smoking, estradiol, metabolism and hormone replacement therapy. *Current Medicinal Chemistry. Cardiovascular and Hematological Agents, 3*(1), 45–54.

Nguyen, N., Walters, S., Wyatt, T., & DeJong, W. (2011). Use and correlates of protective drinking behaviors during the transition to college: Analysis of a national sample. *Addictive Behaviors, 36*(1), 1008–1014.

Pan American Health Organization (PAHO). (2013). *Health authorities pledge to improve access to health care for LGBT people.* Washington, DC. Retrieved from https://www.paho.org/hq/index.php?option=com_content&view=article&id=9056&Itemid=1926.

Parsons, J., Grov, C., & Golub, S. (2012). Sexual compulsivity, co-occurring psychosocial health problems, and HIV risk among gay and bisexual men: Further evidence of a syndemic. *American Journal of Public Health, 102,* 156–162.

Ross, M., & Rosser, B. (1996). Measurement and correlates of internalized homophobia: A factor in analytic study. *Journal of Clinical Psychology, 52,* 15–21.

Saal, D., Dong, Y., Bonci, A., & Malenka, R. (2003). Drugs of abuse and stress trigger a common synaptic adaptation in dopamine neurons. *Neuron, 37,* 577–582.

Silverstein, P. (1992). Smoking and wound healing. *American Journal of Medicine, 93*(1), S22–S24.

Skeer, M., Mimiaga, M., Mayer, K., O'Cleirigh, C., Covahey, C., & Safren, S. (2012). Patterns of substance use among a large urban cohort of HIV-infected men who have sex with men in primary care. *AIDS Behavior, 16,* 676–689.

Substance Abuse and Mental Health Services Administration (SAMHSA). (2010). *Results from the 2009 national survey on drug use and health: Volume 1. Summary of national findings* (Office of Applied Studies, NSDUH Series H-38A, HHS Publication No. SMA 10-4586 Findings). Rockville, MD. Retrieved from http://www.gmhc.org/files/editor/file/a_pa_nat_drug_use_survey.pdf.

Substance Abuse and Mental Health Services Administration (SAMHSA). (2013). *Results from the 2012 National Survey on Drug Use and Health: Summary of National Findings,* NSDUH Series H-46, HHS Publication No. SMA 13-4795.

Rockville, MD. Retrieved from https://www.samhsa.gov/data/sites/default/files/NSDUHresults2012/NSDUHresults2012.pdf.

Talley, A., Hughes, T., Aranda, F., Birkett, M., & Marshal, M. (2014). Exploring alcohol-use behaviors among heterosexual and sexual minority adolescents: Intersections with sex, age, and race/ethnicity. *American Journal of Public Health, 104*(2), 295–303.

Tharp-Taylor, S., Haviland, A., & D'Amico, E. (2009). Victimization from mental and physical bullying and substance use in early adolescence. *Addictive Behaviors, 34*, 561–567.

United States Department of Health and Human Services, Centers for Disease Control and Prevention. (2014). *Tobacco product use among adults—United States, 2012–2013*. Retrieved from https://www.cdc.gov/mmwr/preview/mmwrhtml/mm6325a3.htm.

Van Griensven, F., Kilmarx, P., Jeeyapant, S., Manopaiboon, M., Korattana, S., Jenkins, R., … Mastro, T. (2004). The prevalence of bisexual and homosexual orientation and related health risks among adolescents in Northern Thailand. *Archives of Sexual Behavior, 33*(2), 137–147.

Vellozzi, C., Brooks, J., Bush, T., Conley, L., Henry, K., Carpenter, C., … Holmberg, S. (2009). The study to understand the natural history of HIV and AIDS in the era of effective therapy (SUN study). *American Journal of Epidemiology, 169*, 642–652.

Wang, H., Deng, J., Zhou, X., Lu, C., Huang, J., Huang, G., … He, Y. (2014). The nonmedical use of prescription medicines among high school students: A cross-sectional study in Southern China. *Drug and Alcohol Dependence, 141*, 9–15.

Wilsnack, R., Wilsnack, S., Kristjanson, A., Vogeltanz-Holm, N., & Gmel, G. (2009). Gender and alcohol consumption: Patterns from the multinational GENACIS project. *Addiction, 104*(9), 1487–1500.

Wong, C., Schrager, S., Holloway, I., Meyer, I., & Kipke, M. (2014). Minority stress experiences and psychological well-being: The impact of support from and connection to social networks within the Los Angeles House and Ball Communities. *Prevention Science, 15*, 44–55.

Wray, T., Pantalone, D., Kahler, C., & Monti, P. (2016). The role of discrimination in alcohol-related problems in samples of heavy drinking HIV-negative and positive men who have sex with men (MSM). *Drug and Alcohol Dependence, 166*, 226–234.

CHAPTER 6

Mental Health

PSYCHOLOGICAL DISTRESS

This chapter will discuss the mental health of the LGBT community in the context of psychological distress, suicide, homelessness, reparative therapies, and resiliency and protective factors.

> The thing is, in many cases, mental illness and being queer go hand in hand. It's an uncomfortable but important reality that LGBT youth are four times more likely to kill themselves than their heterosexual counterparts. More than half of individuals who identify as transgender experience depression or anxiety. Even among Stonewall's own staff, people who dedicate themselves to the betterment and improved health of our community, 86% have experienced mental health issues first-hand. It's a morbid point to make, but it makes perfect sense that we, as a community, struggle disproportionately. (Alexander Leon, 2017, Opinion Web Log, *The Guardian*)

Prior research by Hatzenbuehler (2009) found a relationship between the stigma experienced by young adult men who identify as Black, gay, and bisexual (GBM) and health-related problems including poor mental health in the form of higher rates of psychological distress as compared to the general population (e.g., Hatzenbuehler, 2009). Boone, Cook, and Wilson (2016) identify one key source of psychological distress for gay and bisexual men as internalized homophobia, wherein an individual who self-identifies as gay may internalize society's negative attitudes toward homosexuals,

© The Author(s) 2020
S. R. Notaro, *Marginality and Global LGBT Communities,*
Neighborhoods, Communities, and Urban Marginality,
https://doi.org/10.1007/978-3-030-22415-8_6

same-sex attraction, and same-sex sexual behavior. Further, the internalization of these negative attitudes may begin at an early age (e.g., Boone et al., 2016; Herek, 2009). Young black gay and bisexual men (GBM) may experience additional psychological distress resulting from their negotiating of two identities—sexual and racial. Specifically, GBM may feel simultaneously ostracized and rejected by the black community due to their sexual identity, and by the gay community due to their racial identity (e.g., Boone et al., 2016; Choi, Han, Paul, & Ayala, 2011).

Millett, Malebranche, Mason, and Spides (2005) conducted research which further investigated issues and concerns that are more closely aligned with bisexual black men as compared with gay black men. For example, bisexual black men face stereotypes that label them as HIV positive individuals who spread HIV into the heterosexual black community (Millet et al., 2005). In response to these stereotypes, some bisexual black men may conceal their sexual identity which may lead to mental distress and physical health risk (e.g., Wilson, 2008). In contrast to bisexual black men, gay-identified black men may face more direct forms of stigma due to their sexual orientation as they may less able to hide their sexual identity or may choose not to do so (e.g., Malebranche, 2008).

Boone et al. (2016) noted that few prior studies have examined both the impact of internalized homophobia as well as the internalization of HIV/AIDS stigma on psychological distress. Indeed, people with HIV have frequently been the target of discrimination, prejudice, and violence, which can then lead to psychological distress (Boone et al., 2016). Thus, Boone et al. (2016) investigated the relationship of sexual identity to internalized homophobia and HIV/AIDS stigma and the ensuing impact of these stressors on the psychological distress of GBM. A convenience sample of 227 Black gay or bisexual men (GBM) were recruited for this study in New York City (Boone et al., 2016). Participants were included who identified as Black, as being between the ages of 18–35 years old, as gay or bisexual, and as someone who had engaged in oral or anal intercourse with another man in the two months prior to the study. Participants were recruited in a variety of ways including outreach to community-based organizations, social media, flyers, and snowball sampling (Boone et al., 2016). Demographic information indicated that the participants had a mean age of 23.9 years (SD = 4.2 years, range 18–34 years). Self-reported HIV status revealed that approximately 25% of the sample was HIV positive while approximately 75% reported HIV-negative status. In terms of sexual identity, nearly 75% of participants identified as gay or homosexual while the other 25% of the participants identified as bisexual.

Boone et al. (2016) assessed several constructs including internalized homophobia, HIV/AIDS stigma, and psychological distress. The Internalized Homophobia Scale (IHP) included 9 items designed to measure internalized homophobia in men with same-sex sexual attractions and behaviors (Meyer, 1995). A sample item included in the IHP was "I feel alienated from myself because of being gay or bisexual." Respondents were asked to rate how often they felt this way on a Likert scale with responses ranging from 1 (often) to 4 (never). Boone et al. (2016) reported a Cronbach's alpha of .88 for the IHP in this sample. The HIV/AIDS stigma scale was used to measure stigma against HIV and AIDS in men who have sex with men (Diaz, 2006). Two versions of the scales were used—one for HIV-positive men and one for HIV-negative and HIV-status unknown men. Both scales were scored with a 4-point Likert scale. Boone et al. (2016) reported Cronbach alphas of .71 for HIV-positive participants and .77 for HIV-negative and unknown status participants.

Psychological distress was measured via the Kessler Screening Scale of Non-Specific Psychological Distress or the K10 (Kessler et al., 2002). The K10 measures cognitive, affective, and behavioral symptoms of psychological distress. Participants were asked to rate how often they had experienced feelings and emotions (e.g., "I felt hopeless") in the past thirty days with a 4 point Likert scale. Boone et al. (2016) reported a Cronbach's alpha of .92 for the K10 in this sample. Psychological distress was also assessed in this study with the 53 item Brief Symptom Inventory or BSI (Derogatis & Spencer, 1993). Participants rated the severity of the overall incidence of psychological distress along with five subscales focusing on depression, anxiety, interpersonal sensitivity, somatization, and hostility that they had experienced over the 14 days prior to the study. Boone et al. (2016) reported a Cronbach's alpha of .97 for the global severity index and coefficients of .88, .83, .80, .79, and .79, respectively for the five subscales.

Boone et al. (2016) performed multiple linear regression analyses which revealed that internalized homophobia was significantly and positively related to psychological distress. Further analyses revealed an interaction between sexual identity and internalized homophobia such that internalized homophobia was positively and significantly related to psychological distress only for gay/homosexual participants, but not for bisexual participants. Analyses regarding the subscales of the BSI indicated that internalized homophobia was significantly related to four subscales—depression, anxiety, interpersonal sensitivity, and somatization. No interaction was found between sexual orientation and internalized homophobia on any of the BSI subscales.

Boone et al. (2016) extended prior findings that demonstrated a relationship between "enacted" stigma, including discrimination and psychological distress in gay men to include internalized homophobia as an important influence on psychological distress in young Black gay men. These relationships between internalized homophobia and psychological distress were only significant for gay men and not bisexual men. Boone et al. (2016) hypothesize that bisexual men may use relationships with women as a way to decrease the salience or attention paid to their same-sex sexual behavior in their community. In turn, with less focus on their same-sex sexual behaviors, Black bisexual men may then access protective factors including the seeking of support and coping resources that mitigate internalized homophobia.

As for HIV/AIDS and psychological distress, no significant main effects were found between HIV/AIDS stigma and psychological distress; however, there was a significant interaction between HIV status and HIV/AIDS stigma wherein the relationship between psychological distress and HIV/AIDS stigma was significant for HIV-positive men, but not for HIV negative men. Higher levels of HIV/AIDS stigma were related to higher levels of psychological distress in HIV-positive men.

Boone et al.'s (2016) finding of a relationship between HIV/AIDS stigma and psychological distress for HIV-positive men but not for HIV-negative or unsure status men contradicted their hypothesis that this relationship would hold for HIV-negative and unsure status men as well. This hypothesis was based on the evidence that society associates HIV and AIDS with sexual identities and behaviors of young gay black men, even if they are HIV negative. Boone et al. (2016) provide several possible explanations for the lack of association between HIV/AIDS stigma and psychological distress for HIV-negative and unsure status men. First, young black gay and bisexual men in this particular community may not perceive a societal bias that associates sexual identity with HIV. Thus, these men may not experience psychological distress from stigma directed at HIV-positive individuals. Second, it is possible that even if HIV/AIDS stigma has a small negative impact on psychological well-being of gay Black men, these HIV-negative men utilized personal and community resources to reduce its impact. These protective factors are contrasted with the experience of HIV-positive gay black men whose HIV positive status is negatively evaluated by society and whose internalization of HIV/AIDS stigma is associated with psychological distress.

Boone et al. (2016) acknowledged several limitations of their study including the small convenience sample that is not generalizable to the general population. They called for future research that would include black men who identify as both heterosexual and as MSM (men who have sex with men) to allow for comparisons of the experience of HIV/AIDS stigma. Finally, the findings that HIV/AIDS stigma impacted the psychological distress of HIV-positive GBM men establishes targets for public health intervention.

SUICIDE

Suicide attempts are four times more likely among LGBT youth as compared with their heterosexual peers and "questioning" youth or those who are not sure about their sexual identity, are three times more likely to attempt suicide as compared with their heterosexual peers (e.g., Centers for Disease Control and Prevention [CDC], 2011). Specifically, the CDC (2011) reported that for nine states (Delaware, Maine, Massachusetts, Rhode Island, Vermont, Boston, Chicago, New York City, and San Francisco) that assessed attempted suicide one or more times during the 12 months prior to administering the Youth Risk Behavior Surveys, the prevalence of attempted suicide ranged from 3.8 to 9.6% (median: 6.4%) among heterosexual students, from 15.1 to 34.3% (median: 25.8%) among gay or lesbian students, from 20.6 to 32.0% (median: 28.0%) among bisexual students, and from 13.0 to 26.7% (median: 18.5%) among unsure students. Another layer of health disparities is demonstrated by data indicating that racial minority LGBT youth (African American and Latino) attempt suicide at twice the rate of nonminority LGBT youth (CDC, 2011). As death records do not typically record sexual orientation, these findings may actually underestimate mortality among LGBT youth (Sidaros, 2017). In addition to suicide, suicidal ideation or thinking about suicide is almost twice as prevalent among LGBT individuals of all ages as compared with their heterosexual peers (e.g., King et al., 2008).

Data suggests that the risk for suicide among LGBT individuals is related to a greater extent to sexual identity than to sexual behavior, given that mood and anxiety disorders—common correlates of suicidal behavior—are more strongly associated with LGBT identity than with same-sex sexual behaviors (e.g., Bostwick, Boyd, & Hughes, 2010; Sidaros, 2017). Zhao,

Montoro, Igartua, and Thombs (2010) provided further corroboration of these findings in their study which demonstrated that adolescents who experience same-sex attraction or same-sex sexual behaviors, but who identify as heterosexual, do not demonstrate an elevated risk of suicidal behavior as compared to their peers. In terms of chronological age as a risk factor for suicide among the LGBT community, some data suggests that suicide may be more evenly distributed across the lifespan and associated with age of sexual orientation disclosure or "coming out" as compared to the general population wherein suicide is more common in adolescents and young adults (e.g., De Graaf, Sandfort, & Ten, 2006; Paul et al., 2002).

While data consistently demonstrates an association between suicide attempts in LGBT individuals and major depression, generalized anxiety disorder, and substance use, these comorbid psychiatric diagnoses do not fully account for two to three-fold increase in the risk of suicidal behavior in the LGBT population (e.g., Fergusson, Horwood, & Ridder, 2005; Sidaros, 2017). Sidaros (2017) posited that the elevated risk of suicide among LGBT individuals is partially accounted for by bias, discrimination, and prejudice discussed in the minority stress literature (e.g., Meyer, 2007), which identifies stressors that may negatively impact the mental health of LGBT individuals. The minority stress literature investigates both objective or external stressors (e.g., family rejection, housing and job discrimination) and subjective or internal stressors (e.g., internalized homophobia) and corresponding interventions that may alleviate such stressors (e.g., policy changes and cognitive appraisal of stress techniques). Some research has demonstrated that LGBT young adults who experience frequent family rejection are 8 times more likely to attempt suicide as compared to those LGBT young adults who report parental acceptance (e.g., Ryan, Huebner, Diaz, & Sanchez, 2009; Sidaros, 2017). Parental rejection is also associated with homelessness—a health disparity experienced by an estimated 40% of LGBT adolescents in the United States (e.g., Durso & Gates, 2012). An estimated 50% of transgender individuals report job-related discrimination in terms of promotions, hiring, and firing due to their transgender identities with transgender people of color reporting even higher levels of employment discrimination (e.g., Sidaros, 2017).

In terms of interventions, Sidaros (2017) described several foundations and organizations designed to reduce suicide risk among LGBT individuals. These entities attempt to offer culturally appropriate and tailored mental health services. For example, the Trevor Project, the only national crisis and suicide prevention hotline created especially for LGBT and questioning youth, provides in-school workshops, online resources, and advocacy to reduce LGBT stigma (Sidaros, 2017). Several organizations focus on LGBT individuals and their families such as GLSEN (Gay, Lesbian, and Straight Education Network), SAGE (Services and Advocacy for Gay, Lesbian, Bisexual, and Transgender Elders), and PFLAG (Parents, Families, and Friends of Lesbian, Gay, Bisexual and Transgender People). In addition to national organizations, Sidaros (2017) identified a need for culturally sensitive, knowledgeable physicians and therapists with high-level skills in screening, diagnosis, treatment, and self-awareness of potential bias to help LGBT individuals cope with suicidal risk and psychiatric comorbidities. While training to manage psychiatric morbidities and suicidal risk in LGBT patients has not typically been offered to psychiatric residents, the Group for the Advancement of Psychiatry focuses on LGBT mental health by training psychiatric residents to take sexual histories in LGBT patients, prioritize ethical psychotherapy, and learn about the history of psychiatry and homosexuality (Sidaros, 2017). Finally, the Association of American Medical Colleges (AAMC) (2014) and the Gay and Lesbian Medical Association (GLMA) (2013) have created online resources to improve the health care and increase inclusivity for LGBT patients as well as for LGBT students and health professionals.

HOMELESSNESS

According to the United States Department of Housing and Urban Development (USDHUD) (2014), 33% of homeless individuals as of January 2014 identified as children, youth, and young adults (aged 18–24). About one-quarter of these individuals who are younger than 25 years of age reported having no adult, relative, or caregiver to provide them with shelter (USDHUD, 2014). Of the population of runaway and homeless youth (RHY), LGBTQ individuals are overrepresented at 20–40%, a much higher percentage than either heterosexual or cisgender (individuals whose gender identity matches the sex that they were assigned at birth) peers (e.g., Durso & Gates, 2012). Although these data may be an underrepresentation of sexual orientation and gender identity within the homeless population, the USDHUD (2014) conservative estimate of 20% of LGBTQ homeless and unaccompanied individuals under the age of 25 results in 18,082 LGBT individuals out of a total of 45,205 individuals (e.g., Corliss, Goodenow, Nichols, & Austin, 2011; Cray, Miller, & Durso, 2013).

A review of service organizations focused on RHY suggest that these agencies may not adequately meet the needs of LGBTQ RHY due to a lack of knowledge and resources to appropriately assist these individuals with a host of specialized needs (e.g., Maccio & Ferguson, 2016; Shelton, 2015). Agencies focusing on heterosexual and cisgender RHY may not realize that the origins of health disparities within the LGBTQ RHY population may differ according to sexual orientation and gender identity (e.g., Maccio & Ferguson, 2016; Snapp, Hoenig, Fields, & Russell, 2015). Maccio & Ferguson (2016) advocate for services that affirm youth's sexual and gender identity by recognizing bias, discrimination, and other stressors that may influence their homelessness and lack of family support. Maccio and Ferguson (2016) conducted an inventory of LGBTQ RHY resources offered by 19 agencies across the United States. The authors sought to gather information related to existing services and gaps with the hopes of offering suggestions for more customized approaches and policies for LGBTQ RHY. Maccio and Ferguson (2016) employed several strategies to identify the 19 LGBTQ RHY organization and 24 staff for their investigation, including internet searches, snowball sampling or referrals from participating agencies, and resource guide reviews (e.g., Child Welfare League of America, 2012).

Using the above methods, Maccio and Ferguson (2016) identified 32 organizations offering LGBTQ RHY services—either exclusively or as part of general services. Of the 32 agencies identified, 19 agreed to participate in the study (response rate = 59.4%). Of the 19 organizations, 6 served LBGTQ RHY and their allies (considered as LGBTQ-supportive heterosexual individuals); 13 served LGBTQ RHY in general while also offering specific programs for LGBTQ RHY; all 19 agencies provided LGBTQ-affirming versus accepting environments. Maccio and Ferguson (2016) defined LGBTQ-affirming environments as displaying LGBTQ symbols including the gay pride flag, welcome signs and bulletin boards with diversity messages, and workplace non-discrimination policies. Most of the agencies were located in large cities (14/19) with populations greater than 100,000 while more than half of the agencies were located in cities with populations of 1 million or more. All regions in the U.S. were represented with 5 agencies in the Northeast and 5 in the West. The 24 staff who participated in the study either served as executive directors or their designees (e.g., clinicians) and provided oral informed consent. Maccio and Ferguson (2016) conducted one-hour telephone interviews in 2012 with staff. Interview notes were transcribed and coded using template analysis (e.g., King,

1998). Template analysis is a qualitative method which identifies themes by arranging them in a hierarchy wherein broader themes (e.g., educational services) are described by more specific themes (e.g., college preparation) (e.g., King, 1998; Maccio & Ferguson, 2016).

The template analysis resulted in 7 main themes with more specific subthemes illustrating service gaps in LGBTQ RHY agencies. The first theme, housing services, revealed the need for more beds at crisis shelters for LGBTQ RHY. Some staff advocated for completely separate beds for these youth while some stressed the need to avoid isolating or segregating based on sexual and gender identity. The consensus across agencies was that transgender youth should be housed with the gender with which they identified (e.g., Maccio & Ferguson, 2016; Yu, 2010). Maccio and Ferguson (2016) recommend the establishment of more permanent housing designed to serve LGBTQ RHY beyond the age of 18 such as the True Colors Residence in New York City. This facility, containing 30 units for LGBTQ youth aged 18–24, may be the first permanent housing residence for LGBTQ youth in the United States (e.g., Corporation for Supportive Housing, 2011; Maccio & Ferguson, 2016). Housing options such as True Colors are especially relevant for youth who are considered too old for foster care, which is the case for the 28 states that did not pass the 2014 federal legislation, Fostering Connections to Success and Increasing Adoption Act, that extended the foster care age to 21 (National Conference of State Legislatures, 2014). In general, youth who remain in foster care for one additional year to age 19 have additional access to education, health, and mental health services that may increase physical and psychological well-being and financial stability (e.g., Courtney et al., 2005; Maccio & Ferguson, 2016).

The second theme, educational services, suggested the need for alternative educational programming including General Education Development or GED preparation for LGBTQ youth who have dropped out of high school or are at risk for dropping out due to psychological distress associated with bullying and school violence (Maccio & Ferguson, 2016). The analyses identified the additional educational services of college preparation as well as college housing and dining for LGBT RHY. Maccio and Ferguson (2016) argue for increased research examining the college experiences of the overlapping and intersecting populations of college youth who are LGBT, homeless, first generation/and or foster care involved.

Enhanced employment services were identified as the third theme, with one program described as a possible model for LGBTQ RHY clients.

The Green Chimneys program in New York City requires 20 hours work per week among its LGBTQ clients in exchange for assistance with resumes, interviewing, and executing job roles in a professional manner (e.g., Maccio & Ferguson, 2016; Nolan, 2006). According to Nolan (2006), nearly 60% of the youth who left the Green Chimneys shelter had secured a job with that percentage increasing to nearly 70% of the clients who remained at the shelter for more than 6 months. A specialized component of employment services for the LGBTQ RHY population includes youth with criminal backgrounds and substance use problems, as prior research has demonstrated that longer periods of homelessness are positively correlated with unemployment and criminality. Maccio and Ferguson (2016) point out that job training may help youth with these concerns avoid criminal behavior and end homelessness. Some services identified as part of the employment theme focused on community-based economic development or opportunities outside of shelters and housing services such as connecting employers with LGBT youth (Maccio & Feguson, 2016). Finally, within the employment services theme, Maccio and Ferguson (2016) discuss workplace discrimination and harassment, with a special focus on transgender RHY. To combat discrimination aimed at transgender youth in the workplace, agencies recommended the promotion and support of legislation that protects the employment rights of individuals based on sexual orientation and gender identity (e.g., Pizer, Sears, Mallory, & Hunter, 2012).

Increased services focused on families were identified as the fourth theme. Gattis (2013) recommended family therapy for LGBTQ youth who are homeless or at risk of being rejected from their home. One example of such therapy is San Francisco State University's Family Acceptance Project (FAP) which is designed to help families support LGBT children's well-being, and minimize their rejection from family (e.g., Ryan, 2010). Within this theme of family services, Maccio and Ferguson emphasized the need for an assessment of bicultural and multicultural interventions that tailor services according to unique cultural aspects including religion, language, and ethnicity.

The fifth theme related to LGBTQ-affirming services including programs commonly offered in shelters and drop-in centers. One such service identified was the Sylvia Rivera Law Project based in New York City which aids low income, transgender, and gender variant people with issues of discrimination, violence, homelessness, unemployment, and arrests (e.g., Maccio & Ferguson, 2016; Shepard, 2013). Other programs mentioned were based in public libraries and offered LGBTQ RHY the opportunity to take temporary shelter and to search for online resources with minimal engagement with library staff (e.g., Shelton & Winkelstein, 2014). Medical services tailored to LGBTQ youth in general were also identified, including a need for nurses, doctors, and other clinicians to use gender-neutral and nonjudgmental language during patient care. One resource mentioned for LGBTQ RHY seeking appropriate and sensitive medical treatments and standard screenings for a host of health concerns (e.g., mood disorders, PTSD, trauma, and substance use) included the referral lists published and curated by the GLMA (e.g., Coker, Austin, & Schuster, 2010; Keuroghlian, Shtasel, & Bassuk, 2014). Relatedly, the need for more services tailored to LGBTQ youth living with HIV or at risk for HIV was identified along with the services (e.g., case management, mental health services, HIV testing, hormone treatment) provided by Health and Education Alternatives for Teens (HEAT) located in Brooklyn, New York (e.g., Lolai, 2015; Maccio & Ferguson, 2016).

The last two themes—cultural competency and advocacy—have been interspersed throughout the prior themes. Agencies called for increased education on the culture, terminology, and context of LGBTQ youth among homeless shelters and the adoption of policy recommendations put forth by the National Gay and Lesbian Task Force including requirements of cultural competence and LGBTQ awareness for all federally funded agencies, social service workers, and child welfare, and juvenile justice staff (Maccio & Ferguson, 2016). An increase in integration and connections between LGBTQ and heterosexual and cisgender RHY was also encouraged for shelters and agencies that are not specifically tailored to LGBTQ RHY (e.g., Maccio & Ferguson, 2016). The final theme identified the need for advocacy and organizing, especially in smaller and more rural communities with fewer LGBTQ resources. More research examining the experiences of LGBTQ RHY in these environments is warranted, given the lack of shelters located in small, rural communities (e.g., Maccio & Ferguson, 2016).

Maccio and Ferguson (2016) delineated several limitations of their study including its small, nonrepresentative sample size which may have excluded newer organizations, or agencies in rural communities, and those with no websites. Information should be gathered from nonresponders to increase the validity of these findings. Finally, the study did not gather specific data regarding the funding sources for organizations as some of the respondents served as direct and frontline workers who may have lacked knowledge of funding information. This lack of information prevented the authors from considering the impact of funding on service gaps (Maccio & Ferguson, 2016).

In an urban community sample in Chicago, Illinois, researchers Bruce, Stall, Fata, and Campbell (2014) examined the relationships among sexual minority stress variables (e.g., experiencing sexual orientation stigma, internalizing sexual orientation stigma), homelessness, current depression, and substance use in young men (age range 16–24) who have sex with men (YMSM). Overall, Bruce et al. (2014) found that experiencing sexual orientation-related stigma (e.g., being rejected by a friend because of sexual orientation) directly and significant affected major depressive symptoms and indirectly impacted these symptoms through internalized homophobia (e.g., feeling ashamed of one's sexual orientation) and being homeless in the past twelve months. Additionally, being forced out of one's home mediated the impact of experiencing sexual orientation-related stigma on daily marijuana use (Bruce et al., 2014). Bruce et al. (2014) identified several promising avenues of intervention that focus on the family, school, and social media contexts. Helping families accept adolescent and young-adult sexual orientation, providing training and development to bolster support for sexual minorities among teachers and staff in schools, and designing social networking sites that promote positive identity development may help to ameliorate the impact of both the experiences of and internalization of stigma on young adults who have sex with men and other sexual minorities (Bruce et al., 2014).

REPARATIVE THERAPIES

While evidence-based and culturally sensitive interventions designed to increase coping among LGBT individuals are appropriate and necessary, so-called "reparative therapies" have been found to cause physical and emotional harm to those receiving such therapy (e.g., Shidlo & Schroeder, 2002). Therapists attempting to "repair" homosexual orientation practice various forms of reparative therapies (e.g., psychotherapy, electric shock, hypnosis) based on the assumption that homosexual orientation results from a deficiency in personal development and does not represent a normal variant of human sexuality in contrast to the view espoused by the American Psychological Association (APA) (2012). To increase the understanding of specific variables that may be associated with the development of a reparative attitude or therapeutic approach to homosexuality, Lingardi, Nardelli, and Tripoldi (2015) surveyed over 28,000 psychologists who were members of the Italian Psychological Association. Lingardi et al. (2015) chose to examine these attitudes in Italy based on several factors. First, many members of the general population in Italy hold negative views of homosexuality (Lingardi et al., 2015). Second, the location of the Vatican in Italy may support negative perceptions of homosexuality in that the Roman Catholic Church officially views homosexuality as weakening the traditional family unit (Lingardi et al., 2015). Third, there is a lack of civil rights and legal protections for same-sex couples and those victimized by homophobic-related hate crimes in Italy (Lingardi et al., 2015). The authors contrast Italy with Spain and Portugal, both countries whose inhabitants also hold negative views of homosexuality, but which do extend civil and political rights for LGBT individuals including the recognition of marriage among same-sex couples (Lingardi et al., 2015).

Through a partnership with the Italian Psychological Association, Lingardi et al. (2015) distributed an online, password-protected survey to 28,477 Italian psychologists to collect demographic information as well as attitudes toward homosexuality, lesbians, and gay men. The response rate of 11% represented 3135 completed questionnaires. The demographic items on the questionnaire included age, gender, and sexual orientation. Sociocultural items included political orientation (e.g., more conservative to more progressive); religious education (e.g., none to fully); and religious commitment (nonbeliever to believing in God and attending religious services). Professional attributes related to sexual minority clients were measured in terms of the amount and nature of clinical experience with sexual minority clients and self-evaluation of preparation for working with such clients. Assumptions about the origins of homosexuality were measured in terms of the extent of agreement with theories connecting homosexuality with pathology or troubled family interactions as contrasted with the most current and widely accepted view within international health organizations that homosexuality is a normal variation of human sexuality (Lingardi et al., 2015). Another key measure was reparative attitude or whether or not the clinician self-reported having a professional treatment plan that included "repairing" or altering a sexual minority orientation for clients who sought help for distress related to sexual orientation. Responses ranged from no attempt to repair homosexual orientation to only if requested by the client to always attempting to repair homosexual orientation. Finally, the proclivity of clinicians to respond in socially desirable ways was assessed via the short form of the Marlow-Crowne Social Desirability Scale developed by Reynolds (1982).

The survey respondents were overwhelmingly female (86%) with an age range of 25–83 years (M = 38.61; SD = 10.11). Respondents resided in northern, central, and southern Italy and 89% identified as exclusively heterosexual. The vast majority had received religious education while about 38% believed in God, but did not attend religious services. About 16% of respondents reported no political orientation, while the other responses on this item ranged from most conservative to most progressive (5–40%). Of the respondents, 41% were licensed psychotherapists with 65% having received psychotherapy treatment. In terms of the respondents' beliefs about the origins of homosexuality, 76% reported that homosexuality is a normal variant of human sexuality; however, some respondents expressed some combination of views that homosexual orientation is pathological or a deviation from normal sexuality. For example, 3% of respondents reported that homosexuality is a pathology; nearly 10% believed that homosexual orientation stems from an arrested psychological development; and nearly 24% believed that homosexuality results from troubled family interactions.

While approximately 76% of respondents viewed homosexuality as a normal variant of human sexuality, more than half held a reparative attitude toward homosexuality. Lingardi et al. (2015) point out that such views are consistent with those held in the general Italian population according to data from the 2011 National Institute of Statistics. This general population survey ($N = 44{,}000$) found that 74.8% of respondents did not view homosexuality as an illness, but only 43.9% approved of legalizing same-sex marriage and 19% approved of adoption by same-sex couples (National Institute of Statistics, 2012).

Responses regarding the preparation to effectively work with homosexual clients who express anxiety regarding their sexual orientation revealed that most respondents believed that they lacked the appropriate knowledge about the theoretical and clinical issues surrounding homosexuality; indeed, of the 30% of respondents who reported having clients who were worried about their homosexuality, only 15% of them felt adequately prepared to assist with clinical issues related to homosexuality. In terms of therapeutic attitude, 58% of the sample would intervene to change or repair a client's sexual orientation, and of these, 56% would do so only at the request of the client while 2% would pursue a reparative treatment plan even if the client did not request it.

Responses regarding the correlates of holding a reparative attitude toward homosexuality demonstrated that the strongest predictor was the respondent reporting a heterosexual orientation (Lingardi et al., 2015).

Furthermore, some lesbian and gay identified psychologists also hold reparative attitudes, suggesting that these psychologists may be struggling with similar issues of internalized homophobia that impact their clients. Additional correlates of reparative attitude include age, which was a small, significant predictor with older age more associated with reparative attitude, possibly reflecting attitudes of older people in the general population who are more likely to express homophobia. Older psychologists also may have received training during the time when homosexuality was viewed as a mental disorder (Lingardi et al., 2015).

RESILIENCY AND PROTECTIVE FACTORS

The literature examining mental health and psychological well-being of sexual minorities often focuses on deficits and maladaptive processes with less attention and research aimed at understanding the developmental context of the family's impact on healthy sexual identity formation (e.g., Zimmerman, Darnell, Rhew, Lee, & Kaysen, 2015). Zimmerman et al. (2015) posited that the minority stress theory, which investigates the burden of societal discrimination and bias experienced by sexual minorities, could be bolstered by a more comprehensive and developmental examination of the interdependence of overlapping microsystems of individual, family, and society. Specifically, Zimmerman et al. (2015) implored a social-ecological development model to explore the interplay of these systems in the formation of normative sexual minority development and resilience in young adult sexual minority women (SMW). Their study investigated family rejection of SWM as a stressor that potentially interacts with sexual identity development and "outness" or the status of having revealed one's sexual minority status to family, to predict community connectedness and collective self-esteem over a 12-month period.

Zimmerman et al.'s (2015) strengths-based approach and focus on resilience is informed by prior research demonstrating that most SMW women do not show symptoms of mental disorders, despite experiencing societal discrimination and bias; furthermore, most SMW develop a lesbian or bisexual identity during adolescence and young adulthood. SMW typically disclose their identity to family, form connections with sexual minority communities, and develop collective, affiliation-based lesbian or bisexual self-esteem or group pride (e.g., Calzo, Antonucci, Mays, & Cochran, 2011; Savin-Williams & Ream, 2003). Healthy sexual identity formation and family acceptance can then buffer or decrease identity risk factors including self-stigma, internalized homophobia, and motivations to conceal sexual identity (e.g., Zimmerman et al., 2015). Parental acceptance and positive responses to SMW's identity disclosure predict health and well-being as they reduce depression and increase self-esteem (e.g., Legate, Ryan, & Weinstein, 2012; Rosario, Schrimshaw, & Hunter, 2011).

Despite prior findings of mostly healthy sexual minority identity development among SMW, some research has focused on SMW's experiences of family rejection, which is associated with poorer mental health in terms of increased risk for suicide, depression, and substance abuse (Ryan et al., 2009). In a small number of cases, SMW experience severe family rejection, including verbal and physical abuse and attacks (e.g., Zimmerman et al., 2015). Familial rejection may exacerbate societal risks of bias and discrimination as evidenced by research indicating that poor mental health among sexual minorities was accounted for by both perceived societal discrimination, hate crime, and victimization, as well as by family rejection (e.g., Frisell, Lichtenstein, Rahman, & Langstrom, 2009). SMW who are rejected by their families may demonstrate resilience, which is not observed directly, but rather is inferred by responses and adaptations in the context of risk factors and stressors (e.g., Dohrenwend, 2000; Masten, 2001; Zimmerman et al., 2015). Rejected SMW who develop greater community connectedness and collective self-esteem than is typical among non-rejected SMW provide evidence of resiliency and positive coping (e.g., Zimmerman et al., 2015).

Zimmerman et al.'s (2015) conceptual framework is one of protective-enhancing resilience wherein these resilience processes are defined by the interaction between high-risk stressors and adaptations to such stressors. As risk increases, so does the possibility of resilience. Under this model, Zimmerman et al. (2015) expected that resilient young adult (YA) SWM who have a strong sense of sexual identity and identity disclosure or "outness" to family and who are also rejected by family would be even more likely to seek out community resources than would be typical for SMW who are not rejected by their families. Rejected SMW would then demonstrate resilience by adapting to fill their needs for socialization within the community rather than in the family.

Zimmerman et al. (2015) investigated whether sexual identity formation and outness to family predicted sense of community and collective self-esteem over a 12-month period for all SMW or whether an interaction existed such that relationships between individual and community protective factors were moderated by family rejection. The authors recruited a large national sample of SMW through online advertisements featured on Facebook and Craigslist between 2010 and 2011. The final sample consisted of 873 SMW which was comprised of 21% of the SMW who expressed interest in completing the screening tool, who met the study criteria, and who participated in the study at both baseline and at 12-month follow-up. The study retained 77% of its original sample from initial interview to baseline follow-up with eligible participants residing in the United States, possessing a valid email address, self-reporting ages between 18 and 25 (M = 21.4, SD = 2.1), and sexual identity as lesbian or bisexual based on their response to one item asking them to describe their sexual identity. According to one-way ANOVA analyses, there were no differences in respondents who remained in the study at 12 months versus those who dropped out of the study in terms of demographics and study variables (Zimmerman et al., 2015).

The respondents self-reported their sexual identity as bisexual (57%) and lesbian (43%). Approximately 10% of respondents reported a Latina or Hispanic ethnicity, with racial identity reported as White (54.2%), multiracial (16.6%), African American (9.6%), and Asian (3.1%). The majority of respondents lived in a large urban area (31%), with the remainder living in medium-sized cities (26%), smaller cities and towns (29%), suburban areas (9%), and rural areas (5%). Zimmerman et al. (2015) examined several measures that have been previously validated in racially diverse samples of SMW. The age at which individuals disclosed their sexual identity was measured via the Age of Coming Out Questionnaire (e.g., Rosario et al., 2011). Identity risk was assessed at baseline (Cronbach alpha = .80) and at 12 months (Cronbach alpha = .84) via the 27-item Lesbian, Gay, & Bisexual Identity Scale (Mohr & Fassinger, 2000) which focused on 6 identity risk factors (e.g., stigma, concealment of sexual identity, identity uncertainty, internalized homophobia, difficulty with identity development, and identity superiority or denigration of heterosexual identity). Changes in identity risk were assessed over time, with time one scores subtracted from time two scores. Positive values indicated an increase in overall identity risk across the 6 factors.

Family rejection was assessed with 6 items from the Daily Heterosexual Experiences Questionnaire (DHEQ) (Balsam, Beadnell, & Molina, 2012) at baseline (Cronbach alpha = .81) and at 12 months (Cronbach alpha = .82). Specifically, Zimmerman et al. (2015) assessed the family's acceptance of partners, avoidance of discussions related to sexual identity, and rejection by mother, father, siblings, or extended family due to sexual identity. Reponses ranged from never to almost every day with higher scores indicating higher levels of rejection. Disclosure of sexual identity or "outness" was measured via the Outness Inventory (Mohr & Fassinger, 2000) at baseline (Cronbach alpha = .85) and at 12 months (Cronbach alpha = .85). Zimmerman et al. (2015) used 4 items from this inventory to specifically investigate identity disclosure to mother, father, siblings, and extended family to create an "outness to family" measure ranging from no knowledge of the respondent's sexual orientation to openly talking about the respondent's sexual orientation. Changes in outness to family was assessed over the 12 month study period with a score of 0 indicating stable outness relationships and positive values indicating increases in overall outness across relationships.

Connections to the LGBTQ community were assessed with 8 items via the Connectedness to LGBTQ Community Scale (Frost & Meyer, 2012) at baseline (Cronbach alpha = .87) and at 12 months (Cronbach alpha = .90). The 8 items included items measuring community belonging (e.g., "I feel I a m a part of the LGBTQ community") with higher scores indicating higher connectedness. A related measure to LGBTQ connectivity, Collective Self-Esteem, assessed positive self-esteem related to membership in the LGBTQ community with 4 subscales at baseline (Cronbach alpha = .93) and at 12 months (Cronbach alpha = .93). Higher scores reflected higher levels of collective self-esteem.

In this sample, the most frequent response to family rejection items was "never" (range 59–82%), which is consistent with prior findings demonstrating the positive family relationships and family resources to cope with societal bias among young adult SMW (Zimmerman et al., 2015). Despite these mostly positive findings, a subset of respondents (range 10–24%) reported daily family rejection related to sexual minority identity. These individuals' experience of family rejection worsened societal stress related to sexual minority identity. As hypothesized, despite high levels of family rejection, coming out to family was associated with increasing community protective factors 12 months later. This finding of increased community protective factors being associated with coming out to family, despite high levels of family rejection, demonstrates protective-enhancing resilience. This resilience process is inferred from the finding that rejected SMW reported community connectedness that exceeded non-rejected peers (Zimmerman et al., 2015). Despite this resilience, family rejection also increased self-stigma, identity-confusion, internalized homophobia, and other identity risk factors that lowered collective self-esteem. Zimmerman et al. (2015) discussed the importance of connections to the LGBTQ community for young adult SMW in helping them to reduce risks of suicide, homelessness, and violence. For example, the GLBT National Help Center provides young adult peer support via text messages, telephone, and online referrals to LGBTQ centers and resources. Other resources include PFLAG (Parents and Friends of Lesbians, and Gays), Substance Abuse and Mental Health Services Administration (SAMHSA), both of which provide guidelines for helping families support LGBT children, including information on the impact of family rejecting behaviors on substance abuse (e.g., SAMHSA, 2014).

Zimmerman et al. (2015) reported no significant differences in ethnicity, but did find an impact of race such that those respondents who self-identified as multiracial, African American, and Asian American also reported lower community connectedness as compared to those who identified as White. Zimmerman et al. (2015) provided three possible explanations for this finding, based on prior research. First, developing connections with sexual minority communities may be of lower importance for racial minority young adult SMW. Second, racial differences in sexual minority community connectedness may be associated with the salience of sexual minority identity as compared to racial minority identity. Racial minority young adult SMW may not experience similar levels of belonging in the LGBTQ community as compared to their White peers. Zimmerman et al. (2015) pointed out that, as race was not a significant covariate in the collective self-esteem models, racial minority SMW may use strategies that they learned to cope with racial minority discrimination to also ameliorate stresses related to their sexual minority identity (e.g., Neblett, Rivas-Drake, & Umana-Taylor, 2012).

Zimmerman et al. (2015) acknowledged several limitations including possible sampling bias due to recruitment via social network web sites and online data collection. Their findings may generalize less to SMW who do not self-identify an interest in women on their social media profiles. Second, the study collected only self-report data of family rejection from SMW. While this data could be validated by also collecting it from family members, such a strategy might cause additional stress for rejected SMW (Zimmerman et al., 2015). Future research extending the data collection beyond 12 months could help inform an understanding of whether these relationships continue after young adulthood or decrease over time.

Zimmerman et al. (2015) concluded with several strengths including their robust sample size which encompassed a large portion of U.S.

geographical regions and ethnic and racial backgrounds. The authors provided evidence of the resilience process in that the rejected SMW who increased outness to family also reported more community connectedness and collective self-esteem. Such findings add to the small body of research focusing on SMW strengths and resiliency while identifying implications for intervention. Specifically, Zimmerman et al. (2015) suggested that young adult SMW who report internalized homophobia and who conceal their sexual orientation could be at greatest risk for poor mental and physical health—especially in high-rejecting families.

Summary

This chapter explored relationships among mental health, discrimination, stigma, suicide, homelessness, reparative therapies, and resiliency within the LGBT community. For example, Boone et al. (2016) identified internalized homophobia as a key factor in the psychological distress of young black gay and bisexual men due to the internalization of societal negative attitudes toward homosexuals, same-sex attraction, and same-sex sexual behavior. Next, the chapter identified suicide as a health disparity given that suicide attempts are four times more likely among LGBT youth as compared with their heterosexual peers and "questioning" youth (CDC, 2011), and that racial minority LGBT youth (African American and Latino) attempt suicide at twice the rate of nonminority LGBT youth (CDC, 2011). Research findings indicating that the elevated risk of suicide among LGBT individuals is partially accounted for by bias, discrimination, and prejudice as well as from family rejection were reviewed (e.g., Ryan et al., 2009; Sidaros, 2017). Possible interventions designed to reduce suicide risk among LGBT individuals, such as the Trevor Project, the only national crisis and suicide prevention hotline created especially for LGBT and questioning youth, were discussed.

The chapter also focused on homelessness given that the population of RHY is comprised of a 20–40% overrepresentation of LGBTQ individuals, a much higher percentage than either heterosexual or cisgender (individuals whose gender identity matches the sex that they were assigned at birth) peers (e.g., Durso & Gates, 2012). A review of service organizations providing support to RHY suggest that the most effective agencies affirm youth's sexual and gender identity by recognizing bias, discrimination, and other stressors that may influence their homelessness and lack of family support (e.g., Maccio & Ferguson, 2016; Shelton, 2015). An inventory of

LGBTQ RHY resources offered by 19 agencies across the United States identified seven areas for improvement, including housing, education, employment, family, LGBTQ-affirming services, cultural competency, and advocacy (Maccio & Ferguson, 2016).

This chapter also reviewed research focused on the harmful approach of "reparative therapies," designed to repair or change homosexual orientation to heterosexual. In terms of the correlates of clinicians holding a reparative attitude toward homosexuality, one study found that the strongest predictor was the respondent reporting a heterosexual orientation (Lingardi et al., 2015). Furthermore, internalized homophobia among some lesbian and gay identified psychologists may be a factor in their embracing reparative therapies for homosexuality (Lingardi et al., 2015). Finally, the concepts of resiliency and protective factors were reviewed as Zimmerman et al. (2015) discussed the importance of connections to the LGBTQ community for young adult SMW in helping them to reduce risks of suicide, homelessness, and violence.

References

American Psychological Association (APA). (2012). Guidelines for psychological practice with lesbian, gay, and bisexual clients. *American Psychologist, 67*, 10–42.

Association of American Medical Colleges (AAMC). (2014). *Implementing curricular and institutional climate changes to improve health care for individuals who are LGBT, gender non-conforming, or born with DSD (difference of sex development)*. Retrieved from https://www.aamc.org/download/414172/data/lgbt.pdf.

Balsam, K., Beadnell, B., & Molina, Y. (2012). The daily heterosexist experiences questionnaire: Measuring minority stress among lesbian, gay, bisexual, and transgender adults. *Measurement and Evaluation in Counseling and Development, 46*(1), 3–25.

Boone, M., Cook, S., & Wilson, P. (2016). Sexual identity and HIV status influence the relationship between internalized stigma and psychological distress in black gay and bisexual men. *AIDS Care, 28*(6), 764–770.

Bostwick, W., Boyd, C., & Hughes, T. (2010). Dimensions of sexual orientation and the prevalence of mood and anxiety disorders in the United States. *American Journal of Public Health, 100*(3), 468–475.

Bruce, D., Stall, R., Fata, A., & Campbell, R. (2014). Modeling minority stress effects on homelessness and health disparities among young men who have sex with men. *Journal of Urban Health: Bulletin of the New York Academy of Medicine, 91*(3), 568–580.

Calzo, J., Antonucci, T., Mays, V., & Cochran, S. (2011). Retrospective recall of sexual orientation identity development among gay, lesbian, and bisexual adults. *Developmental Psychology, 47*(6), 1658–1673.

Centers for Disease Control and Prevention (CDC). (2011). *Youth risk behavior surveillance.* Atlanta: Centers for Disease Control and Prevention. Retrieved from https://www.cdc.gov/mmwr/preview/mmwrhtml/ss6104a1.htm.

Child Welfare League of America. (2012). *Recommended practices to promote the safety and well-being of lesbian, gay, bisexual, transgender, and questioning (LGBTQ) youth and youth at risk of living with HIV in child welfare settings.* Retrieved from https://www.lambdalegal.org/sites/default/files/publications/downloads/recommended-practices-youth.pdf.

Choi, K., Han, C., Paul, J., & Ayala, G. (2011). Strategies for managing racism and homophobia among U.S. ethnic and racial minority men who have sex with men. *AIDS Education and Prevention, 23*(2), 145–158.

Coker, T., Austin, S., & Schuster, M. (2010). The health and health care of lesbian, gay, and bisexual adolescents. *Annual Review of Public Health, 31,* 457–477.

Corliss, H., Goodenow, C., Nichols, L., & Austin, B. (2011). High burden of homelessness among sexual-minority adolescents: Findings from a representative Massachusetts high school sample. *American Journal of Public Health, 101*(9), 1683–1689.

Corporation for Supportive Housing. (2011, November 11). *True colors provides safe haven for LGBT youth.* Retrieved from https://www.csh.org/2011/11/true-colors-provides-safe-haven-for-lgbt-youth/.

Courtney, M., Dworsky, A., Ruth, G., Keller, T., Havilicek, J., & Bost, N. (2005). *Midwest evaluation of the adult functioning of former foster youth: Outcomes at age 19.* Retrieved from https://www.chapinhall.org/wp-content/uploads/Courtney_Midwest-Evaluation-Adult-Functioning_Report_2005.pdf.

Cray, A., Miller, K., & Durso, L. (2013). *Seeking shelter: The experiences and unmet needs of LGBT homeless youth.* Retrieved from https://www.americanprogress.org/wp-content/uploads/2013/09/LGBTHomelessYouth.pdf.

De Graaf, R., Sandfort, T., & Ten, H. (2006). Suicidality and sexual orientation: Differences between men and women in a general population-based sample from the Netherlands. *Archives of Sexual Behavior, 35*(3), 253–262.

Derogatis, L., & Spencer, P. (1993). *Brief Symptom Inventory: BSI.* Upper Saddle River, NJ: Pearson.

Diaz, R. (2006). In our own backyard: HIV/AIDS stigmatization in the Latino gay community. In N. Teunis & G. Herdt (Eds.), *Sexual inequalities and social justice* (pp. 50–67). Los Angeles: University of California Press.

Dohrenwend, B. (2000). The role of adversity and stress in psychopathology: Some evidence and its implications for theory and research. *Journal of Health and Social Behavior, 41*(1), 1–19.

Durso, L., & Gates, G. (2012). *Serving our youth: Findings from a national survey of service providers working with lesbian, gay, bisexual, and transgender youth who are homeless or at risk of becoming homeless*. Los Angeles: The Williams Institute with True Colors Fund and the Palette Fund. Retrieved from https://williamsinstitute.law.ucla.edu/wp-content/uploads/Durso-Gates-LGBT-Homeless-Youth-Survey-July-2012.pdf.

Fergusson, D., Horwood, J., & Ridder, E. (2005). Sexual orientation and mental health in a birth cohort of young adults. *Psychological Medicine, 35*, 971–981.

Frisell, T., Lichtenstein, P., Rahman, Q., & Langstrom, N. (2009). Psychiatric morbidity associated with same-sex sexual behavior: Influence of minority stress and familial factors. *Psychological Medicine, 40*(2), 315–324.

Frost, D., & Meyer, I. (2012). Measuring community connectedness among diverse sexual minority populations. *Journal of Sex Research, 49*(1), 36–49.

Gattis, M. (2013). An ecological systems comparison between homeless sexual minority youths and homeless heterosexual youths. *Journal of Social Service Research, 39*(1), 38–49.

Gay and Lesbian Medical Association. (2013). *Recommendations for enhancing the climate for LGBT students and employees in health professional schools*. Retrieved from https://www.healthdiversity.pitt.edu/sites/default/files/RecommendationsforEnhancingLGBTClimateinHealthProfessionalSchools.pdf.

Hatzenbuehler, M. (2009). How does sexual minority stigma "get under the skin?" A psychological mediation framework. *Psychological Bulletin, 135*(5), 707–730.

Herek, G. (2009). Hate crimes and stigma-related experiences among sexual minority adults in the Unites States: Prevalence estimates from a national probability sample. *Journal of Interpersonal Violence, 24*(1), 54–74.

Kessler, R., Andrews, G., Colpe, L., Hiripi, E., Mroczek, D., Normand, S., … Zaslavsky, A. (2002). Short screening scales to monitor population prevalences and trends in non-specific psychological distress. *Psychological Medicine, 32*(6), 959–976.

Keuroghlian, A., Shtasel, D., & Bassuk, E. (2014). Out on the street: A public health and policy agenda for lesbian, gay, bisexual, and transgender youth who are homeless. *American Journal of Orthopsychiatry, 84*(1), 66–72.

King, M., Semlyen, J., Tai, S., Killespy, H., Osborn, D., Popelyuk, D., & Nazareth, I. (2008). A systematic review of mental disorder, suicide, and deliberate self-harm in lesbian, gay, and bisexual people. *BMC Psychiatry, 8*(70), 1–17.

King, N. (1998). Template analysis. In G. Symon & C. Cassell (Eds.), *Qualitative methods and analysis in organizational research: A practical guide* (pp. 118–134). Thousand Oaks, CA: Sage.

Legate, N., Ryan, R., & Weinstein, N. (2012). Is coming out always a "good thing"? Exploring the relations of autonomy support, outness, and wellness for lesbian, gay, and bisexual individuals. *Social Psychological and Personality Science, 3*(2), 145–152.

Leon, A. (2017, May 12). *LGBT people are prone to mental illness. It's a truth we shouldn't shy away from* [Web log post]. Retrieved from https://www.theguardian.com/commentisfree/2017/may/12/lgbt-mental-health-sexuality-gender-identity.

Lingardi, V., Nardelli, N., & Tripodi, E. (2015). Reparative attitudes of Italian psychologists toward lesbian and gay clients: Theoretical, clinical, and social implications. *Professional Psychology: Research and Practice, 46*(2), 132–139.

Lolai, D. (2015). "You're going to be straight or you're not going to live here": Child support for LGBT homeless youth. *Law & Sexuality: A Review of Lesbian, Gay, Bisexual, & Transgender Legal Issues, 24,* 35–98.

Maccio, E., & Ferguson, K. (2016). Services to LGBTQ runaway and homeless youth: Gaps and recommendations. *Children and Youth Services Review, 63,* 47–57.

Malebranche, D. (2008). Bisexually active black men in the United States and HIV: Acknowledging more than the "down low". *Archives of Sexual Behavior, 37*(5), 810–816.

Masten, A. (2001). Ordinary magic: Resilience processes in development. *American Psychologist, 56*(3), 227–238.

Meyer, I. (1995). Minority stress and mental health in gay men. *Journal of Health and Social Behavior, 36,* 38–56.

Meyer, I. (2007). Prejudice, social stress, and mental health in lesbian, gay, and bisexual populations: Conceptual issues and research evidence. *Psychological Bulletin, 129*(5), 674–697.

Millet, G., Malebranche, D., Mason, B., & Spikes, P. (2005). Focusing "down low": Bisexual black men, HIV risk and heterosexual transmission. *Journal of the National Medical Association, 97*(Suppl. 7), S52–S59.

Mohr, J., & Fassinger, R. (2000). Measuring dimensions of lesbian and gay male experience. *Measurement and Evaluation in Counseling and Development, 33,* 66–90.

National Conference of State Legislatures. (2014). *Fostering Connections Act: State action.* Retrieved from http://www.ncsl.org/research/human-services/fostering-connections-state-action.aspx.

National Institute of Statistics. (2012). *The homosexual population into the Italian community: Year 2011.* Retrieved from https://www.istat.it/it/archivio/62168.

Neblett, E., Rivas-Drake, D., & Umana-Taylor, A. (2012). The promise of racial and ethnic protective factors in promoting ethnic minority youth development. *Child Development Perspectives, 6*(3), 295–303.

Nolan, T. (2006). Outcomes for a transitional living program serving LGBTQ youth in New York City. *Child Welfare, 85*(2), 385–406.

Paul, J., Cantania, J., Pollack, L., Moskowitz, J., Canchola, J., Mills, T., … Stall, R. (2002). Suicide attempts among gay and bisexual men: Lifetime prevalence and antecedents. *American Journal of Public Health, 92*(8), 1338–1345.

Pizer, J., Sears, B., Mallory, C., & Hunter, N. (2012). Evidence of persistent and pervasive workplace discrimination against LGBT people: The need for federal legislation prohibiting discrimination and providing for equal employment benefits. *Loyola of Los Angeles Law Review, 45*(3), 715–779.

Reynolds, W. (1982). Development of reliable and valid short forms of the Marlowe-Crowne social desirability scale. *Journal of Clinical Psychology, 38,* 119–125.

Rosario, M., Schrimshaw, E., & Hunter, J. (2011). Different patterns of sexual identity development over time: Implications for the psychological adjustment of lesbian, gay, and bisexual youths. *Journal of Sex Research, 48*(1), 3–15.

Ryan, C. (2010). Engaging families to support lesbian, gay, bisexual, and transgender youth: The family acceptance project. *Prevention Researcher, 17*(4), 11–13.

Ryan, C., Huebner, D., Diaz, R., & Sanchez, J. (2009). Family rejection as a predictor of negative health outcomes in white and Latino lesbian, gay, and bisexual young adults. *Pediatrics, 123*(1), 346–352.

Savin-Williams, R., & Ream, G. (2003). Sex variations in the disclosure to parents of same-sex attractions. *Journal of Family Psychology, 17*(3), 429–438.

Shelton, J. (2015). Transgender youth homelessness: Understanding programmatic barriers through the lens of cisgenderism. *Children and Youth Services Review, 59,* 10–18.

Shelton, J., & Winkelstein, J. (2014). Librarians and social workers: Working together for homeless LGBTQ youth. *Young Adult Library Services, 13*(1), 2024.

Shepard, B. (2013). From community organization to direct services: The Street Trans Action Revolutionaries to Sylvia Law Project. *Journal of Social Service Research, 39*(1), 95–114.

Shidlo, A., & Schroeder, M. (2002). Changing sexual orientation: A consumers' report. *Professional Psychology: Research and Practice, 33,* 249–259.

Sidaros, R. (2017). Current challenges in the management of LGBT suicide. *Psychiatry Online, 12*(1), 8–10.

Snapp, S., Hoenig, J., Fields, A., & Russell, S. (2015). Messy, butch, and queer: LGBTQ youth and the school-to-prison pipeline. *Journal of Adolescent Research, 30*(1), 57–82.

Substance Abuse and Mental Health Services Administration (SAMHSA). (2014). *A practitioner's resource guide: Helping families to support their LGBT children.* Rockville, MD: Substance Abuse and Mental Health Services Administration.

United States Department of Housing and Urban Development (USDHUD). (2014). *The 2014 annual homeless assessment report (AHAR) to Congress.*

Retrieved from https://www.hudexchange.info/resources/documents/2014-AHAR-Part1.pdf.

Wilson, P. (2008). A dynamic-ecological model of identity formation and conflict among bisexually-behaving African-American men. *Archives of Sexual Behavior, 37*(5), 794–809.

Yu, V. (2010). Shelter and transitional housing for transgender youth. *Journal of Gay & Lesbian Mental Health, 14*(14), 340–345.

Zhao, Y., Montoro, R., Igartua, K., & Thombs, B. (2010). Suicidal ideation and attempt among adolescents reporting "unsure" sexual identity or heterosexual identity plus same-sex attraction or behavior: Forgotten groups? *Journal of the American Academy of Child and Adolescent Psychiatry, 49*(2), 104–113.

Zimmerman, L., Darnell, D., Rhew, I., Lee, C., & Kaysen, D. (2015). Resilience in community: A social ecological developmental model for young adult sexual minority women. *American Journal of Community Psychology, 55,* 179–190.

CHAPTER 7

Violence

INCARCERATION: VIOLENCE AND SEXUAL ABUSE IN THE UNITED STATES

This chapter will discuss violence inflicted upon the LGBT community, with a focus on the vulnerable populations of incarcerated individuals and young abused boys in Afghanistan. Examining violence within U.S. prisons necessitates a discussion of the Prison Rape Elimination Act (PREA), federal legislation which was sponsored by former U.S. Attorney General Jeff Sessions and unanimously passed by both chambers of Congress in 2003.

> In prison, it's hard. But being gay in prison makes it ten times harder. (G. Guzman, personal interview, Johnson, 2017, *Inmates Tell of Abuse, Use of Solitary*)

PREA sought to identify and analyze the incidence and prevalence of prison rape in federal, state, and local prisons and jails throughout the United Sates, and to provide information, recommendations, and funding to eliminate prison rape (National PREA Resource Center, 2018). PREA provided a mandate and requisite funding for research conducted by the United States Bureau of Justice Statistics through the National Institute of Justice. PREA also created the National Prison Rape Elimination Commission whose charge was to draft standards for the elimination of prison rape. A subset of those standards, which were finalized by the Department of Justice on August 20, 2012, mandated that prison officials must screen

S. R. Notaro, *Marginality and Global LGBT Communities*,
Neighborhoods, Communities, and Urban Marginality,
https://doi.org/10.1007/978-3-030-22415-8_7

all inmates upon admission and transfer to assess their risk for experiencing sexual abuse in the facility (National PREA Resource Center, 2018). The rules were put in place to protect transgender inmates and specifically required that "genital status" not be used to determine a transgender inmate's housing in a men's or women's prison; rather, PREA required the determination of a housing decision be made on a case-by-case basis, taking into account the preferences of transgender inmates (National PREA Resource Center, 2018).

The National Inmate Survey-3 or the NIS-3 was administered by the Research Triangle Park, North Carolina between February 2011 and May 2012 in 233 state and federal prisons, 358 jails, and 15 facilities operated by Immigration and Customs Enforcement (ICE), the U.S. military, and Indian reservations (Beck, Berzofsky, Caspar, & Krebs, 2013). The surveys were collected from 91,177 adult prison and jail inmates and 1738 juveniles aged 16–17 incarcerated in adult prisons and jails via computer-assisted self-interview (ACASI), which involved a touch screen to interact with the computer-assisted questionnaire. Allegations of sexual victimization and other forms of violence were confidential and anonymous to increase response rates; however, Beck et al. (2013) cautioned that both under-and over-reporting may have occurred as there was no independent review to substantiate abuse. Results of the survey, which used weights to provide national and facility level estimates, indicated that 4.0% of prison inmates reported experiencing one or more incidents of sexual victimization in the past 12 months or since admission into the facility if less than 12 months (Beck et al., 2013). As indicated in Table 7.1, results demonstrated large and statistically significant ($p < 0.05$) differences in sexual victimization among inmates based on their sexual orientation whereby prison inmates identifying as lesbian, gay, bisexual, and transgender reported higher rates of inmate-on-inmate sexual victimization as well as abuse from prison staff as compared with heterosexual inmates (e.g., Beck et al., 2013).

The data in Table 7.1 provide evidence that transgender prisoners may be most at risk of sexual victimization during incarceration, when compared with individuals identifying as heterosexual, lesbian, gay, and other. Indeed, reports of abuse suffered by transgender inmates abound, such as the case of Jules Williams, a transgender woman who reported multiple instances of sexual and physical assault and harassment while incarcerated in the Allegheny County Jail in Pittsburgh, Pennsylvania between 2015 and 2017. While Williams is recognized by the state of Pennsylvania on her identification card as a woman, she was incarcerated with men; fur-

Table 7.1 Percent of adult prison inmates reporting sexual victimization in the United States

Sexual orientation	Source of victimization inmate-on-inmate (%)	Staff sexual misconduct (%)
Heterosexual	1.2	2.1
Lesbian, gay, other	12.2	5.4
Transgender	33.2	15.2

Note Author created using information adapted from Table 8, prevalence of sexual victimization, by type of incident and inmate sexual characteristics, National Inmate Survey, 2011–2012, Beck et al. (2013) and Table 2, prevalence of sexual victimization among transgender adult inmates, by type of victimization, National Inmate Survey, 2007, 2008–2009, and 2011–2012, Beck (2015)

thermore, although the jail's policy requires transgender prisoners to be housed in single cells, this policy was violated when the jail officials placed Williams and other transgender women in holding cells with 10–15 men for up to 72 hours while waiting to transfer these inmates to the main areas of the jail (Cowart, 2017).

In September 2015, Williams was arrested and incarcerated in Allegheny County Jail where she was placed in a holding cell with male prisoners. After reporting harassment from male prisoners and corrections officers, Ms. Williams requested protective custody which typically translates to solitary confinement. Instead of granting her request, jail officials transferred Williams to a cell with one male prisoner whom Williams alleges raped her repeatedly for four days, while guards ignored her pleas and screams for help. Williams also alleges that guards referred to her in derogatory terms such as "faggot" and forced her to shower and change clothes in the presence of mail prisoners. The assignment of Williams to a male prison violates PREA's (2003) mandate that transgender prisoners be assigned to men's or women's correctional facilities on a case-by-case basis that considers the prisoners' beliefs of where they will be safest. On behalf of Williams, the American Civil Liberties Union (ACLU) of Pennsylvania and a private attorney sued Allegheny County for trauma and abuse that she suffered in jail after guards refused to house her with other female inmates (Cowart, 2017). The litigation is ongoing.

In a similar case of alleged sexual violence within prisons, Deon "Straw-berry" Hampton, a transgender woman serving a 10-year sentence in Illinois for burglary, filed a lawsuit in March 2017 against the Illinois Department of Correction (IDOC) requesting a transfer to the woman's prison in Lincoln, Illinois. Hampton was quoted as saying "I feel inhu-man" after reporting denial of her ability to represent herself as a female, numerous sexual assaults, verbal and physical harassment, and beatings in two Illinois men's prisons (Brady-Lunny, 2018). According to IDOC, 80 inmates who are incarcerated in Illinois prisons have self-identified as trans-gender women (Brady-Lunny, 2018). In response to Hampton's lawsuit, which is based upon violations of PREA, U.S. district court judge Nancy Rosenstengel ordered the state of Illinois to submit a training plan regard-ing the appropriate treatment of transgender prisoners within 14 days for its correction officers. The decision of whether to grant Hamptons' request for a transfer to a women's prison will be made by IDOC's Transgender Care Review Committee based on evidence both for and against the trans-fer (Brady-Lunny, 2018).

The judge further ordered that Hampton be permitted to attend a transgender support group within the men's prison—a privilege she had been denied due to her housing in segregation or solitary confinement. The judge's ruling noted that although three of Hampton's sexual com-plaints had been substantiated, the assistant warden of operations at the men's prison where she was incarcerated could not provide evidence that any measures had been implemented to protect Hampton after her claims were substantiated (Brady-Lunny, 2018). Additionally, the judge's ruling referred to her understanding that the IDOC transgender committee had not met with Hampton nor had they considered her complaints or her per-sonal sense of safety. In response, IDOC officials maintained that Hamp-ton's basic needs were met, that she was housed in a safe environment, that some of their mental health-focused staff received specialized training in transgender issues, and that training for all IDOC staff was underway (Brady-Lunny, 2018).

The debate over transferring transgender women from men's prisons to women's prisons has taken on another layer in countries such as England. The issue is whether or not transgender women should be permitted to transfer to women's prisons if they have been convicted of committing violent crimes against women and if they have not legally changed their gender to female (Topping, 2018). According to England's Ministry of Justice, 125 transgender prisoners are incarcerated in England and Wales, with 60 of these 125 prisoners having been convicted of one or more sexual offenses (Topping, 2018). The consideration of transfers for transgender women prisoners to women's prisons was recently brought to the forefront in England, when Karen White, a transgender woman prisoner who had been convicted for multiple rapes and other sexual assaults against women, was transferred upon her request to New Hall prison for women (Topping, 2018). After the transfer, White was accused of four sexual assaults against female inmates, which then precipitated a second transfer to a men's prison (Topping, 2018).

White subsequently admitted to sexually assaulting two female inmates while she was incarcerated at the women's prison. Some women prison's advocates, such as Frances Cook, Chief Executive of the Howard League for Penal Reform, stress that situations in which a transgender woman prisoner's prior offending history of violent crimes against women as well as the decision not to legally change gender to female should disqualify such prisoners from transferring to a female prison. Cook and other groups who support her viewpoint on these issues, argue that allowing self-identification of gender as opposed to legally changing gender, would give a subset of men posing as transgender access to women in women's prisons (Topping, 2018).

England's Ministry of Justice apologized for the decision to transfer White to a women's prison, admitting that the typical protocol wherein the transgender case board considers all previous offending history in the transfer request of a transgender person whose legal gender does not match their self-identified gender was not followed in White's case (Topping, 2018). While Cook acknowledged that the transgender case board does carry out its review process appropriately in some cases resulting in the denial of transfer requests from self-identified transgender women with histories of sexual assault against women, the case of Karen White points out the need to standardize the transgender case board's decision-making process (Topping, 2018). The consideration of legal gender and self-identified gender is further complicated by the fact that legally changing gender in accordance with England's Gender Recognition Act can take up to 5 years—a circumstance that has prompted a review and possible reform of this Act to decrease the time frame and complexity of the process (Topping, 2018). In another attempt to influence transgender prison policy, some women's prison advocacy groups have initiated legal action related to the Labor Party's policy of formally including self-identifying transgender women on female prison short-lists (Topping, 2018).

Turning back to the United States, in light of the importance of PREA in determining the housing preferences and potential transfer of transgender inmates, many LGBT activists are outraged with the Trump administration's May 2018 rollback of the PREA mandate that all transgender inmates must be screened at admission or upon transfer to determine the safest environment in which to house them (Burns & Dreier, 2018). The Trump administration's new policy encourages all prisoners to be housed based upon their "biological sex," which is not a defined legal term, but is presumed to refer to a prisoner's assigned sex at birth (Burns & Dreier, 2018). This policy change has been challenged by several advocacy groups including the National Center for Transgender Equality as well as by 67 members of the United States Congress. These 67 members of Congress signed a letter drafted by Representative Jerrold Nadler (D-NY), the ranking member of the House Judiciary Committee, and Representative Robert Scott (D-VA). The letter was addressed to the head of the United States Bureau of Prisons demanding a return to the PREA policy of considering the housing of transgender inmates according to self-identified gender identity (Burns & Dreier, 2018).

Another issue of concern in the treatment of transgender inmates is their frequent housing in "segregated" or "restrictive" housing which can take several forms including disciplinary and administrative segregation and solitary confinement within prisons and jails. Data from the U.S. Department of Justice's Bureau of Justice Statistics (Beck, 2015) indicates that on an average day during the calendar year of 2011–2012, up to 4.4% of state and federal inmates and 2.7% of jail inmates were held in restrictive housing. In terms of demographic differences in restrictive housing, younger inmates, those without a high school diploma, and those identifying as LGB were significantly ($p < 0.05$) more likely to report time spent in restrictive housing as compared to older inmates, those with a high school diploma or more school, and those identifying as heterosexual (Beck, 2015).

Restrictive housing is difficult to measure as there is no uniform definition or classification system within the prison system and wide variations in the duration and conditions of restrictive confinement exist (Beck, 2015). Disciplinary segregation is typically imposed for violating a facility rule as compared to administrative segregation which is considered non-punitive and imposed while an inmate is awaiting a transfer or a hearing (Beck, 2015). Solitary confinement, which can keep an inmate in a small cell for up to 23 hours per day, may be imposed as punishment or for a prisoner's protection as is the case with some transgender inmates who report sexual assaults in prison; however, in some cases solitary confinement is applied as harassment and is meted out disproportionately to transgender inmates (e.g., Brammer, 2017).

Most prison reformers assert that solitary confinement is associated with emotional distress as well as denial of services and programs (e.g., Brammer, 2017). According to the U.S. Department of Justice's Bureau of Statistics, restrictive housing was associated with inmate mental health problems as evidenced by the estimates that 29% of prison inmates and 22% of jail inmates who reported current symptoms of serious psychological distress also reported spending time in restrictive housing over the past 12 months (Beck, 2015).

Prisons with higher rates of restrictive housing also reported higher levels of facility "disorder" including self-reported prisoner accounts of fighting among inmates and between inmates and staff, worry about being assaulted by other inmates, possession of weapons by other inmates, gang activity, and theft of possessions by inmates (Beck, 2015). Relatedly, prisons with higher rates of restrictive housing also housed larger percentages of inmates who self-reported mental health problems and identified as LGB—note that gender identity was not assessed (Beck, 2015).

The case of Chelsea Manning, a transgender woman and former Army soldier convicted of leaking military intelligence information to WikiLeaks, highlights the toll that solitary confinement can take on an inmate who is also harassed and abused partly due to a transgender identity. Until Manning's sentence was commuted by former President Barack Obama in January 2017, she was housed in solitary confinement in Kuwait and at Quantico where she was reportedly stripped naked daily and denied access to basic essentials including toilet paper (e.g., Brammer, 2017). Eventually, Manning attempted suicide twice during her incarceration, partially attributed to her placement in solitary confinement as well as the Army's denial of her request for gender-affirmation surgery (e.g., Brammer, 2017).

INCARCERATION AND GOVERNMENT BIAS: VIOLENCE AND SEXUAL ABUSE GLOBALLY

Reports of police and law enforcement's harassment of LGBT people in countries around the world demonstrate the ubiquity of the unfair treatment of this community. In Egypt, 57 arrests, primarily for promoting sexual deviancy, were precipitated in September 2017 when a subset of concert attendees waived the rainbow LGBT flag in support of the band's lead singer, who is one of the few openly gay performers in the Middle East (e.g., Youssef, 2017). After the initial arrests and subsequent arrests made after raids on cafes and homes associated with LGBT people, Egypt's Supreme Council for Media Regulation issued a statement labeling homosexuality as a disease and banning the discussion of LGBT issues in the media, except for cases in which the LGBT person showed repentance (e.g., Youssef, 2017). These arrests are indicative of the approximately 300 other arrests that have occurred since 2013 when Abdel Fatah al-Sisi took control of Egypt's government and its media (e.g., Youssef, 2017). As homosexual acts in public in Egypt are illegal but homosexuality itself is not, most of the arrests have been for charges such as debauchery. Some advocates for LGBTQ rights claim that the Egyptian government's consideration of criminalizing homosexuality and imposing a prison sentence of up to 15 years is an attempt to distract the public from the countries' social and economic problems (e.g., Youssef, 2017). LGBT people who have been incarcerated in Egyptian jails report sexual harassment from other inmates as well as from guards.

In the Indonesian province of Banda Aceh in May 2017, a Sharia Court sentenced two gay men to 85 public lashes for breaking the Sharia law prohibiting sodomy after members of the public followed them to an apartment, filmed them, and burst into the room while they were engaged in sex (e.g., Dearden, 2017). The men were arrested by local Sharia police and sentenced to a public beating based upon the sharia morality code whereby up to 100 lashes may be imposed for offenses such as adultery, gambling, women wearing tight clothes, and same-sex sexual behavior for men and for women (e.g., Dearden, 2017). Sharia law stipulates that members of the public and sharia police may publicly detain and identify anyone suspected of breaking its rules (e.g., Dearden, 2017). Currently, Banda Aceh is the only province within Indonesia practicing Sharia law (e.g., Dearden, 2017). The national government agreed to allow Sharia law in this province to end a war with separatists (e.g., Dearden, 2017). Across Indonesia, the United Nations and other human rights advocacy groups have reported a recent increase in police raids, LGBT-activist arrests, and media censorship and bans on broadcasts and information that portray LGBT people as non-deviant (e.g., Dearden, 2017).

Brazil

Brazil, a country with the largest gay pride parade in the world and where gay marriage has been legal since 2013, experienced a sudden, large increase in violent deaths of LGBT people in 2017 (e.g., Cowie, 2018). The vast majority of the estimated 445 deaths were attributed to homophobia and represented a 30% increase in such deaths as compared to 2016 (e.g., Cowie, 2018). Even given the reputation of Brazil as a violent country, this sharp one-year increase in violence directed towards the LGBT community is alarming. Some victims of anti-gay hate crimes claim that police often refuse to record these crimes as acts of homophobia and decry the current lack of training programs designed to educate police officers on bias and hate crimes and the especially heinous crimes committed against transgender Brazilians (e.g., Jacobs, 2016). Even when arrested, the perpetrators of homophobic-fueled violent crimes are often treated leniently, receiving minimal jail time and paying small fines for crimes as serious as attempted murder (Jacobs, 2016).

The president of the LGBT rights group Grupo Gay de Bahia in Brazil asserts that the rise in violence against LGBT people is directly influenced by the homophobic views of ultraconservative politicians who are supported by Brazil's evangelical caucus in the Brazilian congress (e.g., Cowie, 2018). While the Brazilian population is comprised of approximately 25% evangelical citizens, the Brazilian congress includes more than 60 evangelicals out of the 513 members of the lower house—a number that has doubled since 2010 (e.g., Jacobs, 2016). This caucus, referred to as the "B.B." or Bullets, Beef, and Bible caucus, is unified and disciplined, voting consistently in a block, as compared to the remaining, fractured legislature (Jacobs, 2016). The BB caucus is purported to have blocked proposed legislation that would have punished homophobic acts, discrimination, and hate crimes (e.g., Jacobs, 2016). Several other factors may play into this rise in violence in Brazil aimed at LGBT people. In September 2017 a Brazilian judge approved gay conversion therapy, designed to change the sexual orientation of LGB people to heterosexual (e.g., Jacobs, 2016). The media and its portrayal of LGBT people is also influenced by the religious leaders who have purchased hundreds of television and radio stations in recent years (e.g., Jacobs, 2016).

Papua New Guinea (PNG)

In addition to violence, another health disparity impacting incarcerated LGBT people is the risk of HIV. One study that focused on HIV risk and homophobia in incarcerated populations within Papua New Guinea (PNG) demonstrated the negative impact of violence, discrimination, and bias on individuals identifying as LGBT and/or as those engaging in male-to-male and female-to-female sexual behaviors (Kelly-Hanku, Kawage, Vallely, Mek, & Mathers, 2015). In 2010, prisons in PNG were identified as a key cite for increased HIV transmission for incarcerated individuals. This focus on the association between increased HIV risk and prisons is widespread among international health organizations including the World Health Organization (WHO, 2014) as a result of prison-related activities including consensual sex, rape, intravenous drug use, and tattooing.

Within PNG, Kelly-Hanku et al. (2015), conducted 116 semi-structured in person interviews with male (35) and female (21) prisoners and key informants (36 men, 24 women) in police holding cells and prisons to probe possible gender differences in HIV-related risks in both types of facilities. Key informants included staff from government and nongovernment organizations, international donor agencies, and researchers (Kelly-Hanku et al., 2015). Participants were approached by a third party and informed of the opportunity to participate in the study. Informed consent was obtained prior to the interviews which were audio-recorded, transcribed, and translated from Tok Pisin into English. Data were thematically coded.

Results demonstrated that police holding cells (which had no female guards and were positioned directly in front of all-male guards) placed women at more risk of rape as compared to men by police personnel, although official reports by female victims were rare (Kelly-Hanku et al., 2015). One woman interviewed about her experience in police holding cells explained that she was raped repeatedly every night for three consecutive weeks by a police officer. The study describes the culture surrounding these types of attacks in prison holding cells as one of victim-blaming wherein other female inmates refer to female rape victims as "acting like dogs who get pregnant with bastard children" (Kelly-Hanku et al., 2015).

In contrast to prison holding cells, prisons were associated with higher HIV risk for men than for women. A number of factors contributed to this differential risk profile for men versus women, with one of the most salient being nonconsensual anal sex between male prisoners. The culture of denial of such activities, under or no reporting of rape, the fact that male-to-male sex is illegal in PNG, and a violent culture of exchanging sex for commodities such as food contributed to the HIV-related risks of incarcerated individuals. Most of the key informants, including guards and higher-ranking prison officials, denied that male prisoners engaged in sexual contact with each other. Some informants suggested that prison rehabilitation practices offering religious fellowship programs to male prisoners were responsible for the lack of sexual contact between male prisoners (Kelly-Hanku et al., 2015). Some prisoners also denied the occurrence of sexual behavior between men, sometimes citing the availability of pornography via websites as mitigating men's desire for sex in prison. Despite denials of sexual acts between men, there were numerous reports of such acts, with most regarded as nonconsensual and perpetuated by men serving long-term sentences.

The reporting of non-consensual male-to-male sexual behavior in prisons was uncommon, as victims of rape feared retribution and even death from the perpetrators. Guards and wardens reiterated these concerns with one warden stating that "the men who were raped in prison could not report such crimes, as they would be a dead man" (Kelly-Hanku et al., 2015, p. 995). One male prisoner who requested to speak with the research team reported that he had notified an international nongovernmental agency of his experience of being raped in prison, but had not received any follow-up communication from the agency. Women in prisons reported almost no instances of sex with men or rape by men as all men were denied access to female prisons; however, once women were transferred back to police holding cells for court appearances, the women again became vulnerable to rape.

Despite the prevalence of non-consensual sex in prisons and the endorsement of the availability and distribution of condoms by the Papua New Guinea Correctional Services HIV/AIDS Policy and Management Guidelines, condoms were not actually provided to male or female prisoners. Only one prison, led by a commander who was a member of the Provincial AIDS Committee, provided limited access to condoms for male inmates during weekend release from prison, but not within the prison facility. Key informants including guards and wardens discussed their refusal to distribute condoms as upholding the law against sodomy and sexual acts between men. They viewed condom distribution as condoning illegal sexual behavior. None of the key informants discussed their reasoning for denying condoms to female prisoners. A final barrier to condom distribution in prisons within Papua New Guinea is the influence of conservative faith-based organizations who offer literacy programs and other resources within prisons but who also object to homosexuality and condom use.

HIV and STI testing were not mandatory and did not occur due to a lack of financial resources and trained personnel, despite the endorsement of several regional commanders at various prisons and the official policy requiring health screenings upon admission to prisons (Kelly-Hanku et al., 2015). One commander further stated that the lack of trained health workers prevented the monthly inspection of prisons by medical officers, as required by the Corrections Act. Some prisons offered voluntary, confidential HIV testing, ranging from a stand-alone accredited voluntary counseling and testing center to mobile units sponsored by faith-based agencies or hospitals. Several of the prisoners indicated that they had received voluntary HIV testing and that the prison officials had kept their results confidential. Several prisoners in two of the prisons were living with HIV and most of these individuals along with guards and wardens indicated that inmates with HIV were treated well despite being denied access to nutritional food including fresh fruit.

Kelly-Hanku et al. (2015) concluded with their assertion that the culture of violence, homophobia, and gender inequality within the prison system in Papua New Guinea and other prisons globally exacerbate the risk of HIV, STIs, and unwanted pregnancies. Their study demonstrated the continued abuse of power by male police officers. The researchers encouraged an examination and possible implementation of an intervention practiced in some U.S. prisons that has demonstrated significantly fewer reported cases of rape and coerced sexual acts (e.g., D'Alessio, Flexon, & Stolzenberg, 2013). Their most urgent recommendations called upon government agencies who administer the prison system to require the distribution of condoms to all prisoners, both male and female, to protect against the transmission of HIV and STIs and to make greater and sustained efforts to prevent rape and coerced sexual acts within prisons and prison holding cells. Kelly-Hanku et al. (2015) pointed out that the most pressing challenge in achieving these changes is the lack of political will and related resources, a culture that condones sexual violence in prisons and in society, and a failure to view inmates as patients whose human rights warrant protection.

HUMAN TRAFFICKING AND PEDOPHILIA: YOUNG BOYS IN AFGHANISTAN

Similar to the violence experienced by vulnerable members of the LGBT community, is the common practice of sexual abuse and human trafficking of young boys by men in Afghanistan, many of whom are members of the Afghan National Defense and Security Forces (Drury, 2016).

> Bacha bazi is pervasive sexual slavery of children, seen widely as a cultural practice and not a crime. (C. Hogg, personal interview, Chopra, 2016, *The Taliban Is Using Child Sex Slaves to Catch and Kill Afghan Police*)

Although this custom referred to as bacha bazi or "boy play" has been practiced for centuries, it is illegal under Afghan law as it is a violation of Islam; however, the laws are seldom enforced as the perpetrators are commonly Afghan military forces and powerful warlords supported by the United States Department of Defense (DOD) and Department of State (Nordland, 2018) in the quest to defeat the Taliban and hold territory (Drury, 2016). An interview with a Grand Mullah, a religious cleric in Afghanistan, revealed his view of bacha bazi as unacceptable in Islam and a form of child abuse that continues because the Afghan criminal justice system is dysfunctional (Qobil, 2010).

This secret culture of abuse revolves around the rape, kidnap, and trafficking of young boys and young men who are also referred to as chai (tea) boys or bacha bereesh (men without beards) ranging in age from 10 to 17, before signs of puberty emerge (Goldstein, 2015). Most of these boys, as in the case with many children in Afghanistan, live in extreme poverty and are either orphaned, kidnapped, or sold by their desperate families for money (Drury, 2016). The men who engage in this practice view it as a sign of their wealth and prestige and often keep several young boys at once as sex slaves, trading them among their friends who rape the boys after parties (Drury, 2016). Perpetrators of this abuse who do admit to having sex with young boys and young men insist that the practice is not homosexuality because they are not in love with the boys, and are therefore not gay. Regardless of the sexual orientation of the abusers, the sexual violence and forced sexual enslavement inflicted upon the young, impoverished, vulnerable boys of Afghanistan, is a health disparity and gross violation of human rights that has not been adequately addressed (Nordland, 2018).

Bacha bazi was outlawed as punishable by death under Taliban rule (1996–2001) but resurfaced in 2001 after the U.S.-led invasion ousted the Taliban (Drury, 2016). The United States military's quest to defeat the Taliban was supposedly partly due to the Taliban's gross violation of human rights; however, the practice of bacha bazi and sexual abuse of young boys calls into question the U.S. support of the Afghan's government and its military forces who violate the human rights of young boys via sexual violence and kidnapping (Goldstein, 2015).

One reporter from the BBC World Service spent several months investigating the practice of bacha bazi in Afghanistan, gaining the trust of several abused boys or bacha bereesh and a few of the abusers (Qobil, 2010). One young boy told the reporter that he started dancing at wedding parties when he was ten-years-old to help support his widowed mother and his two younger brothers after his father was killed in a landmine explosion. The boy gave his meager earnings from dancing at the parties to his mother who purchased rice to keep the family just out of reach of starvation (Qobil, 2010). The Independent Human Rights Commission in Kabul has discussed some of the contributing factors of bacha bazi as secrecy and shame of the victims as well as their families who rarely accept the boys back into their homes, even after escape from the abuse, as well as the extreme poverty of an estimated 65,000 children who work on the streets of Afghan cities polishing shoes, begging, and reselling plastic bottles (Qobil, 2010).

At a bacha bazi party that took place less than one mile from the Afghan government's headquarters, a reporter spoke with a master or bacha baz who proudly proclaimed to have three dancing boys ranging in age from 15 to 18 years of age. The master discussed paying the boys to dance at parties in women's clothing for the entertainment of himself and his friends and admitted to hugging and kissing the boys; however, he denied having sexual contact with any of them (Qobil, 2010). He told the reporter that "some people like dog fighting, some practice cockfighting. Everyone has their hobby, for me, it's bacha baze" (Qobil, 2010).

No studies have been conducted to determine how many children are sexually abused across Afghanistan. In terms of the United States government, there are reports from U.S. soldiers that they have been instructed by their commanding officers to ignore the sexual abuse of young boys perpetrated by members of the Afghan army (e.g., Goldsten, 2015; Nordland, 2018). Some members of the U.S. military even claim to have been dismissed from service after complaining about the sexual abuse, some of which is alleged to have occurred on military bases, as they were told by officers that such practices were accepted in Afghan culture (Goldstein, 2015). In one instance, former Special Forces captain Dan Quinn claims to have been relieved of his command and removed from Afghanistan for getting into a fight with an American-backed militia commander (Goldstein, 2015). Captain Quinn and another Marine attacked the Afghan military commander for allegedly keeping a young boy chained to a bed as a sex slave and for beating the boy's mother when she attempted to end the abuse (Goldstein, 2015). Former Captain Quinn, who has since left the military, stated that:

> The reason we're here is because we heard the terrible things the Taliban were doing to people, how they were taking away human rights. But we were putting people into power who would do things that were worse that the Taliban did—that was something village elders voiced to me. (Goldstein, 2015, *New York Times*)

The United States Congress, whose attention to the abuse of young boys by Afghan military was captured by the 2015 *New York Times* report detailing former Captain Quinn's allegations (Goldstein, 2015), requested an investigation into the practice of bacha bazi by Afghan security forces supported and funded by the United States military (Nordland, 2018). Since fiscal year 2002, the United States has provided more than $71.2 billion in assistance to the Afghan Security Forces Fund (ASFF) (SIGAR, 2018). The Special Inspector General for Afghanistan Reconstruction (SIGAR) conducted and published the heavily redacted results of its investigation in June 2017 and a less redacted version in January 2018 (SIGAR, 2018). The investigation was particularly focused on determining whether a group of federal laws commonly referred to as the "Leahy Laws" were being violated by the practice of bachi bazi. The Leahy Laws prohibit the DOD and the Department of State (State) from providing funds to a foreign security force if knowledge exists that the force has committed a gross violation of human rights (SIGAR, 2018). A complicating matter in the enforcement of the Leahy Laws is the existence of a clause within the Afghan Security Forces Fund provision within the Department of Defense's Appropriations Act which specifically stipulates that aid to Afghan military forces should be available "notwithstanding any other provision of law" (SIGAR, 2018). The SIGAR report asserted that the notwithstanding clause has been used repeatedly to avoid the cessation of military aid to Afghan security forces, despite credible allegations of gross human rights abuses, including the rape of young boys by members of the Afghan forces (SIGAR, 2018).

The SIGAR report also asserted that a number of factors preclude a full and complete understanding of the extent of child sexual abuse among Afghan security forces, including the lack of details within incident reports, the reluctance of individuals with knowledge to provide information, and the lack of training and protocol among soldiers related to reporting incidents (SIGAR, 2018). Additional impediments in understanding and addressing this abuse is the lack of coordination and consistency in investigating alleged abusers among the Afghan government's Ministry of Defense and Ministry of Interior, as well as among the United States DOD and Department of State. Protocols, investigative techniques, training, and tracking of incidents all vary among both the Afghan and United States government entities charged with addressing allegations of gross violations of human rights including child rape (SIGAR, 2018). One example of these inconsistencies in the United States government is the fact that the State Department considers allegations reported in the *New York times* as "credible information" that may be used to launch an investigation, whereas the DOD requires independent corroboration of the allege incident and additional details of the facts of the case (SIGAR, 2018).

The SIGAR report included several overarching recommendations. First, the Special Inspector General urged the United States Congress to consider prohibiting the DOD from using the notwithstanding clause to avoid complying with the Leahy Law. Second, the DOD and State departments should reiterate to all department personnel and contractors in Afghanistan that gross violations of human rights, including child sexual assault, are prohibited. Third, both departments should provide transparent training and guidance on the reporting of these allegations. Fourth, all existing and future contract clauses must stipulate the mandatory reporting of such allegations by military contractors to the Leahy Law point of contact. Fifth, both departments should coordinate their activities such that both units can work with the Afghan Attorney General's Office on allegations of gross violations of human rights, including child sexual abuse by Afghan security forces. Sixth, both departments should consistently participate in and sustain a Leahy forum specifically established to review compliance with the Leahy Law to allow for the coordination of all relevant stakeholders. Seventh, the DOD and State departments should collaborate on a single, accessible tracking system for all allegations of human rights allegations. Finally, the report recommended the creation or designation of a specific position within the DOD charged with overseeing both departments' implementation of the Leahy Law in Afghanistan. The DOD and State Departments provided comments on the SIGAR report, indicating their overall agreement with the recommendations and plans for implementation, with the exception of designating a specific position to oversee the Leahy Law in Afghanistan. The DOD did commit to clarifying the roles and responsibilities of all DOD units engaged in the implementation of the recommendations.

The aftermath of bacha bazi is disastrous for most victims of this abuse. When the dancing boys are no longer valued (e.g., become too old and show signs of puberty) by their masters or escape despite threats of violence and murder, they have no place to turn as they are stigmatized and shamed by Afghan society and labelled as "gay". This practice of victimizing young boys is a life sentence, with many of the boys turning to drugs and alcohol. Those who manage to keep their past a secret have an opportunity to marry while others become perpetrators themselves and continue the cycle of abuse (Drury, 2016) A report on the practice of bacha bazi by the Independent Human Rights Commission in 2015 (Drury, 2016) attracted the attention of the ministries of justice and religion who have now instituted the first law which outlaws bacha bazi and empowers police to make arrests. It is the goal of the Independent Rights Commission that a home for the former chi boys be established (Drury, 2016).

SUMMARY

Chapter 6 reviewed violence as a health disparity among the LGBT community that is exacerbated by discrimination, homophobia, and a disregard for the lives of children. The chapter began with a discussion of the violence and sexual abuse experienced by incarcerated LGBT individuals in both the United States and throughout the globe. The chapter summarized federal legislation (the Prison Rape Elimination Act or PREA), which provided a mandate and funding for research conducted by the United States Bureau of Justice Statistics through the National Institute of Justice. Results of the National Inmate Survey-3 (NIS-3) revealed that prison inmates identifying as lesbian, gay, bisexual, and transgender reported statistically significantly higher rates of inmate-on-inmate sexual victimization as well as abuse from prison staff as compared with heterosexual inmates (Beck et al., 2013).

This chapter also presented specific examples illustrating the evidence that transgender prisoners may be most at risk of sexual victimization during incarceration, when compared with individuals identifying with sexual orientations of heterosexual, lesbian, gay, and other. The chapter discussed the individual cases of several transgender women in the United States who are pursuing litigation to transfer from a men's prison to a women's prison, given their reports of alleged harassment and physical and sexual abuse suffered at the hands of prison officials and prisoners (e.g., Cowart, 2017; Brady-Lunny, 2018).

Next, this chapter summarized several global reports of police harassment of LGBT people in countries including Egypt, Indonesia, and Brazil (e.g., Dearden, 2017; Youssef, 2017). The chapter also examined incarceration and homophobia as correlates of another health disparity impacting LGBT—the risk of HIV. A study conducted by Kelly-Hanku, Kawage, Vallely, Mek, and Mathers in 2015 focused on HIV risk and homophobia in incarcerated populations within Papua New Guinea (PNG). Kelly-Hanku et al. (2015) asserted that the culture of violence, homophobia, and gender inequality within the prison system in Papua New Guinea and other prisons globally exacerbate the risk of HIV, STIs, and unwanted pregnancies. The researchers urged prison administrators to distribute condoms to both male and female prisoners to decrease the transmission of HIV and STIs and to make sustained efforts to prevent rape within all incarcerated environments.

This chapter ended with a discussion of the common, secret, and illegal practice of bacha bazi, the sexual abuse and human trafficking of young boys by men in Afghanistan, many of whom serve in the United States-supported Afghan National Defense and Security Forces (Drury, 2016). Most of the victims of bacha bazi are boys and young men who experience extreme poverty as a result of years of war and violence (Drury, 2016). Perpetrators of this abuse, who express pride in this practice as it affords them prestige and power, do not label their sexual behaviors with the young boys and young men as homosexual. Chapter 6 argues that regardless of the sexual orientation of the abusers, this rampant and devastating sexual abuse ruins the lives of countless impoverished and powerless boys of Afghanistan (Nordland, 2018).

This chapter concluded with an overview of the recent SIGAR report investigating the practice of bacha bazi and the involvement of the United States DOD and State Department. The SIGAR report issued several recommendation, with the overall themes of ending bacha bazi, increasing accountability for perpetrators, and ensuring coordinated responses from the DOD and Department of State (SIGAR, 2018). The final note on the victims of bacha bazi is one of ruin, desperation, and a repetitive cycle of abuse.

References

Beck, A. (2015). *PREA data collection activities, 2015.* National Inmate Survey, 2013. Department of Justice, Office of Justice Programs, Bureau of Justice Statistics. Retrieved from https://www.bjs.gov/content/pub/pdf/pdca15.pdf.

Beck, A., Berzofsky, M., Caspar, R., & Krebs, C. (2013). *Sexual victimization in prisons and jails reported by inmates, 2011–12.* National Inmate Survey, 2011–2012. U.S. Department of Justice, Office of Justice Programs, Bureau of Justice Statistics. Retrieved from https://www.bjs.gov/content/pub/pdf/svpjri1112.pdf.

Brady-Lunny, E. (2018, November 13). Transgender inmate claims abuse, wants transfer to Lincoln women's prison. *Herald and Review.* Retrieved from https://herald-review.com/news/state-and-regional/transgender-inmate-claims-abuse-wants-transfer-to-lincoln-women-s/article_7cbd784c-fdb8-535b-8bc6-8583d173212e.html.

Brammer, P. (2017, May 17). *LGBTQ people face unique challenges in the criminal justice system* [Web log post]. Retrieved from https://www.nbcnews.com/feature/nbc-out/lgbtq-people-face-unique-challenges-criminal-justice-system-n760881.

Burns, K., & Dreier, P. (2018, August 2). Members of Congress: Trump administration's prison policy could lead to 'significant discrimination' for trans people. *Rewire.News.* Retrieved from https://rewire.news/article/2018/08/02/members-of-congress-trump-administrations-prison-policy-could-lead-to-significant-discrimination-for-trans-people/.

Chopra, A. (2016, June 16). *The Taliban is using child sex slaves to catch and kill Afghan police* [Web log post]. Retrieved from https://www.businessinsider.com/afp-taliban-use-honey-trap-boys-to-kill-afghan-police-2016-6.

Cowart, D. (2017, November 13). *Transgender prisoners face sexual assault and discrimination in Pittsburgh jail* [Web log post]. Retrieved from https://www.aclu.org/blog/lgbt-rights/criminal-justice-reform-lgbt-people/transgender-prisoners-face-sexual-assault-and.

Cowie, S. (2018, January 22). Violent deaths of LGBT people in Brazil hit all-time high. *The Guardian.* Retrieved from https://www.theguardian.com/world/2018/jan/22/brazil-lgbt-violence-deaths-all-time-high-new-research.

D'Alessio, S., Flexon, J., & Stolzenberg, L. (2013). The effect of conjugal visitation on sexual violence in prison. *American Journal of Criminal Justice, 38*(1), 13–26.

Dearden, L. (2017). Sharia court in Indonesia sentences two gay men to 85 lashes each after being caught having sex. *The Independent.* Retrieved from https://www.independent.co.uk/news/world/asia/islamic-court-indonesia-gay-men-85-lashes-sex-caught-homosexuality-laws-first-time-khairil-jamal-a7740626.html.

Drury, F. (2016, January 7). The secret shame of Afghanistan's bacha bazi 'dancing boys' who are made to dress like little girls, then abused by pedophiles. *DailyMail.com*. Retrieved from https://www.dailymail.co.uk/news/article-3384027/Women-children-boys-pleasure-secret-shame-Afghanistan-s-bacha-bazi-dancing-boys-dress-like-little-girls-make-skirts-abused-paedophiles.html.

Goldstein, J. (2015, September 20). U.S. soldiers told to ignore sexual abuse of boys by Afghan allies. *The New York Times*. Retrieved from https://www.nytimes.com/2015/09/21/world/asia/us-soldiers-told-to-ignore-afghan-allies-abuse-of-boys.html#story-continues-1.

Jacobs, A. (2016, July 5). Brazil is confronting an epidemic of anti-gay violence. *The New York Times*. Retrieved from https://www.nytimes.com/2016/07/06/world/americas/brazil-anti-gay-violence.html.

Johnson, H. (2017, June 28). *'Being gay in prison is ten times harder': Inmates tell of abuse, use of solitary* [Web log post]. Retrieved from https://progressive.org/dispatches/%E2%80%98being-gay-in-prison-is-ten-times-harder%E2%80%99-inmates-tell-of-ab/.

Kelly-Hanku, A., Kawage, T., Vallely, A., Mek, A., & Mathers, B. (2015). Sex, violence and HIV on the inside: Cultures of violence, denial, gender inequality and homophobia negatively influence the health outcomes of those in closed settings. *Culture, Health, & Sexuality, 17*(8), 990–1003.

National PREA Resource Center. (2018). *Prison Rape Elimination Act*. Retrieved from https://www.prearesourcecenter.org/about/prison-rape-elimination-act-prea.

Nordland, R. (2018, January 23). Afghan pedophiles get free pass from U.S. military, report says. *The New York Times*. Retrieved from https://www.nytimes.com/2018/01/23/world/asia/afghanistan-military-abuse.html.

Qobil, R. (2010, September 8). The sexually abused dancing boys of Afghanistan. *BBC World Service*. Retrieved from https://www.bbc.com/news/world-south-asia-11217772.

Special Inspector General for Afghanistan Reconstruction (SIGAR). (2018, January 18). *Child sexual assault in Afghanistan: Implementation of the Leahy Laws and reports of assault by Afghan Security Forces*. Retrieved from https://www.sigar.mil/pdf/inspections/SIGAR%2017-47-IP.pdf.

Topping, A. (2018, September 9). Sexual assaults in women's prisons reignite debate over transgender inmates. *The Guardian*. Retrieved from https://www.theguardian.com/uk-news/2018/sep/09/sexual-assaults-in-womens-prison-reignite-debate-over-transgender-inmates-karen-white.

Youssef, A. (2017, October 8). LGBT people in Egypt targeted in wave of arrests and violence. *The Guardian*. Retrieved from https://www.theguardian.com/world/2017/oct/08/lgbt-people-egypt-targeted-wave-arrests-violence.

World Health Organization (WHO). (2014). *People in prisons and other closed settings*. Retrieved from https://www.who.int/hiv/topics/prisons/en/.

CHAPTER 8

A Framework for the Future

Coinciding with the 50th anniversary of the 1969 Stonewall uprising, *Marginality and Global LGBT Communities: Conflicts, Civil Rights and Controversy* has demonstrated that despite significant gains in LGBT rights, the purposeful, systematic decisions to withhold equitable civil and political rights from LGBT individuals in the United States and globally as well as efforts to reverse gains in such rights will continue to be associated with bias, stigma, discrimination, and death within this community. The volume also highlighted the strength, resiliency, and courage of LGBT persons who have fought for the recognition of their humanity and right to exist (e.g., Zimmerman, Darnell, Rhew, Lee, & Kaysen, 2015).

> There will not be a magic day when we wake up and it's now okay to express ourselves publicly. We make that day by doing things publicly until it's simply the way things are. (Tammy Baldwin, First Openly Gay U.S. senator, "Never Doubt" speech at the Millennium March for Equality, 2000, N. Rivero, 2017, *15 Inspiring Quotes from LGBT Leaders*)

Importantly, this volume reviewed research and conceptual models (e.g., Meyer, 1995, 2003, 2010) that seek to understand and decrease the deleterious impacts of bias, discrimination, and stigma on the health disparities of the LGBT population. The volume provided a historical and contemporary overview of the tremendous gains that ensued from the Stonewall Inn riots and the empowerment of a forgotten and hidden community (e.g., Carter, 2004).

© The Author(s) 2020
S. R. Notaro, *Marginality and Global LGBT Communities*,
Neighborhoods, Communities, and Urban Marginality,
https://doi.org/10.1007/978-3-030-22415-8_8

Chapter 2 provided ample evidence that the denial of legal rights continue to plague the LGBT community in the arenas of employment, housing, education, public accommodations, military service opportunities, refugee protections, and remedies for hate crimes based on sexual orientation and gender identity. The continued struggle to simply exist, without fear of hatred-fueled violence, is expressed by Kirsten Beck, the first openly transgender former U.S. Navy Seal.

> I don't want you to love me. I don't want you to like me. But I don't want you to beat me up and kill me. You don't have to like me, I don't care. But please don't kill me. (K. Beck, personal interview, Cooper, 2013)

Chapter 3 shed light on the renewed challenges to accessing health care for LGBT persons under the Trump administration—challenges that make it likely that the U.S. Supreme Court will again weigh in on the overall legality of the Affordable Care Act with possible negative consequences and impacts on health disparities experienced by marginalized populations such as the LGBT community. Chapter 4 described historical cultural, structural, and legal barriers to comprehensive, life-saving HIV/AIDS prevention and care for persons most vulnerable to HIV. At a structural level, domestic and global funding must increase for community based clinics and health services, as well as integrated, comprehensive programs targeting HIV-related stigma, discrimination, and societal and legal bias.

Although there is only limited research available from which to assess the rates of LGBT substance abuse as well as the specific treatment needs, Chapter 5 reviewed the evidence of associations among discrimination and substance use and abuse (e.g., alcohol, cigarettes, and prescription drugs) and sexual orientation. Research demonstrated that LGBT status is associated with minority stress and other prejudices that can lead to drug use as a coping mechanism and create disincentives to seek drug recovery services. Chapter 6 explored the importance of connections to the LGBTQ community, as well as concepts of resiliency and protective factors in reducing the risk of suicide, homelessness, and damaging reparative therapy practices that seek to force those who identify as LGBT to adopt heterosexual sexual orientations.

Chapter 7 provided an overview of the severe and enduring violence that is so often inflicted among LGBT incarcerated persons as well as the horrifying custom of child sex slavery or bacha bazi that is commonly practiced in some regions of Afghanistan. The chapter concluded with a solemn view of the lives of victims of bacha bazi—ruin, desperation, and a repetitive cycle of abuse. The remainder of this chapter will focus on the foremost questions that have arisen from the volume's review of the historical, social, and political context of the LGBT experience in the United States and globally. Where will the struggle for LGBT equality go from here? What are the next phases in the fight for humanity and the struggle to live and love freely?

Perhaps the first step is to acknowledge, celebrate, and encourage more of the brave voices who have managed to come out of the shadows, to embrace their identity, and to share their struggles and triumphs with the world. Charles M. Blow, journalist, commentator, and columnist for the *New York Times* is one such individual whose 2014 memoir, *Fire Shut Up in My Bones*, formed the foundation of an opera based on his life. Below, Blow reflected on how identifying himself as bisexual was the beginning of his escape from the darkness of hiding both his sexual identity and the childhood sexual abuse that he suffered. During Pride Month, the celebration of LGBT communities held annually in June across the globe, Blow shared words of hope with other queer people who are searching for acceptance, for community, and for the strength to love themselves:

> I had to simply say that I was a bisexual man in order for me to begin to not only accept that but to celebrate it, to begin to see that my sexual identity was distinct from my sexual abuse…It is about agony — world-afflicted and self-imposed — and anger, but also love and beauty. It is about grappling and wrestling with who and what one is and coming at long last to accept, embrace and love that person. So, during this Pride Month, I want to say what countless others have said: 'It gets better.' And, I want to say that to the throngs of people who are not necessarily today's most celebrated queer narratives: those who come out late in life, those whose families are not affirming, those whose identities don't necessarily adhere to the sexual binary or may well be fluid, those queer people who still feel out of place even when they are in the queer community. (Charles M. Blow, It Got Better. That's My Testimony, *New York Times*, Op. Ed., June 16, 2019)

Blow's affirmative message of hope is a testament to the importance of self-love in the struggle for basic human rights and to the realization that marginalization of any group of people is an affront to the rights of all people.

Going forward, this basic principle of humanity for all people must be affirmed by institutions and formal structures that hold power over the daily lives of LGBT persons. Recently during Pride Month progress was made on this front as the New York City police commissioner, James O'Neill, apologized for the New York City Police Department's (NYPD) misconduct that occurred fifty years ago at the Stonewall Inn uprising:

> The actions taken by the NYPD were wrong, plain and simple. The actions and the laws were discriminatory and oppressive, and for that, I apologize. (J. McNeil, interview at police headquarters, B. Allyn and D. Matia, 2019, *NYPD Commissioner Apologizes for 'Oppressive' 1969 Raid on Stonewall Inn*)

O'Neill's apology was issued under pressure from LGBT activists and local politicians as New York City prepares to host World Pride on June 30, 2019 in honor of the 50th anniversary of the Stonewall uprising. Despite the circumstances of the apology, Corey Johnson, a New York City Councilman who is gay, viewed O'Neill's statement as "very emotional and moving…It is a big moment in having further healing and reconciliation." Other voices who weighed in on the apology let it be known that the NYPD's admission of wrongdoing was long overdue, as was the case with Mark Segal, a gay journalist who remembers well the Stonewall Inn raid:

> It took 50 years to get an apology for this? It's just amazing. It's unfathomable to me. (M. Segal, personal interview, B. Allyn and D. Matia, 2019, *NYPD Commissioner Apologizes for 'Oppressive' 1969 Raid on Stonewall Inn*)

Segal and other activists pointed out that although the NYPD have provided security for the annual gay-rights parade commemorating Stonewall, the lack of a formal apology was still a source of tension between the police department and the LGBT community. Segal relayed his hope that one meaningful result of the apology would be to make LGBT youth feel welcome and encouraged to consider a career in law enforcement. Segal's request that O'Neill appear in person to issue an apology at the June 30, 2019 World Pride parade has so far not been granted, even though in Segal's estimation, the personal gesture could inspire police departments in other cities with a similar fraught relationship with the LGBT community to "realize that if the commissioner in New York can make an apology after 50 years, maybe they can do a little better on their end."

Similarly, James Fallarino, a staff member and spokesperson for NYC Pride which organizes the annual parade, expressed his sentiment in a statement that although one apology could not erase years of tense and discriminatory interactions between the NYPD and the LGBT community, that moving forward LGBT persons would "continue to demand better treatment by and improving relationships with the NYPD and other branches of law enforcement...That relationship has reached a turning point, and we hope that this gesture will allow for even more dialogue moving forward."

Moving from the more local structures of police departments to the broader scope and jurisdiction of the courts, brings us to a consideration of future court cases that will impact the civil rights and daily lives of the LGBT community both in the United States and globally. First, an examination of the United States Supreme Court's possible future stance on LGBT rights is illuminating and troubling to those concerned with preserving LGBT rights. President Trump's recent appointment of conservative Justice Brett Kavanaugh to the U.S. Supreme Court as the replacement for former Justice Anthony Kennedy who voted in the majority in the *Obergerfell v. Hodges* decision legalizing gay marriage has left many LGBT activists nervously anticipating the possible unraveling and overturning of LGBT protections. Several areas of concern include transgender rights, employment, religious justifications for discrimination, and even marriage equality itself.

In terms of transgender anti-discrimination protections in health care within the United States, Chapter 3 described several provisions in the Affordable Care Act (ACA or Obamacare) which provided LGBT persons with protections based on gender identity and sexual orientation including that preventive services are available for all patients, regardless of gender identity, sex assigned at birth, or recorded birth. On May 24, 2019, the Trump administration released its proposed rule that would repeal the ACA's discrimination protections for transgender people as well as women seeking care after abortions (Stern, 2019). This latest erosion of transgender rights extends the conscience rights (also discussed in Chapter 3 of this volume) of health care providers and insurance companies allowing them to refuse to treat transgender individuals (Stern, 2019). Transgender rights groups, who are preparing civil litigation to fight this new rule which is based on the Trump administration's definition of "sex" as "biological sex," warn that the roll-back in protections will not only increase discrimination against transgender people within the health care system, but it may deter them from seeking care in the first place, resulting in possible dire health consequences (Stern, 2019). The key to the future of protections for LGBT persons, and especially transgender people, in the United States lies with the Supreme Court, as the justices will likely soon consider the question of the definition of "sex" in an analogous sex discrimination case.

The precarious arena of employment protections for LGBT people was discussed in Chapter 2 of this volume. Federal legislation prohibiting discrimination in employment does not include the categories of sexual orientation or gender identity and fewer than half of the states have added these classes to their anti-discrimination laws. Given the lack of federal protections in employment, LGBT activists have argued that the ban on sex discrimination in Title VII of the Civil Rights Act of 1964 should apply to those who identify as LGBT. Advocates have made the case that firing a person for identifying as LGBT is a form of gender discrimination and punishment for failure to conform to expectations of dress and behavior associated with their sex assigned at birth. Federal courts, as well as the Equal Employment Opportunity Commission, have accepted this argument and currently interpret Title VII's prohibition of sex discrimination as forbidding any employment discrimination based on gender identity or sexual orientation. Despite this history and current interpretation of Title VII by the EEOC, a conservative ruling in the case of *EEOC v. R.G. & G.R. Harris Funeral Homes* could end the EEOC's protection of LGBT employment rights. This EEOC case involves Aimee Stephens, a transgender woman who was fired from a Michigan funeral home job after coming out as a gay woman. In March 2018, the Sixth Circuit ruled that the funeral homeowners violated Title VII because they fired Stephens for failure to conform to sex stereotypes. LGBT activists anticipate that this case will make its way to the U.S. Supreme Court which is now much more likely to strike down current interpretations of Title VII as extending federal employment protections to LGBT persons, leaving only individual state laws to prohibit employment discrimination for this community. Importantly, LGBT advocates are gearing up for a battle as the justices have agreed to decide in the near future whether federal civil rights law protects people from job discrimination because of their sexual orientation or gender identity.

The issue of religious justifications for discriminating against LGBT persons has been playing out in the arena of wedding services requested by same-sex couples in several states, including Colorado, Oregon, and Washington. On July 17, 2019 the U. S. Supreme Court threw out an Oregon court ruling (*Klein, dba Sweet Cakes by Melissa v. Oregon Bureau of Labor and Industries*) against bakers who refused to make a wedding cake for a same-sex couple, directing the appellate judges in Oregon to consider the 2018 U.S. Supreme Court ruling (*Masterpiece Cakes v. Colorado Civil Rights Commission*) in favor of a baker from Colorado who cited religion reasons for refusing to make a cake for a same-sex wedding. The U.S. Supreme court's ruling in the Colorado case was limited in its findings, leaving open the broader question of religious justifications for refusing service to same-sex couples. The U.S. Supreme Court is likely to soon take up the case of *Arlene's Flowers Inc. v. Washington*, which involves a florist from Washington state who refused to create flower arrangements for a same-sex wedding.

An issue that is related to religious justifications for refusing services to same-sex couples is that of the equal rights and protections extended to same-sex married couples under the Supreme Court's 2015 *Obergefell v. Hodges* ruling. Even if *Obergefell v. Hodges*, which legalized same-sex marriage nationwide, is upheld in the future, the issue of the granting of the same rights afforded to married opposite-sex couples as to same-sex couples may be attacked and eroded. A Texas case (*Pidgeon v. Turner*) that dealt with this issue could land in the U.S. Supreme Court in the near future. In 2013, a minister and an accountant from Dallas, Texas successfully sued the city of Houston over the payment of benefits to same-sex city employees, arguing that taxpayers should not have to pay for the benefits. Despite the *Obergefell* ruling, the Texas Supreme Court ruled that the legalization of same-sex marriage did not resolve the issue of benefits for same-sex couples. As of December 2017, the U.S. Supreme Court has refused to hear the city of Houston's challenge to the Texas Supreme Court's decision. LGBT advocates fear that if this case or a similar one should return to the U.S. Supreme Court, the justices may decide to permit states to limit or eliminate benefits for same-sex couples while still technically allowing same-sex marriage to remain legal—effectively overturning *Obergefell* in everything but name only.

Turning a global lens to recent court rulings that have significant consequences for LGBT rights brings us to African nations such as Kenya, whose punitive laws outlawing homosexually were ushered in my Britain during the beginning of the colonial period during the late nineteenth and early twentieth centuries. Indeed, in April 2019 British Prime Minister Theresa May acquiesced to pressure from U.K. LGBT activists and apologized for Britain's introduction of anti-homosexuality laws to its former colonies and encouraged leaders of now independent nations to repeal such laws. Although progress continues on this front as evidenced by the legalization of same-sex marriage in South Africa in 2006 and Malta in 2017, LGBT activists in African countries are fighting to change the culture and views that homophobia and not homosexuality was introduced to Africa by British colonizers. If this altered view on homosexuality can be realized, then advocates hope that the laws will change accordingly.

A setback on this front occurred in May 2019 when Kenya's High Court unanimously ruled that the country's law criminalizing homosexuality or "unnatural acts," does not violate the country's 2010 constitution which guarantees equal protection to all people, freedom of expression, and freedom from discrimination. Charles Kanjama, a lawyer for the Kenya Christian Professionals Forum, has argued that the majority of Kenyans believe that homosexuality should remain illegal as they view homosexuality as "a very moral perversion—a taboo" (Kushner, 2019). The belief that homosexuality is "un-African" and introduced by foreigners is evident in statements from other Kenyans such as Vincent Kidada who support the criminalization of homosexuality:

> The devil in the name of foreign agents comes and introduces an alternative sex. "Foreigners are the people who are nurturing our very locals to this act." (Kushner, 2019)

This latest ruling in Kenya is consistent with the fact that other rights extended to LGBTQ people such as same-sex marriage and same-sex adoption are not even on the agenda of Kenya's courts. Despite these recent retrenchments, artists and writers such as Kenyan writer Mukoma Wa Ngugi have not given up the fight for LGBT rights or the struggle to reject laws remaining from colonial-era penal codes. At an African literature festival held in Berlin in 2017, Ngugi said:

> The British empire in one sense ended, but its language is now the language of the world. That's a sentiment I've heard LGBTQ-rights defenders echo and reframe to criticize not just colonial language, but the morals espoused through it. (Kushner, 2019)

Expressing a similar sentiment, Kari Mugo, the operations manager at the National Gay and Lesbian Human Rights Commission of Kenya said that "we have undo the notion of what culture is, as well as what it means to be African" (Kushner, 2019). The movement to repeal laws which criminalize homosexuality is in some ways a reimagining of and reclaiming of acceptance for LGBT people in Kenya, Uganda, and other former British colonies that was made impossible by over a century of colonial-imported homophobia (Kushner, 2019).

Moving to another region of the globe—Latin America—provides additional insights into the future of LGBT rights. On June 13, 2019 the Supreme Federal Court (STF), Brazil's Supreme Court, voted to criminalize homophobia, or what they label "homotransphobia," an important sign of progress for LGBT persons living in one of the most dangerous countries for sexual minorities in the world. The STF took this action as the country waits for the Brazilian Congress, which is governed by a conservative evangelical majority, to pass a law prohibiting discrimination based on sexual orientation and gender identity. One of the judges who voted for the new measure, Carmen Luzia, expressed the sentiment of the Court's majority opinion:

> All prejudice is violence. All discrimination is a cause of suffering. But I learned that some prejudices cause more suffering than others. (AFP, 2019a)

Although Brazil now joins several other countries (e.g., Argentina, Colombia, Uruguay, and Ecuador) throughout Latin America that have passed laws, including same-sex marriage, protecting LGBT rights, Judge Ricardo Lewandowski expressed the sentiment of all three Brazilian STF judges who voted against the homotransphobia measure when he said that only "Congress can pass laws on criminal conduct" (AFP, 2019a). The STF's decision faces opposition from conservative members of the Brazilian Congress who fear that church leaders may be penalized for using religious texts to reject same-sex unions. These fears are entrenched despite the STF's explicit assurance that religious freedom will not be curtailed as a result of criminalizing homotransphobia, as long as churches refrain from promoting hate speech that incites discrimination, hostility, or violence based on sexual orientation or gender identity.

Adding to the opposition to the new LGBT protection is none other than Brazil's conservative President Jair Bolsonaro who criticized the Supreme Court's decision in a statement on Friday, June 14, 2019 claiming that it could "hurt" gays by deterring companies from hiring them. Bolsonaro argued that employers would "think twice" before hiring a gay person for fear they could be accused of homophobia (AFP, 2019b). Bolsonaro went further by raising again his threat of nominating an evangelical judge to the STF to help "balance" the bench. LGBT advocates were not surprised by Bolsonaro's remarks regarding the new law, as his statements are in line with prior declarations that he would prefer his son to die than to be gay. For now, due to the actions of the SFC, the newly defined crime of homotransphobia carries a penalty in Brazil of one to three years in prison or a fine, as is the case with the crime of racism. The question for the future is whether or not changes in the political landscape of the Brazilian SFC, Congress, or the Presidency will impact the lives of millions of LGBT Brazilians by either supporting, weakening, or repealing the law prohibiting homophobia.

In conclusion, this volume provided a foundation and a framework for considering some of the lived experiences, triumphs, and challenges of LGBT persons across the globe. Progress in securing LGBT rights is moving forward; however, society must grapple with and identify ways in which to continue the struggle for LGBT civil and political rights with a reduced cost and burden to mental, physical, and emotional well-being. A deeper understanding of ways to intervene in LGBT health disparities is sorely needed, being mindful of and harnessing the protective factors and supports that exist within the diverse LGBT community. Ending the entrenched societal and structurally based discrimination and bias levied upon the LGBT community will require the moral and political will of every nation throughout the world. Going forward, the questions for society are twofold. What are the human costs of continued marginalization for any group of people? Do these costs matter enough to bring about change?

References

AFP. (2019a, June 14). *Brazil Supreme Court criminalizes homophobia* [Web log post]. Retrieved from https://www.msn.com/en-nz/news/world/brazil-supreme-court-criminalizes-homophobia/ar-AACSv0A.

AFP. (2019b, June 14). *Brazil's President says criminalizing homophobia could 'hurt' gays* [Web log post]. Retrieved from https://www.msn.com/en-us/news/world/brazils-president-says-criminalizing-homophobia-could-hurt-gays/ar-AACTE1J.

Allyn, B., & Matia, D. (2019, June 6). *NYPD Commissioner apologizes for 'oppressive' 1969 raid on Stonewall Inn* [Web log post]. Retrieved from https://www.npr.org/2019/06/06/730444495/nypd-commissioner-apologizes-for-oppressive-1969-raid-on-stonewall-inn.

Arlene's Flowers, Inc. v. Washington, No. 91615-2 (2017).

Blow, C. (2019, June 16). *It gets better. That's my testimony* [Opinion Editorial]. Retrieved from https://www.nytimes.com/2019/06/16/opinion/pride-it-gets-better.html.

Carter, D. (2004). *Stonewall: The riots that sparked the gay revolution.* New York, NY: St. Martin's Griffin.

Cooper, A. (2013, June 6). Anderson Cooper's exclusive interview with transgender former Navy SEAL Kristen Beck pt. I. CNN Pressroom. Retrieved from http://cnnpressroom.blogs.cnn.com/2013/06/06/part-i-of-andersoncoopers-exclusive-interview-with-transgender-former-navy-seal-kristen-beck/.

EEOC v. R.G. & G.R. Harris Funeral Homes, No. 16-2424 (2018).

Klein, dba Sweet Cakes by Melissa v. Oregon Bureau of Labor and Industries, 289 Or. App. 507 (2017).

Kushner, J. (2019, May 25). *The British Empire's homophobia lives on in former colonies* [Web log post]. Retrieved from https://www.msn.com/en-xl/africa/kenya/the-british-empires-homophobia-lives-on-in-former-colonies/ar-AABTiHA?li=BBKxOeh&MSCC=1544122609&ocid=spartanntp.

Masterpiece Cakes v. Colorado Civil Rights Commission, 584 U.S.__ (more) 138 S. Ct. 1719; 201 L. Ed. 2d35.

Meyer, I. (1995). Minority stress and mental health in gay men. *Journal of Health and Social Behavior, 36*, 38–56.

Meyer, I. (2003). Prejudice, social stress, and mental health in lesbian, gay and bisexual populations: Conceptual issues and research evidence. *Psychological Bulletin, 129*, 674–697.

Meyer, I. (2010). Identify, stress, and resilience in lesbians, gay men, and bisexuals of color. *Counseling Psychologist, 38*(3), 1–9.

Obergefell v. Hodges, 576 U.S. __ (2015).

Pidgeon v. Turner, 549 S.W.3d 130 (2016).

Rivero, N. (2017, June 28). *15 inspiring quotes from LGBT leaders* [Web log post]. Retrieved from http://mentalfloss.com/article/502121/15-inspiring-quotes-lgbt-leaders.

Stern, M. (2019, May 24). *The Trump administration releases its plan to let health care providers refuse to treat transgender people* [Web log post]. Retrieved from https://slate.com/news-and-politics/2019/05/trump-administration-releases-plan-to-let-health-care-providers-refuse-to-treat-transgender-people.html.

Zimmerman, L., Darnell, D., Rhew, I., Lee, C., & Kaysen, D. (2015). Resilience in community: A social ecological developmental model for young adult sexual minority women. *American Journal of Community Psychology, 55*, 179–190.

Index

© The Editor(s) (if applicable) and The Author(s) 2020
S. R. Notaro, *Marginality and Global LGBT Communities*, Neighborhoods, Communities, and Urban Marginality, https://doi.org/10.1007/978-3-030-22415-8